高等院校特色课程英语系列教材

英伦视听100篇

孙少华　编著

苏州大学出版社
Soochow University Press

图书在版编目(CIP)数据

英伦视听100篇/孙少华编著. —苏州：苏州大学出版社，2022.1
高等院校特色课程英语系列教材
ISBN 978-7-5672-3657-8

Ⅰ.①英… Ⅱ.①孙… Ⅲ.①英语-听说教学-高等学校-教材 Ⅳ.①H319.9

中国版本图书馆CIP数据核字(2021)第274134号

Yinglun Shiting 100 Pian
书　　名：英伦视听100篇

编　　著：孙少华
责任编辑：沈　琴
封面设计：刘　俊

出版发行：苏州大学出版社(Soochow University Press)
社　　址：苏州市十梓街1号　邮编：215006
印　　装：苏州市深广印刷有限公司
网　　址：www.sudapress.com
邮　　箱：sdcbs@suda.edu.cn
邮购热线：0512-67480030
销售热线：0512-67481020

开　　本：787 mm×1 092 mm　1/16　印张：18.25　字数：422千
版　　次：2022年1月第1版
印　　次：2022年1月第1次印刷
书　　号：ISBN 978-7-5672-3657-8
定　　价：49.80元

凡购本社图书发现印装错误，请与本社联系调换。服务热线：0512-67481020

Preface

一、本书简介

这是一本全英式英语视听教材，共 100 课，每课时长约 2～5 分钟，取材于近四年英国主流电视新闻。教材突出课程思政理念，所选题材弘扬主旋律。练习包含问答、填空、听写、翻译及课后任务，旨在全方位提升学习者对英式英语的听力理解能力，锻造纯正的英伦音，并帮助他们深入了解今天的英国社会与文化。本书用途广泛，可用作英语专业高级视听说教材，非英语专业学生和广大英语爱好者泛听学习或模仿英音的教材；专家学者可借助此书研究英式英语、英国文化和英文媒体；雅思考生和赴英留学生可用于浸润式听力训练；中高级口译爱好者可用作英汉口译强化训练。

二、本书特色与创新

1. 课程思政理念为先导。本教材的选材主题极为广泛，充分体现建设人类命运共同体的思想，如环保（伦敦超低排放区、收取拥堵费、推行清洁能源、推广电动汽车、轻松回收、快递包装盒等）、野生动物保护（昆虫减少、拯救白鲸、野化乡村等）、医学重大进步（HIV 基因疗法、胎儿先天脊髓缺陷修补、已故女性子宫移植、AI 诊断眼病、机器人手术等）、交通（伦敦地铁、英国高铁、自行车道、智能限速、无人机危害等）、新式住房（铁轨上建新房、水上新房等）、饮食（纤维之益、蜂蜜的妙用、糖过量、食品安全等）、健康（瘦基因、肥胖与癌症等）、教育（无屏校园等）、科技（基因测序、数字化石、超级黑洞等），以及对中国社会发展的报道等。上述主题完全切合我国新时代背景下的学生培养理念，有助于潜移默化地培养识大体、顾大局、不出国门而熟知西方前沿、关心人类命运共同发展的一代新人。

2. 课程量大，练习设计更人性化。市面上大量的视听教程内容偏少，练习设计偏应试。本书秉持高强度训练有利于培养优秀人才的理念，少讲技巧，多做训练，每课有听写，同一话题也可多次出现，但来自不同时间、视角和媒体。经过对本教材的深入学习和坚持不懈的训练，学习者的积极词汇量将大幅度增长，英语爱好者英语听说能力将大幅度提升，各类英语水平测试通过率也将明显提高。

3. 充实国内英语专业英式英语视听类教材。本教材内容取自英国两大主流电视台 BBC 和 ITV 的新闻报道。长期以来，中国英语学习者看、听 BBC 的语料主要来自 BBC

World Service，主题偏重于世界各地的政治、军事、灾难等。实际上，我们需要一本多角度展现英国的英语视听教材，让学习者真实地认识英国，了解英国人工作、学习、生活的方方面面。与以往类似教材相比，本书编排注重从单元数、课程时长、词汇深度、主题广度及媒体来源方面推陈出新。本教材语料中的新闻主播和记者，大多语音纯正，叙述沉稳，有助于培养学习者的学科素养和表达能力。

三、本书编排方案

本教材共收录73篇BBC新闻和27篇ITV新闻。主题涵盖22类，其中篇幅占5篇以上的主题有：环保(9)、医疗(8)、健康(8)、旅游(7)、运动(7)、交通(7)、科技(6)、名人(6)、民生(5)、社会(5)、趣闻(5)，占5篇以下的主题包括：艺术、中国、住房、历史、动物、经济、商业、影视、皇室、政治和教育等。

全书共分4部分，每部分含25篇，按标题首字母顺序排列。各部分的划分依据是音频时长：Part Ⅰ，90～140秒；Part Ⅱ，141～160秒；Part Ⅲ，161～180秒；Part Ⅳ，181～300秒。总体上遵循由易到难的原则，词汇和练习难度逐步提升，但语速并没有明显不同。

每课按照字母顺序列出了生词表，附词性与中文词义。

每课设计了含8～15个空缺的填空练习，每个空缺填入1～3个单词。

每课设计了70～120个单词的听写练习，取自各语篇的精华部分。

每课设计了英译汉练习，选取语篇中较难的句子进行翻译。

课后任务形式多样。部分单元设计了课后练习，如故事复述、深度调研；部分单元设计了课堂讨论的话题。

部分单元提供了地名、人名、历史事件、英国文化等信息的背景解读，置于词汇表之前。

四、推荐学习方案

建议教师和学习者按照以下顺序讲授或自学：

1. 每课开始，先观看视频2～3遍，不看词汇表，不看文本，适当做笔记。
2. 口头回答教材设计的问题；如回答不了，建议重看视频，直到大致找到问题的答案。
3. 对照文本，播放视频或声音；难度较大部分，应反复看或听。
4. 对照词汇表，查词典，做笔记，找到生词的上下文，深入理解词汇和新闻内容。
5. 完成填空练习、听写练习、翻译练习。
6. 积极参与课堂讨论。
7. 复习词汇表。
8. 反复朗读文本，注意模仿重要的语段。
9. 每周滚动播放语音文件，始终让耳朵浸润在纯英文环境里。

五、本书出版前的使用情况

本书出版前，大部分内容作为泛听学习资料用于苏州城市学院（原苏州大学文正学院）16级英语、17级英语、18级英语、18级英语"专转本"、19级英语"专转本"、20级英语"专转本"，苏州大学外国语学院17级法语、18级法语、18级西班牙语等班级的视听教学，总人数达400人左右。学生普遍反映良好。

本书能够最终出版，要感谢多方面的帮助。感谢苏州大学外国语学院、苏州大学出版社对本教材的出版给予的大力支持。感谢苏州城市学院18级和19级英语"专转本"核心听力组学生完成所有ITV电视新闻的文字初稿。感谢所有学过本教材课程的学生在泛听学习过程中对本教材内容提出的修改意见。

由于笔者水平有限，谬误之处在所难免，恳请读者批评指正。

孙少华

2021年12月

Contents

Part I

1. Archie McInnes / **2**
2. Bungee 40 years / **4**
3. Changing Behaviour / **6**
4. Cleared of HIV / **8**
5. Cycle Routes / **10**
6. Emmy Awards / **13**
7. Golf at Church / **15**
8. Great Swimmer / **17**
9. Guest Editor / **19**
10. Herdwick Farming / **21**
11. Hotspur New Stadium / **23**
12. House of Commons / **26**

13. Kate's Brand / **28**
14. London's ULEZ / **30**
15. New Business / **32**
16. Noisy Supercars / **34**
17. Ole Solskjaer / **36**
18. Pound Devaluation / **39**
19. Right Direction / **41**
20. Serial Returners / **43**
21. Sniffing Out Covid / **46**
22. Top Tourist Attractions / **48**
23. Toxic London / **50**
24. Treasure Trove / **52**
25. Young Gamblers / **55**

Part II

26. Armistice Day / **60**
27. Artificial Organ / **62**
28. Buy Before You Die / **65**
29. Captain Sir Tom Moore / **67**
30. Cardboard Cut-down / **69**
31. Digital Fossils / **72**
32. Female Conductor / **74**
33. Fibre Benefit / **77**
34. Football Finances / **79**
35. Gross Footage / **82**
36. HIV Breakthrough / **85**
37. Honey and Health / **87**

38. Intelligent Speed Assistance / **90**
39. Jetpack for Paramedics / **92**
40. New Green Initiative / **95**
41. Roadside Eyesight Test / **97**
42. Spina Bifida Repair / **100**
43. Stonehenge Puzzle Solved / **102**
44. Sugar Warning / **104**
45. The Scream / **107**
46. Titanic Wreckage / **109**
47. Wet Wood Ban / **112**
48. Wildlife Photographer of the Year / **114**
49. Without Pain / **117**
50. Womb Transplant / **119**

Part III

51. Aston Martin Bulldog / ***124***
52. Blackout Report / ***126***
53. Breastfeeding Support / ***129***
54. Brexit Deal Done / ***131***
55. Congestion Fees / ***134***
56. Discoverer Discovered / ***136***
57. Elizabethan Maps / ***139***
58. Fares to Rise / ***142***
59. Floating Home / ***145***
60. Future Houses / ***147***
61. Healthy Diet / ***150***
62. High Street Decline / ***153***

63. Incentivising Cycling / ***155***
64. Insects in Decline / ***157***
65. Lyme Disease / ***160***
66. Museum of the Year / ***163***
67. New Homes over Rails / ***166***
68. Record Summer Heat / ***168***
69. Running for NHS / ***171***
70. Saving the Beluga Whales / ***174***
71. Screen Time Out / ***176***
72. Sir Sean Connery / ***179***
73. Skinny Genes / ***182***
74. The Mariana Trench / ***185***
75. The New £50 Note / ***187***

Part IV

76. Admiralty Arch / 192
77. AI Eye Diagnosis / 195
78. Boris Johnson's Journey / 198
79. Cancer Treatment / 201
80. Chaotic Train Service / 204
81. China Moon Landing / 207
82. Commuter Safety / 209
83. Dirty Streaming / 212
84. Drone Disruption / 214
85. Easier Recycling / 217
86. Fake Products / 220
87. Fake Takeaway / 224

88. Focus on Farming / 226
89. Food Safety / 229
90. Genome Sequencing / 232
91. Gymnastic Abuse / 235
92. Importance of Sculpture / 238
93. Judith Kerr / 241
94. Lady Hale / 243
95. London's Future Skyline / 246
96. Mosquito Research / 249
97. Netflix Expansion / 251
98. Supermassive Black Hole / 254
99. Tackling Climate Change / 257
100. V & A Dundee / 260

Glossary / 263

Part I

扫码看视频

扫码填空

扫码听写

1. Archie McInnes

ALASTAIR: And finally, Churchill called the pilots who won the Battle of Britain "The Few". Their number has fallen further with the death of Flight Lieutenant Archie McInnes. He flew a Hurricane during the epic aerial conflict and died just hours after celebrating his 100th birthday. The Chief of the Air Staff said he was part of an extraordinary band of selfless aviators to whom we owe the freedoms that we enjoy today. Geraint Vincent reports on a wartime hero.

GERAINT: One of those young men to whom so many owe so much. The Battle of Britain was already a month old when Archie McInnes completed his pilot training.

RADIO: Hitler hopes to gain the mastery of the air, but to a lot of the British Empire breeds men like these...

GERAINT: Immediately he was commissioned into the Royal Air Force and he flew into mortal danger in the skies above Southern England. Archie was a Hurricane pilot, who was shot down later in the war over North Africa and lost an arm. (*Tail comes up.*) 77 years later, Flight Lieutenant McInnes found himself in a Hurricane cockpit once again, when his biographer took him to the home of the Battle of Britain Memorial Flight.

JONNY: (*Then carry on.*) Archie never tended to dwell on the darker side of conflict too much. He just very much had such a passion for the experience of flying. You know, you have to conjure up the memory of just being on his own in a single-seater fighter, flying in and playing up in the clouds by himself, and that was always his fondest memory.

GERAINT: There was another reunion in the 100th year of Archie's life. Last autumn, this time at Biggin Hill where the veteran was taken up in a two-seater Spitfire to meet an old friend in the sky—a Hurricane came alongside, to Archie's obvious delight. He was a modest man who did his extraordinary duty a lifetime ago, and left it to others to remember his heroism.

ALASTAIR: Battle of Britain hero Flight Lieutenant Archie McInnes who has died. (*ITV-20190802*)

Notes

Biggin Hill：比金山，位于伦敦附近的飞机场，第二次世界大战期间英国皇家空军战斗机由此向德国出击。

Words and Expressions

aerial *adj.* 空中的
aviator *n.* 飞行员
breed *n.* （人的）类型；种类
cockpit *n.* 驾驶舱
commission *vt.* 任命军职
conjure up 想象
dwell on 唠叨
epic *adj.* 艰苦卓绝的；漫长而艰难的
flight lieutenant *n.* （英国空军）上尉
Hurricane *n.* 飓风式战斗机
mastery *n.* 控制权
mortal *adj.* 致命的；极度的
single-seater *n.* 单座机
Spitfire *n.* 喷火式战斗机
two-seater *n.* 双座机
veteran *n.* 老兵

Questions

1. How old was Archie when he became a pilot?
2. Did he suffer any injury during the war?
3. What are the main types of British fighter jets in World War II?
4. Did Archie love to talk a lot about his fighting experience?

Gap-filling

GERAINT: Immediately he was ______________ into the Royal Air Force and he flew into ______________ danger in the skies ______________ Southern England. Archie was a Hurricane ______________, who was shot down later in the war over North Africa and lost ______________. 77 years later, Flight Lieutenant McInnes found himself in a Hurricane ______________ once again, when his ______________ took him to the home of the ______________ of Britain Memorial Flight.

JONNY: Archie never tended to ______________ the darker side of conflict too much. He just very much had such a(n) ______________ for the experience of flying. You know, you have to ______________ the memory of just being on his own in a single-seater fighter, flying in and playing up ______________ by himself, and that was always his ______________ memory.

Dictation

And finally … enjoy today.

Translation

1. He was part of an extraordinary band of selfless aviators to whom we owe the freedoms that we enjoy today.
2. Hitler hopes to gain the mastery of the air.
3. A Hurricane came alongside, to Archie's obvious delight.

Post-class task

Do a research on the Battle of England and write a report in no less than 200 words.

2. Bungee 40 years

MARY: Finally, 40 years ago today, police officers in Bristol were called to what they thought was an April Fool's show—a group of men were going to jump off the Clifton Suspension Bridge, attached to some elastic rope. Not only did the daredevil safely carry out the stunt, they also invented bungee jumping. Returning to the bridge today, the man told Rupert Evelyn about the historic leap.

RUPERT: Someone had to be first, and that honor belongs to David Kirke. Back in front of the Clifton Suspension Bridge where he launched a sport.

There wasn't much room for fear that day, he says, except perhaps for his parents' reaction.

DAVID: I climbed over the balcony there with rails, clutching a top hat with a handkerchief around my face, because I didn't want my mother to recognize me. We worked out that that bridge is 240 feet tall. We would leap to rates about 120 feet. Then you'll fall down, and you'll surface just above the water.

RUPERT: The phrase "Don't try this at home" could have been created for David and his friends of the Dangerous Sports Club who pioneered bungee jumping. Their other creations had merits but didn't become a global phenomenon.

Although bungee jumping is now commonplace around the world, 40 years ago, it was simply an idea. The Dangerous Sports Club had done the theory and they were confident of the mathematics. But it was still a leap into the unknown. The police initially thought the jump was an April Fool's, but when it happened, they arrested the men for breaking the local bylaws.

DAVID: They couldn't have been nicer and they let us off with a 50-quid fine. And I said, "Oh, thank God, we got away with that."

RUPERT: Since 1979, millions have made the heart-stopping jump from some of the world's tallest structures. Free falling, sometimes with absolute precision. Others like 007 seemingly flying gracefully through the air, all thanks to British eccentric innovators. Rupert Evelyn, ITV News, Bristol.

MARY: Not for me, thanks. Julie is here at 10, but from me and all the team, have a great evening. Bye-bye. (*ITV-20190401*)

Words and Expressions

a leap into the unknown 冒险举动
balcony *n.* 栏杆外平台
bylaw *n.* (地方)法规
clutch *vt.* 紧握
commonplace *adj.* 普遍的
daredevil *n.* 冒失鬼
eccentric *adj.* 古怪的
elastic *adj.* 有弹性的
get away with 受到从轻发落
initially *adv.* 起初
innovator *n.* 创新者
let sb. off 从轻处罚
merit *n.* 价值
quid *n.* 一英镑
stunt *n.* 特技;惊险动作
suspension bridge 悬索桥
top hat 高顶礼帽
work out 算出

Questions

1. Why did David cover his face when he jumped?
2. Why did the police arrest David?
3. How was David punished by the police?
4. Is bungee jumping David's only innovation?

Gap-filling

RUPERT: Someone had to be first, and that ________________ belongs to David Kirke. Back in front of the Clifton Suspension Bridge where he ______________ a sport. There wasn't much ________________ for fear that day, he says, ________________ perhaps for his parent's reaction.

DAVID: I climbed over the ________________ there with rails, ________________ a top hat with a handkerchief around my face, ________________ I didn't want my mother to recognize me. We ________________ that bridge is 240 feet tall. We would ________________ to rates about 120 feet. Then you'll fall down, and you'll ________________ just above the water.

Dictation

The phrase ... the local bylaws.

Translation

1. Their other creations had merits but didn't become a global phenomenon.
2. They couldn't have been nicer and they let us off with a 50-quid fine.
3. Thank God, we got away with that.

Post-class task

Pair work: Talk with your neighbour about the craziest sport you have ever done.

3. Changing Behaviour

ALICE: A church in Greenwich is one of several that have managed to double the amount raised in donations, thanks to contactless payments. As the use of cash declines, the Church of England says it wants to ensure it can still benefit from people's generosity, as Alison Earle explains.

ALISON: A service of song, prayer and reflection. So far, so traditional. But it's when it comes to the collection at Christ Church, East Greenwich, that things get a bit different. It's one of around a dozen Church of England places of worship trialling a digital collection box.

MARGARET: Using it makes us feel like we're part of the 21st century; we're not stuck in the kind of musty past. So it kind of feels really appropriate. We allow people to give to the work of the church in whatever way they can, and whichever way is easiest.

ALISON: Gone are the days of rooting around for loose change. The way the device works, well, you choose from four different amounts, then simply use a smartphone or card to tap.

And, overall, it's gone down well.

WOMAN 1: It is easier, and I don't have to keep going in my bag. I just need to bring out my phone and use it.

WOMAN 2: I prefer to use cash most of the time, whatever I'm doing.

MAN 1: It represents the church kind of moving forward with the times.

MAN 2: I rarely find myself with money in my pocket, so ... but I've got my card on me, so it's great to be able to use that in church as well.

ALISON: It seems notes and coins have fallen from grace. Figures from the trade body UK Finance show debit cards are now the more popular way to pay, with contactless now possible on transport, or buskers, and the Mayor's scheme to donate to homeless charities. And the Church of England is benefiting from our changing behaviour.

PETER: Because of the decrease that we're seeing in cash usage, we're definitely providing them with a solution now, where their current congregation can use a card. The direct impact was the 97% increase that we saw from before the solution to after the solution.

ALISON: There are now plans to extend the trial to other C of E churches as we move closer to an era where cash is no longer king. Alison Earle, BBC London News. (*BBC-20190210*)

Words and Expressions

be king 最为重要;极具影响
busker *n.* 街头艺人
C of E = Church of England 英国国教
contactless payment 非接触支付
fall from grace 失去恩宠
generosity *n.* 慷慨
go down well 反应很好
musty *adj.* 陈腐的
root around for sth. 翻寻
scheme *n.* 计划;方案

Questions

1. What new technology has enabled some churches to keep up with the times?
2. Does everyone welcome the new device?
3. What effect has been achieved with the change?
4. Apart from the church, where else is this convenience particularly in need?

Gap-filling

MARGARET: Using it makes us feel like we're ________________ the 21st century; we're not ________________ in the kind of ________________ past. So it kind of feels really ________________. We allow people to give to the work of the church in ________________ way they can, and ________________ way is easiest.

ALISON: Gone are the days of rooting around for ________________ change. The way the ________________ works, well, you choose from four different ________________, then simply use a smartphone or card to ________________. And, ________________, it's gone down well.

Dictation

A church in Greenwich ... a digital collection box.

Translation

1. It seems notes and coins have fallen from grace.
2. Gone are the days of rooting around for loose change.
3. We move closer to an era where cash is no longer king.
4. Overall, the digital collection box has gone down well.

Post-class task

Discussion: Are there any disadvantages when we go cashless?

4. Cleared of HIV

GEORGE: A patient in the UK has become only the second person in the world to be declared clear of HIV. His remission followed a stem cell transplant, part of the treatment for a cancer which he also developed. The donor was resistant to the virus. Experts say it's too early to say he's been cured. Our medical correspondent Fergus Walsh is here with the details. Fergus.

FERGUS: Well, George, this case gives a tantalising glimpse of how, in rare instances, HIV might be defeated. The patient had cancer and underwent a bone marrow transplant at London's Hammersmith Hospital. His donor had a mutation in both copies of the CCR5 gene—this makes them resistant to HIV infection. About 1% of people of north European descent have this immunity. That resistance was passed to the patient, and for the past 18 months he's been off all antiretroviral therapy, clear of HIV, but it's too early to know if he is cured. Now this is just the second time a patient has had prolonged remission from HIV—the first was the so-called "Berlin patient", Timothy Brown. He's now more than a decade clear of HIV.

IAN: I think it proves that the first patient, the so-called "Berlin patient", wasn't a fluke. They did get cured of HIV and this is another potential cure. So it shows that the CCR5 molecule is actually crucial as a means to target preventative strategies to stop people getting infected with HIV.

FERGUS: Three years ago, I reported from San Francisco on another approach to try to defeat HIV—Matt's immune cells were edited to confer the CCR5 mutation—he'd been off HIV meds for two years. Now researchers, writing in the journal *Nature*, say the bone marrow transplant is aggressive, complex and expensive, so it's not suitable for the vast majority of HIV patients who are better off on daily HIV medication, which is highly effective. But it confirms that the CCR5 mutation is crucial for researchers trying to target new ways to treat HIV. George.

GEORGE: Fergus, thank you. (*BBC-20190305*)

Words and Expressions

aggressive *adj.* 激进的
antiretroviral *adj.* 抗逆转录病毒的
bone marrow 骨髓
confer *vt.* 赋予
crucial *adj.* 至关重要的;关键性的
descent *n.* 血统
develop *vt.* 患(病)
donor *n.* 捐赠者
fluke *n.* 偶然
immunity *n.* 免疫力
molecule *n.* 分子
mutation *n.* 变异
preventative *adj.* 预防(性)的
remission *n.* 缓解期
resistant *adj.* 抵抗的
tantalising *adj.* 诱人的;令人向往的
transplant *n.* 移植

Questions

1. How many patients are cleared of HIV so far?
2. How is it possible to clear HIV through stem cell transplant?
3. Why are scientists so excited about such a rare instance?
4. What are feasible ways to cure HIV patients? And which one is the most commonly adopted?

Gap-filling

FERGUS: Well, George, this case gives a tantalising ____________ of how, in rare instances, HIV might be defeated. The patient had cancer and ____________ a bone marrow transplant at London's Hammersmith Hospital. His ________________ had a mutation in both copies of the CCR5 ________________—this makes them resistant to HIV ________________. About 1% of people of north European ________________ have this ________________. That ________________ was passed to the patient, and for the past 18 months he's been off all antiretroviral ________________, clear of HIV, but it's too early to know if he is ________________. Now this is just the second time a patient has had prolonged ________________ from HIV—the first was the ________________ "Berlin patient", Timothy Brown. He's now more than a ________________ clear of HIV.

Dictation

Three years ago ... to treat HIV.

Translation

1. His remission followed a stem cell transplant, part of the treatment for a cancer which he also developed.
2. The donor was resistant to the virus.
3. This case gives a tantalising glimpse of how, in rare instances, HIV might be defeated.

Post-class task

Do a research on bone marrow transplant and write a short report in about 150 words.

5. Cycle Routes

ALICE: After criticism of delays to the cycle superhighway, Sadiq Khan has unveiled plans to rebrand current cycle routes to make it more straightforward to work out your best journey. Our political editor, Tim Donovan, has the story.

TIM: With the role comes all kinds of responsibilities, and today it meant him getting on a bike in Edmonton and pedalling along a cycle lane recently installed and segregated on a busy roundabout.

There is a push from the Mayor's man in charge of cycling to get more people using bikes in outer London. But schemes like this are taking time to put in place. Some object to the loss of parking and the effect, initially at least, on local business.

NESIL: Some of it is about cultural change and also making sure people recognise it. You know, places like Enfield have got huge health inequalities, huge health inequalities, and so we need to make sure that the way that we live our lives helps to improve our health and well-being, and being active is part of that.

TIM: The Mayor's been criticised for delays, but work on two new cycle superhighways will start next year—one from Tower Bridge to Greenwich, the other from Olympia to Brentford. The Mayor accepts more needs to be done online and with a new app to lure people onto two wheels.

KHAN: We are going to release all the data about where the cycle parking is, where the specialist junctions are, where the cameras are. And so these designers will come up with apps, so you as a cyclist can know where are places you can hire a bike, where it's easy to cycle from A to B. So the idea is to make it easy for you with this information to have a lifestyle that means you cycle more than you currently do.

TIM: Campaigners approve, but they want the wheels turning faster.

SIMON: We can understand the concerns, we can understand some of the delays, and there are perfectly reasonable and legitimate reasons why some things haven't happened quite as fast as they should have done. But at the same time the overall pattern is a bit too slow, and it needs to hurry up.

TIM: Now we wait for what will effectively be a rebranding of all cycle routes in the capital in the new year. Tim Donovan, BBC London News. (*BBC-20181217*)

Words and Expressions

come up with 想出;拿出
cycle lane 自行车专用道
cycle route 自行车道
cycle superhighway 自行车高速路
in place 在正确位置;就绪
outer *adj.* 外围的
pedal *vi.* 骑自行车
rebrand *vt.* 重塑……的形象
roundabout *n.* 环行交通枢纽
segregate *vt.* 隔离;使分开
specialist junction 专用枢纽
unveil *vt.* 公布;推出
well-being *n.* 幸福

Questions

1. What is the purpose of installing cycle superhighways?
2. What kind of data about cycling will be released by the Mayor and why does he want to do so?

3. What else can be done to attract more cyclists according to the Mayor?

Gap-filling

KHAN: We are going to ________________ all the data about where the cycle parking is, where the specialist ________________ are, where the ________________ are. And so these designers will come up with ________________, so you as a(n) ________________ can know where are places you can ________________, where it's easy to cycle from A to B. So ________________ to make it easy for you with this information to have a(n) ________________ that means you cycle more than you ________________ do.

TIM: Campaigners ________________, but they want the wheels turning faster.

SIMON: We can understand the ________________, we can understand some of the ________________, and there are perfectly reasonable and ________________ reasons why some things haven't happened ________________ they should have done. But at the same time the ________________ pattern is a bit too slow, and it needs to ________________.

Dictation

With the role ... on local business.

Translation

1. The Mayor has unveiled plans to rebrand current cycle routes to make it more straightforward to work out your best journey.
2. He is pedalling along a cycle lane recently installed and segregated on a busy roundabout.
3. The Mayor accepts more needs to be done online and with a new app to lure people onto two wheels.

Post-class task

Discussion: What else can be done to attract more cyclists?

6. Emmy Awards

SOPHIE: British stars had a good night at the Emmys, America's biggest TV awards, last night with Claire Foy, Thandie Newton and Matthew Rhys among those picking up prizes. But it was an American director with a surprise proposal who really stole the show, as James Cook reports from Los Angeles.

JAMES: TV may be changing, with debates about diversity and a surge in streaming services, but some affairs are eternal, like Hollywood's passion for a party and its love for a British accent.

PRESENTER: Claire Foy, *The Crown*.

JAMES: This was her first Emmy, and her last chance to win it for portraying the Queen.

CLAIRE: I had the most extraordinary two-and-a-half years of my life. I'm not going to cry on this programme. I was given a role that I never thought I would ever get a chance to play, and I met people who I will love for ever and ever and ever.

JAMES: Fellow Brit Thandie Newton was also honoured for *West World*.

THANDIE: I don't even believe in God, but I'm going to thank her tonight.

JAMES: There was British success, too, for writer Charlie Brooker as well as director Stephen Daldry and satirist John Oliver. *Game of Thrones*, which certainly sounds British, regained its Best Drama crown.

MAN: The Emmy goes to Matthew Rhys!

JAMES: The Welsh actor Matthew Rhys triumphed in Cold War thriller *The Americans*. So, the remarkable, outsize influence of British actors on the entertainment industry continues. But that is not what everyone's talking about here.

GLENN: Jan, you are the sunshine in my life.

JAMES: It was this director's speech which stole the show.

GLENN: You wonder why I don't like to call you my girlfriend, because I want to call you my wife.

JAMES: Glenn Weiss making drama of his own.

GLENN: Will you marry me?

JAMES: She said yes, thank goodness, leaving this happy couple the toast of Tinseltown. James Cook, BBC News, Los Angeles.

SOPHIE: Wonderful! (*BBC-20180918*)

Words and Expressions

Brit *n.* 英国人
eternal *adj.* 永恒的
outsize *adj.* 极大的
satirist *n.* 讽刺作家
steal the show 吸引更多的注意;抢风头
streaming service 流媒体服务
surge *n.* 暴增
the toast of ... 有口皆碑的人
thriller *n.* 惊险剧
Tinseltown *n.* 星光熠熠之城(好莱坞的谐称)
triumph *vi.* 获胜

Questions

1. What does Hollywood always like when it comes to show business?
2. For what TV series was Claire Foy awarded an Emmy?
3. For what TV series was Thandie Newton awarded an Emmy?
4. What is the winner of Best Drama?
5. Do you know the nickname of Hollywood?

Gap-filling

JAMES: So, the remarkable, ____________________ influence of British actors on the entertainment industry _________________. But that is not what everyone's talking about here.

GLENN: Jan, you are the _________________ in my life.

JAMES: It was this director's speech which _________________.

GLENN: You _________________ why I don't like to call you my girlfriend, because I want to call you my wife.

JAMES: Glenn Weiss making _________________ of his own.

GLENN: Will you marry me?

JAMES: She said yes, ___________________, leaving this happy couple the _____________________ Tinseltown.

Dictation

TV may be changing ... ever and ever.

Translation

1. It was an American director with a surprise proposal who really stole the show.

2. *Game of Thrones* regained its Best Drama crown.

Post-class task

1. **Discussion**: The wonderful British or American TV series you particularly like and why.
2. Do a research on the categories of Emmy Award and write a report in about 200 words.

7. Golf at Church

MARY: And finally tonight, how a medieval church is trying to tee up a whole new congregation. Rochester Cathedral has turned its nave into a crazy golf course to try to attract young people. But using the thousand-year-old building in this way does not have everyone's blessing, as Ivor Bennett explains.

IVOR: It's not unusual for golfers to seek some divine intervention, but Rochester Cathedral's taken that to the next level: nine holes designed to encourage a younger generation through its doors, whether it's to pray or just play.

MATTHEW: What are the reasons that people go into church? There's all sorts of reasons, and I wouldn't want to judge them for that. I'm really glad that they're here; I'm really glad that they're having fun and that they're engaging and being part of the 1,400-year-old story of this place.

IVOR: So if they're only coming in to play nine holes, that doesn't bother you?

MATTHEW: Absolutely fine. People come in, you know, just to listen to the music.

IVOR: The free course has only been open since the weekend but already has 200 people teeing off a day.

BOY 1: We don't usually come to the Cathedral, but now they've got an event on like this. It's fun.

IVOR: Does this make you want to go to more cathedrals?

BOY 2: Yeah.

IVOR: What does it make you want to play more golf?

BOY 2: As long as they have golf or something in them, I ain't sitting there listening to words.

IVOR: Now, instead of the usual windmills and tunnels, this course is based around bridges which, as well as providing some tricky putting, the cathedral hopes will help people to build bridges in their own lives.

But it's not connecting with everyone. A priest who says he was ordained in Rochester, one of many people to criticise the idea, calling it an embarrassing shambles.

Rochester is not the only cathedral doing things differently. Liverpool's hosted yoga, while Norwich will soon house a helter-skelter, part of a drive to connect cathedrals to their communities.

Services at Rochester will continue as normal while the golf course's here, and even those who aren't religious may well find themselves praying, but to the golfing gods. Ivor Bennett, ITV News, in Rochester. (*ITV-20190730*)

Words and Expressions

blessing *n.* 赞同
cathedral *n.* 大教堂
congregation *n.* 教区全体教徒
divine intervention 上帝之祐
engage *vi.* 参加;参与
golf course 高尔夫球场
helter-skelter *n.* 螺旋滑梯
medieval *adj.* 中世纪的
nave *n.* 教堂正厅
nine holes 九洞高尔夫球
ordain *vt.* 任命为牧师
putting *n.* (高尔夫球)轻击入洞;推杆
shambles *n.* 混乱局面
tee off 发球
tee up 将(高尔夫球)置于球座上;准备击球
tricky *adj.* 难对付的
windmill *n.* 风车

Questions

1. Why does the church introduce golf into its nave?
2. Why is Priest Matthew not bothered even if some people come only to play golf?
3. What does "building bridges in one's own life" really mean?
4. Is Rochester the only church to make some changes to connect communities?

Gap-filling

IVOR: It's not ________________ for golfers to seek some ________________ intervention, but Rochester Cathedral's taken that to the next level: ________________ designed to encourage a younger generation through its doors, whether it's ________________ or just play.

MATTHEW: What are the reasons that people ________________ church? There's all sorts of reasons, and I wouldn't want to ________________ them for that. I'm really glad that ________________; I'm really glad that they're having fun and that they're __________________ and being part of the 1,400-year-old story of ____ ______________.

Dictation

Now, instead of ... to their communities.

Translation

1. It's not unusual for golfers to seek some divine intervention.
2. A priest calls it an embarrassing shambles.
3. Even those who aren't religious may well find themselves praying, but to the golfing gods.

Post-class task

Discussion: What message is hidden behind the news report? Do you think the aim of the churches will finally be achieved?

8. Great Swimmer

MISHAL: An adventurer from Lincolnshire has become the first person to swim almost 1,800 miles around Great Britain. Ross Edgley left Margate on June 1, swimming for up to 12 hours a day. He's been up against strong tides and currents as well as storms and jellyfish. John Maguire went to meet him as he walked back onto shore.

JOHN: This is the moment Ross Edgley set a new world record, became the first person to swim around Britain, and set foot on dry land for the first time in more than five months.

ROSS: Great Britain's big, isn't it?

JOHN: You tell me—you swam round it!

ROSS: Yeah, it's much bigger than I thought. Scotland's big. You know, people don't realise how big that is. The highs are so high but the lows are so low. Scotland is probably the best example. Just amazing, the scenery is stunning. But it's also very humbling, just getting slapped in the face by jellyfish every single day. So, it feels weird now to sort of be looking back and almost reflecting because, for 157 days, I almost didn't allow myself to do that. So now it feels quite nice.

JOHN: Swimming twice a day, every day, for up to 12 hours, both day and night, he's battled storms, exhaustion, and waters seething with jellyfish. On Margate Beach this morning, where he first set off in June, well-wishers who'd followed his progress joined friends and family to welcome him home.

RICHARD: Absolutely immense. I mean he's a man who's always had character and he's shown that over the last five months.

JOHN: He lived on board throughout the 2,000-mile swim, consuming more than a million calories to fuel his endeavour. As for what's next, Ross says he is keen to take on yet another swimming challenge, but that's after he gets his land legs back.

ROSS: Thank you, thank you. Stop it. I'm going to cry!

JOHN: John Maguire, BBC News, Margate. (*BBC-20181104*)

Words and Expressions

adventurer *n.* 冒险家	keen *adj.* 渴望的
current *n.* 水流	seethe with 布满
endeavour *n.* 努力	slap *vt.* 拍
fuel *vt.* 维持	stunning *adj.* 极漂亮的
immense *adj.* 巨大的	take on 决定做
jellyfish *n.* 水母	weird *adj.* 怪异的
humbling *adj.* 令人惭愧的	well-wisher *n.* 祝福者

Questions

1. Hong long did Ross swim around Britain?
2. What is the distance he swam around Britain?
3. Did he swim on the night?
4. What problems did he go through during the swim?
5. How much did he eat in total to sustain the swim?

Gap-filling

ROSS: Yeah, it's much bigger than I ____________________. Scotland's big. You know, people don't ____________________ how big that is. The highs are so high but the lows are so low. Scotland is probably the ____________________. Just amazing, the scenery is ____________________. But it's also very ____________________, just getting slapped in the face by jellyfish ____________________. So, it feels ____________________ now to sort of be looking back and almost __________________ because, for 157 days, I almost didn't __________________ to do that. So now it feels quite nice.

Dictation

Swimming twice a day … last five months.

Translation

1. He's been up against strong tides and currents as well as storms and jellyfish.
2. He consumed more than a million calories to fuel his endeavour.

Post-class task

Do a research on any adventurer you like and tell the story about him or her later on in class.

9. Guest Editor

CLIVE: The Duchess of Sussex has been revealed as the guest editor of *Vogue* magazine for its September issue, regarded as the most important edition of the year, and rather than be photographed herself, she chose to put 15 women on its front cover, all of whom she describes as trailblazing change-makers.

These are the women chosen by the Duchess of Sussex to grace the cover of British *Vogue*, from New Zealand's Prime Minister, Jacinda Ardern, to the teenage climate change campaigner Greta Thunberg. She described them as fearless and breaking barriers.

JAMEELA: My force for change is Yara Shadidi.

FRANCESCA: For me, I think Chimamanda is incredibly inspiring.

CLIVE: All remarkable women with a space reserved on the cover for the reader. Meghan Markle chose not to grace the cover herself, saying it would be boastful. Instead, she selected 15 women, each championing a cause.

JACINDA: One change that I've noticed over the course of my career is just how polarised the world is now. I do think there is a solution to that, though, and that's ultimately us coming back to the humanity that we all share.

CLIVE: She's often criticised in the media, but the Duchess said working with British

Vogue editor in chief, Edward Enninful, had been rewarding, and said she hoped their collaboration will steer the fashion magazine's focus onto values and causes represented by the women.

SALMA: I think my force for change is me.

CLIVE: The new edition of *Vogue*. (*BBC-20190729*)

Words and Expressions

boastful *adj.* 自夸的
champion *vt.* 捍卫
collaboration *n.* 合作
editor in chief 主编
grace *vt.* 荣登;使荣耀
issue *n.* (杂志或报纸的)一期;期号
polarised *adj.* (使)两极化的
steer *vt.* 引导
trailblazing *adj.* 开创性的

Questions

1. Why did Meghan choose these 15 women?
2. Why did Meghan refuse to put herself on the magazine cover?
3. What does the New Zealand's Prime Minister advocate?
4. Does this report mean Meghan has changed her career into a magazine editor?

Gap-filling

CLIVE: All remarkable women with a space ________________ on the cover for the reader. Meghan Markle chose not to ________________ the cover herself, saying it would be __________. Instead, she selected 15 women, each ________________ a cause.

JACINDA: One change that I've noticed __________ my career is just how __________ the world is now. I do think there is a(n) ________________ to that, though, and that's ________________ us coming back to the humanity that we all ________________.

CLIVE: She's often ________________ in the media, but the Duchess said working with the British *Vogue* editor in chief, Edward Enninful, had been ________________, and said she hoped their collaboration will ________________ the fashion magazine's focus onto values and ________________ represented by the women.

Dictation

The Duchess of Sussex has ... breaking barriers.

Translation

1. Meghan describes the 15 women as trailblazing change-makers.
2. They were chosen by Meghan to grace the cover of British *Vogue*.

Post-class task

Do a research on the 15 women that were chosen for the magazine cover, and select one and report her story in class.

10. Herdwick Farming

ANNABEL: Now Herdwick sheep have been an iconic part of the Lake District for a thousand years, but numbers are declining—they've fallen by more than 50% over the past century. Farmers blame government policy, but the Lake District National Park says it recognises their cultural value. Judy Hobson reports.

JUDY: Herdwick sheep have grazed the Lake District fells for centuries and shaped the incredible landscape. Isaac Benson's family has farmed this breed for generations.

ISAAC: The Lake District is a by-product of agriculture, and it is the Herdwick sheep that have delivered this landscape. And without the sheep it would look completely different to how you see it today.

JUDY: Beatrix Potter fought to protect Herdwick sheep but their numbers are dwindling. Over the past century, flock numbers have fallen from 359 to just 157. There are several reasons for the decline, but farmers here say it's mainly down to the government's environmental policy, a view that fewer sheep help to protect the environment and encourage rewilding, but Lakeland farmers say this is their heritage.

ISSAC: What they want to see is more habitat regeneration, and they don't look at the sheep as being able to provide that in the current stock in density. So what they want to see is reductions of the Herdwick sheep throughout the Lake District.

JUDY: In recent years 115 Herdwick farms have been sold.

AMANDA: I think it's very important that we recognise the importance of these rural communities and the Herdwick farmers working in those rural communities and that we don't continue this decline.

JUDY: Isaac Benson has opened a visitor centre to help explain why breeds like the Herdwick are so important. And the symbol of this iconic breed is everywhere.

ISSAC: The livestock, in particular the Herdwick sheep, is my identity. It is what binds me to the land. And if there is a role for me and my family, there has to be a role for my flock and my identity.

JUDY: He says Herdwick farming isn't just a livelihood; it's a way of life. (*BBC-20200908*)

Notes

Beatrix Potter：碧翠克丝·波特(1866—1943)，英国儿童文学作家与插画家，其创作中最知名的角色是彼得兔。

Lake District：湖区，即英国湖区国家公园，是世界自然遗产，位于英格兰西北部坎布里亚郡，方圆 2 300 平方千米。湖区是英国人的心灵之乡，其美景激发了许多作家和诗人的创作灵感。

Lakeland：即 Lake District，湖区。

Words and Expressions

breed *n.* (动植物的)品种
by-product *n.* 副产品
down to 由……引起(或造成)
dwindle *vi.* (逐渐)减少
fell *n.* 小山
graze *vt.* (在草地上)吃青草
habitat *n.* 栖息地
heritage *n.* 遗产
iconic *adj.* 符号的；标志性的；偶像的；非常出名或受欢迎的
livestock *n.* 牲畜
regeneration *n.* 复兴
rewilding *n.* (大片土地的)野化；恢复原始样貌

Questions

1. What is the relationship between the Lake District and agriculture?
2. What is the value of Herdwick farming?
3. How many flocks of Herdwick sheep remain today?
4. Why does the government's policy contribute to the decline of Herdwick flocks?

Gap-filling

JUDY: Herdwick sheep have ________ the Lake District ________ for centuries and ________ the incredible landscape. Isaac Benson's family has farmed this ________ for generations.

ISAAC: The Lake District is a(n) ________ of agriculture, and it is the Herdwick sheep that have ________ this landscape. And without the sheep it would look completely different to how you see it today.

JUDY: Beatrix Potter ________ to protect Herdwick sheep but their numbers are ________. Over the past century, flock numbers have fallen from 359 to just 157. There are several reasons for the ________, but farmers here say it's mainly down to the government's environmental policy, a view that ________ ________ sheep help to protect the environment and encourage ________, but Lakeland farmers say this is their ________.

Dictation

Isaac Benson has opened a visitor centre ... it's a way of life.

Translation

1. Herdwick sheep have grazed the Lake District fells for centuries and shaped the incredible landscape.
2. The Herdwick sheep is what binds me to the land.
3. Herdwick farming isn't just a livelihood; it's a way of life.

Post-class task

Discussion: Which side are you on, the government or the farmers? And why?

11. Hotspur New Stadium

ASAD: After almost a season's delay, Tottenham Hotspur has had a match played in its new £1 billion stadium. It was a test event ahead of the official opening in ten days' time. Chris Slegg was there.

BUS: We are now approaching White Hart Lane ...

CHRIS: Or Tottenham Hotspur Stadium, as the ground is now known until a sponsor is confirmed. For many fans, this was a first glimpse of their new home.

FAN 1: It's just awesome, it's huge. As you come down the station and it comes into view, it's like ...

FAN 2: I'm 50 this year, and I feel like a kid again. Just look at the smile, look at the smile. It's absolutely awesome.

CHRIS: A technical problem at the turnstiles meant the gates opened a little late, but when you've waited this long, what's an extra ten minutes?

FAN 3: Absolutely amazing. It'll be better when everything works properly. A few teething problems today, but that's what you'd expect, I guess, for a first event.

CHRIS: With 62,000 seats, right now this is the second biggest ground in the country behind only Manchester United's Old Trafford. Up to 30,000 will attend this first test event, an under-18s fixture. Next Saturday, 45,000 will be present for an exhibition game. And if all goes well, Tottenham can then officially open the ground for a Premier League fixture against Crystal Palace on April 3.

Everyone should be able to get served in the half-time rush, with technology to deliver 10,000 pints a minute. The Goal Line Bar, at 65 metres, is the longest in the UK. The new ground overlaps the site of the former one, with the old White Hart Lane centre spot marked here. The south stand alone holds 17,500 fans, making it one of the largest single-tier stands in Europe, designed to try and generate an atmosphere to rival the very best.

FAN 4: I love the fact that you can see the whole thing, you can see everybody. The noise when this stadium is going is going to be magnificent.

MUM: It's huge, massive. What do you think, Jess?

JESS: Good!

MUM: Yeah? You love it?

JESS: Yes!

CHRIS: Now to wait for the thumbs-up from the council—then Tottenham Hotspur will be coming home. Chris Slegg, BBC London News. (*BBC-20190324*)

Words and Expressions

fixture *n.* 体育赛事
massive *adj.* 巨大的
overlap *vt.* 与……重叠
pint *n.* 一品脱啤酒
Premier League （英国）超级联赛
rival *vt.* 与……相匹敌；比得上
sponsor *n.* 赞助商
stand *n.* 看台
teething problem 初期问题；萌芽期的困难
thumbs-up *n.* 批准
tier *n.* 层
turnstile *n.* 旋转栅门

Questions

1. Did the new stadium complete the construction according to the schedule?
2. Did everything go well in the first test event?
3. How many fans can be allowed in this new stadium?
4. How many fans can its largest single-tier stand accommodate?
5. Why do some fans prefer to watch a match on the spot instead of on TV?

Gap-filling

CHRIS: Everyone should be able to ____________ in the half-time rush, with technology to ____________ 10,000 pints a minute. The Goal Line Bar, at ____________ metres, is the longest in the UK. The new ground ____________ of the former one, with the old White Hart Lane centre spot ____________ here. The south stand alone holds 17,500 fans, making it one of the largest ____________ stands in Europe, designed to try and ____________ an atmosphere to ____________ the very best.

FAN 4: ____________ that you can see the whole thing, you can see everybody. The noise when this ____________ is going is going to be ____________.

Dictation

With 62,000 seats … April 3.

Translation

1. A few teething problems today, but that's what you'd expect for a first event.
2. Up to 30,000 will attend this first test event, an under-18s fixture.

3. The south stand is designed to try and generate an atmosphere to rival the very best.

Post-class task

Talk in class and share your experience of watching an exciting match on the spot.

12. House of Commons

MARY: So this time tomorrow, then MPs will be preparing for that historic vote, and our political correspondent Carl Dylan has been given special access to the House of Commons to explain how it's all going to happen.

CARL: The Prime Minister will wrap up the debate on her EU withdrawal agreement here at about 7 o'clock tomorrow night. And then it will be decision time. MPs will have a number of decisions to make that could easily be a couple of hours' worth of voting on amendments before the main vote on the agreement itself. At that point, they will all troop out here to the division lobbies. Those who agree with the Prime Minister, however reluctantly, will go through those doors. Those who disagree with the Prime Minister, and there may be many, will walk through these doors. Now, this is one of the most important places in the country, and yet we're hardly ever allowed to show you it. This is one of the two division lobbies of the House of Commons where decisions are made that affect people's lives, day in day out, but the decision MPs will make here tomorrow night, will be one of the most momentous that many of them have ever made in their careers. To cast their votes, they walk through the door that we just walked through or through one of these side doors and down here to where the clerks at the desks will take their names. Then they go through these doors where two tellers will count the number of votes, and that's it—they've voted, and everyone goes back into the chamber. And here we are behind the Speaker's Chair this time to hear the result. Now at that point, you may hear cheering from one side of the other because MPs will already know who's won once they see the tellers line up, because the tellers from the winning side always stand on this side of the Dispatch Box. And at that point, they will announce the result, and we will know whether the Prime Minister has carried the day or whether she's lost and has three days to come back here with a new plan. And we are potentially facing an almost unprecedented period—a political uncertainty. (*TFV-20190114*)

Notes

Dispatch Box：议会厅案头公文箱，英国下议院中央置于大臣站立发言处旁边的箱子。
House of Commons：（英国）下议院。

Words and Expressions

amendment *n.* 修订
carry the day 胜利；成功
chamber *n.* 会议厅
day in day out 日复一日
division lobby （英国议会的）分组表决厅
line up 排成一行
momentous *adj.* 重要的
reluctantly *adv.* 勉强地
teller *n.* 计票员
troop *vi.* 列队行进
unprecedented *adj.* 前所未有的
withdrawal *n.* 退出
wrap up 圆满完成

Questions

1. What has to be completed before the Brexit vote?
2. Will there be MPs who unwillingly vote for the Prime Minister?
3. How can MPs know the result of vote even before it is officially announced?

Gap-filling

CARL: The Prime Minister will ______________ the debate on her EU ____________ ____ agreement here at about ______________ tomorrow night. And then it will be decision time. MPs will have a number of decisions to make that could ________ ______ be a couple of hours' ______________ voting on ______________ before the main vote on the agreement itself. At that point, they will all ________ _____ here to the division lobbies. Those who agree with the Prime Minister, however ______________, will go through those doors. Those who disagree with the Prime Minister, and ______________, will walk through these doors.

Dictation

This is one of … into the chamber.

Translation

1. At that point, they will all troop out here to the division lobbies.

2. MPs will already know who's won once they see the tellers line up.
3. We will know whether the Prime Minister has carried the day or whether she's lost.

Post-class task

Do a research on the structure of the UK Parliament and write a short report in about 150 words.

13. Kate's Brand

JULIE: One of the Duchess of Cambridge's favorite fashion brands L. K. Bennett is on the brink of collapse tonight. It sets the high-end of high street, selling £300 dresses to women who can afford them, but it seems there aren't enough of those to sustain the business in this current form. So unless an investor steps in, the retailer once nicknamed "Kate's Closet" is poised to go into administration.

IVOR: She's been photographed in their outfits dozens of times, giving the royal seal of approval to L. K. Bennett on engagements all over the world. In the months after marrying William, Kate was rarely seen without the brand's trademark beige heels. It's even provided the now famous footwear worn by the Prime Minister on her first day in the job. But it seems high-profile fans are no longer enough on today's high street where experts say high-end is increasingly the wrong end to be pitching.

CATHERINE: Well, I think if you are a duchess, it's a great place to go shopping. For most normal women like myself, it's a little bit on the expensive side. So they're higher than the normal high street, a bit lower than Bond Street prices, but their prices have really gone up, so those dresses we see in the window are selling for about £325, and shoppers are just rejecting that as a price point.

IVOR: The brand has 41 shops in Britain and nearly 500 staff whose jobs are now at risk unless the company can secure urgent investment. Its most recent result showed an operating loss of nearly 6 million pounds.

It was founded in 1990, with the aim of bringing a bit of Bond Street luxury to the high street, but as costs rise and consumer confidence falls, the formula's fallen out of fashion.

Why do you not shop here?

WOMAN 1: Mm … So I think it's just too expensive for me. Mm … I am a nurse. I wouldn't be able to afford to shop here.

WOMAN 2: I think anything more than sort of £60 on a dress is pretty too much for me.

IVOR: Many of the dresses worn by Kate over the years have cost five times that. It used to be the case they'd sell out within hours of being seen on her. But what's fit for a duchess is no longer, it seems, fit for the high street. Ivor Bennet. News at Ten. (*ITV-20190301*)

Words and Expressions

beige *adj.* 米黄色的
collapse *n.* 倒闭
engagement *n.* 约会;约定;安排
footwear *n.* 鞋类
formula *n.* 方案;方法
go into administration 进入行政接管程序
heels *n.* 女高跟鞋
high-end *adj.* 高档的
high-profile *adj.* 引人注目的;高调的
high street *n.* 大街;主要街道
nickname *vt.* 给……起绰号
on the brink of 濒于
out of fashion 过时
outfit *n.* 全套服装;装束
pitch *vi.* 推销
poised (to do sth.) 准备好
retailer *n.* 零售商
seal of approval 批准;认可
trademark *adj.* 典型的;特有的

Questions

1. When and for what purpose was L. K. Bennett founded?
2. Why is this once famous brand unpopular today?
3. Is it possible for the brand to revive?
4. What is the acceptable price of a dress for normal UK women?
5. How influential was Kate in fashion?

Gap-filling

IVOR: She's been photographed in their ________________ dozens of times, giving the royal ________________ of approval to L. K. Bennett on ________________ all over the world. In the months after marrying William, Kate was ________________ seen without the brand's trademark ________________. It's even provided the now famous ________________ worn by the Prime Minister on her first day ________________. But it seems high-profile

__________________ are no longer enough on today's high street __________ ________ experts say high-end is increasingly the wrong end to be pitching.

CATHERINE: Well, I think if you are a(n) __________________, it's a great place to go shopping. For most normal women like __________________, it's a little bit on the expensive side. So they're higher than the normal high street, a bit ____ ______________ than Bond Street prices, but their prices have really ______ ____________, so those dresses we see in the window are selling for about __________________, and shoppers are just rejecting that as a price point.

Dictation

One of the Duchess ... go into administration.

Translation

1. Unless investors step in, the retailer is poised to go into administration.
2. She gave the royal seal of approval to the brand on engagements all over the world.
3. She was rarely seen without the brand's trademark beige heels.

Post-class task

Discussion: What is your favorite brand when purchasing a dress/lipstick/handbag, etc.?

14. London's ULEZ

RIZ: Good evening, and welcome to BBC London News, on Day One of the Mayor's new Ultra Low Emission Zone, or ULEZ, to help clean up the capital's air. It'll currently affect the same area as the congestion charge zone in central London from today. However, that'll be extended in two years' time, to include the area within the North and South Circular. Drivers of the most polluting cars, motorbikes and vans will be charged £12.50 a day. And for some lorries, £100. So, more specifically, if you drive a diesel over four years old or if you have a petrol car that's around 14 years old, you'll have to pay. Here's our transport correspondent Tom Edwards.

TOM: A dank Monday morning, and while most won't notice any changes, today the capital took a bold step in cleaning up its air.

Not everyone welcomes it, though. Sean Fitzgerald is a florist. He had to change his

old diesel van or pay the £12.50 a day to drive in central London.

SEAN: People are, like, really not happy with it. They just see it as a cash cow.

TOM: The Ultra Low Emission Zone was given the go-ahead by the previous mayor, Boris Johnson. But the current mayor brought it forward a year. These maps show the high pollution levels now. By 2025, London should be compliant with legal limits for pollutants like nitrogen dioxide. At the moment the zone only covers central London. But from 2021, the zone will expand to areas like Eltham.

We are right where the ULEZ boundary will be in 2021, but it cuts Eltham right in half. On that side of the boundary you won't have to pay, but on this side of the boundary, £12.50 a day if you drive your car if it's not compliant.

We showed the locals if they'd have to pay extra. Many weren't happy.

LOCAL: I don't want to change the car because there's nothing wrong with it. It's got quite a low mileage. So I just don't really know what I'm going to do.

TOM: City Hall says there's already been an increase in cleaner vehicles over the last two years ahead of the ULEZ. It says expanding the zone is necessary. Tom Edwards, BBC London News. (*BBC-20190408*)

Words and Expressions

boundary *n.* 边界
cash cow 摇钱树
circular *n.* 环线
compliant *adj.* 符合的
congestion *n.* 拥堵
dank *adj.* 阴冷潮湿的
diesel *n.* 柴油;柴油车
emission *n.* 排放
florist *n.* 花店店主
go-ahead *n.* 批准
mileage *n.* 里程数
nitrogen dioxide *n.* 二氧化氮
pollutant *n.* 污染物

Questions

1. What is the Mayor's purpose of introducing ULEZ?
2. What will be the charge for a polluting vehicle within ULEZ?
3. Why are some Londoners not happy about this new policy?

Gap-filling

RIZ: Good evening, and welcome to BBC London News, ____________________ of the Mayor's new Ultra Low ____________________ Zone, or ULEZ, to help clean up the capital's air. It'll currently ________________ the same area as the ____________ ________ zone in central London from today. However, that'll be ________________ in two years' time, to include the area within the North and South ________________. Drivers of the most polluting cars, motorbikes and ________________ will be charged ________________ a day. And for some ________________, £100. So, more specifically, if you drive a(n) ________________ over four years old or if you have a ________________ car that's around 14 years old, you'll have to pay.

Dictation

The Ultra Low Emission Zone … not compliant.

Translation

1. London should be compliant with legal limits for pollutants like nitrogen dioxide.
2. Many Londoners just see ULEZ as a cash cow.

Post-class task

Discussion: Do you think ULEZ is recommendable in big cities in China?

15. New Business

ASAD: A business in North London is celebrating a new multi-million-pound deal to supply sports equipment to China. They say they were prompted to look at new markets because of uncertainty over Brexit. But the firm says it still fears a no-deal breakaway in October. Here's Luke Hanrahan.

LUKE: At the sharp end, factory output has fallen at the fastest rate in seven years, as the risks posed by a no-deal Brexit rise. Here at London's oldest fencing-equipment manufacturer, they've worked tirelessly to ward off what they see as the worst-case scenario, now celebrating a multi-million-pound deal to supply China.

BEN: It's been a very difficult task for anyone to try and predict the millions of different possible outcomes.

LUKE: But it's fair to say, as a result of this unsettling period, it's pushed you to try and do this deal?

BEN: Yes, absolutely, yes, 100%—it's forced us to look outside our what I would call

regular European market.

LUKE: Hard work, but here at Leon Paul they acknowledge luck played its part. This facility, funded by London Olympic legacy money, coinciding with China's first fencing Olympic medal at the 2012 Games, which has seen the sport explode in popularity. At the moment, 40% of this British company's turnover comes from France and the rest of the European Union, but here they're worried that, in a no-deal scenario, that profit could evaporate, which is why this deal with China has come at such a fortuitous time, replacing 20% of that lost revenue.

BOYA: I think, for many British companies, their products have a huge market potential in China, but I think that British manufacturers need to further understand the market, understand the customers.

LUKE: A London business with longevity, doing its best to adapt to Brexit uncertainty by taking up opportunities elsewhere. Luke Hanrahan, BBC London. (*BBC-20190821*)

Words and Expressions

at the sharp end 关键时刻（在文中作双关语）
breakaway *n.* 脱离
coincide (with) 同时发生
evaporate *vi.* （逐渐）消失；消散
fencing *n.* 击剑运动
fortuitous *adj.* 幸运的
longevity *n.* 持久
popularity *n.* 受欢迎；普及
prompt *vt.* 促使
scenario *n.* 可能发生的事；可能出现的情况
unsettling *adj.* 令人紧张（不安）的
ward off 防止
worst-case *adj.* 最不利的

Questions

1. What is this fencing company's market share in Europe?
2. What percentage of market share will China offer?
3. Why is fencing booming in China?
4. What implication does this company's case bring to other British companies?

Gap-filling

LUKE: Hard work, but here at Leon Paul they ____________ luck played its part. This facility, ____________ by London Olympic legacy money, ____________ with China's first fencing Olympic ____________ at the 2012 Games, which has seen the sport ____________ in popularity.

At the moment, 40% of this British company's __________________ comes from France and the rest of the European Union, but here they're worried that, in a no-deal __________________, that profit could __________________, which is why this deal with China has come at such a(n) __________________ time, replacing 20% of that lost __________________.

Dictation

At the sharp end ... to supply China.

Translation

1. They've worked tirelessly to ward off what they see as the worst-case scenario.
2. They acknowledge luck played its part.
3. Their products have a huge market potential in China.

Post-class task

Retell the story.

16. Noisy Supercars

SONJA: There are calls to take a stronger action against drivers of noisy supercars in Kensington & Chelsea. Some residents say they're fed up with the roar of revving engines outside their homes. The council wants to trial new acoustic cameras to catch those responsible. Marc Ashdown has this report.

MARC: The supercar season is under way. This corner of West London has long been the favoured playground of the millionaire petrolhead. The noise from revving engines, however, has long caused anger among some residents. Perhaps, not for long. The government is trialling acoustic cameras to tackle ear-splitting engines.

They'll work just like a normal speed camera. As cars go past, a microphone picks up excessive noise; a camera then takes a picture of the license plate. The motorist could get a fine of up to £100.

Kensington & Chelsea is desperate to be part of the upcoming trials.

CLLR: We are hearing from residents all the time that say the noise is just completely intolerable. On a North Street summer's night, there has been an independent investigation that said the noise it can reach is sort of the average level of a rock concert, up to 130 decibels.

MARC: The Department for Transport told us it hasn't decided where these prototype cameras will be trialled, but it welcomes Kensington & Chelsea's enthusiasm.
Will the cameras be welcome?

LADY: They really rev it up, and they're having fun. I can understand that—they are young. But, you know, there are people with families living in this area. It would be quite nice if it was a bit more peaceful.

MAN: In general, it's not a big nuisance. I live in the area. To be honest ...

MARC: Do you think it will make a difference? I mean these guys are millionaires. If they got fined, would it stop them?

MAN: No, plus also I mean there are regulations in place already about how much noise a car can make, so I don't think it is going to make a big difference.

MARC: Love them or loathe them, the council doesn't want them to be seen, perhaps a bit less heard. Marc Ashdown, BBC London. (*BBC-20190818*)

Words and Expressions

acoustic *adj.* 声音的
decibel *n.* 分贝
desperate *adj.* 非常需要的;非常想要的;极想
ear-splitting *adj.* 震耳欲聋的
enthusiasm *n.* 热情;热心;热衷的活动
fed up (with) 厌烦
intolerable *adj.* 无法忍受的
license plate 车牌
loathe *vt.* 厌恶
motorist *n.* 驾车者
nuisance *n.* 麻烦事
petrolhead *n.* 车迷
prototype *n.* 样机
rev *vt.* & *vi.* (发动机)加快转速
roar *n.* 轰鸣声
trial *n.* & *vt.* 试用
under way 已经开始;在进行中

Questions

1. How noisy can some supercars be?
2. What device is going to be used to catch those responsible?
3. Is such move supported by the British government?
4. Will the fine deter those millionaire petrolheads?

Dictation

The supercar season ... up to £100.

Gap-filling

CLLR: We are hearing from ________________ all the time that say the noise is just completely ________________. On a North Street summer's night, there has been an independent investigation that said the noise ________________ is sort of the average level of a(n) ________________, up to 130 ________________.

MARC: The Department for Transport ________________ it hasn't decided where these ________________ cameras will be ________________, but it welcomes Kensington & Chelsea's ________________.

Translation

1. Some residents are fed up with the roar of revving engines outside their homes.
2. They really rev it up.
3. In general, it's not a big nuisance.

Post-class task

Discussion: Are you also annoyed by supercar noises? Why (not)?

17. Ole Solskjaer

SOPHIE: Manchester United have appointed Ole Gunnar Solskjaer as permanent manager on a three-year contract. The Norwegian arrived at Old Trafford on an interim basis in December to replace Jose Mourinho. He spent 11 seasons as a United player, scoring the winning goal in the 1999 Champions League final. Our sports editor Dan Roan has more.

DAN: As a player, he was super sub, and as a coach, he came on loan. But today, Ole Gunnar Solskjaer became the main man at Manchester United, handed one of the biggest jobs in world football on a permanent basis.

OLE: I always had that dream in my mind to have this responsibility for this huge, fantastic, family of a football club. I'm so honoured and privileged to be given this fantastic responsibility to lead us forward.

DAN: Jose Mourinho's toxic reign at Old Trafford came to an end in December, sacked amid fallouts with key players. With a modest coaching track record, Solskjaer came as a temporary measure, most assuming there'd be a big name replacement this summer. But the Norwegian transformed United's fortunes, winning 14 of the 19 games he's managed, and masterminding one of the club's greatest ever victories against PSG—a win that effectively secured him the job.

ANDY: The way he started, the way he's gone about his business, got results. They play football, the smile on the players' faces, and the staff and everyone. It's like, wow, you know he's done something special.

DAN: Solskjaer becomes the fourth manager in six years, tasked with reviving the glory days of the Sir Alex Ferguson era. In short time he's reinvigorated the spirit of this club and promoted young players. But now the true test begins, and some believe the appointment of a director of football and some new signings are needed to help him succeed in the long term.

Solskjaer won everything as a player here, his injury time winner in the 1999 Champions League final ensuring a legendary status. The hope now that he delivers similar success from the dugout in this, his dream job. Dan Roan, BBC News, Old Trafford. (*BBC-20190328*)

Notes

Jose Mourinho：何塞·穆里尼奥，2016—2018 年任曼联主教练，因战绩不佳而提前下课。

Old Trafford：老特拉福德球场，曼联主场，英国第二大足球场，约有 76 000 个观众座位。

PSG：巴黎圣日耳曼队。

Sir Alex Ferguson：亚历克斯·弗格森爵士，前曼联主教练，执教长达 27 年，率领曼联夺得 13 次英超联赛冠军、2 次欧洲冠军联赛冠军、5 次英格兰足总杯冠军等 38 项冠军，并在 1998—1999 赛季帮助曼联实现“三冠王”，1999 年被英国皇室授予下级勋位爵士。

Words and Expressions

amid *prep.* 在……之中
dugout *n.* 球员席
fallout *n.* 不良影响
injury time （英式足球等运动）伤停补时
interim *adj.* 暂时的
legendary *adj.* 传奇的
mastermind *vt.* 策划
privileged *adj.* 幸运的
reign *n.* 主宰
reinvigorate *vt.* 使再振作
sack *vt.* 解雇
signing *n.* 签约球员
super sub 超级替补
track record 业绩记录
winner *n.* 制胜的一记入球

Questions

1. Do you know Ole's glorious past?
2. Did Ole come to MU as a permanent manager in the beginning?
3. What achievements helped secure his new job?
4. What is Ole's reaction to the new appointment?
5. What is the name of MU's home ground?

Gap-filling

DAN: Solskjaer becomes the fourth manager in six years, ________________ with reviving the glory days of the Sir Alex Ferguson ________________. In short time he's ________________ the spirit of this club and promoted young players. But now the ________________ begins, and some believe the appointment of a(n) ________________ of football and some new ________________ are needed to help him succeed in the long ________________.

Solskjaer won everything as a player here. His injury time ________________ in the 1999 Champions ________________ final ensuring a legendary ________________. The hope now that he ________________ similar success from the dugout in this, his dream job. Dan Roan, BBC News, Old Trafford.

Dictation

Jose Mourinho's … him the job.

Translation

1. As a player, he was super sub, and as a coach, he came on loan.
2. With a modest coaching track record, he came as a temporary measure.
3. Most people assumed there'd be a big name replacement this summer.

Post-class task

Do a research on Manchester United and write a report about its glorious history.

18. Pound Devaluation

ASAD: So, the pound has hit a two-year low against the dollar and the rate against the euro, well, that's not much better. Holiday-makers heading abroad are feeling the pinch, but on the flip side, tourists coming to London are deciding to spend, spend, spend. But it's not good news for everyone, as Tolu Adeoye found out.

TOLU: There is food and drink from all over Europe here at Borough Market. With the pound falling to a two-year low against the euro and the dollar yesterday, traders who rely on imports are nervy.

MAN: In the last two years, due to the devaluation of the pound, we are definitely under a lot of pressure.

TOLU: Amy's family business has been at the market for 20 years.

AMY: This is definitely the hardest time, just dealing with all of our products being paid for in euros. The exchange rate is a real issue and our suppliers in France are anxious about the future as well.

TOLU: The Federation of Small Businesses say many are struggling and could go bust if no plan is in place come Brexit day in October.

SUE: What needs to happen is we are really urging the Government and the Bank of England to stabilise the pound, keep it absolutely stable, that's crucial, because 31 October might be too late for some of these businesses.

TOLU: They say there are two sides to every story, and while a weaker pound is bad news for companies that rely on importing, it can be good news for tourists that are spending money here in London.

The Bernardo family are visiting from Italy. They say getting more pounds for their euros makes London a more attractive destination.

BERNARDO: It's important, because you can buy more things here.

TOLU: And there are businesses like this tour bus company that say the weaker pound has meant more customers.

ANDY: In the last couple of years we have seen really good sales figures. Because of low value of the pound, it's brought a lot of additional international tourists into London.

TOLU: The pound has already recovered some from yesterday's dip, but many worry there is worse to come if we leave the EU without a deal. Tolu Adeoye, BBC London. (*BBC-20190731*)

Notes

Borough Market：波若市场，伦敦最著名的食品市场，有千年历史，坐落在伦敦大桥南端，出售传统英国食物和世界各国的特色食物，食材新鲜，品种丰富。

Words and Expressions

come *prep.* 当……到来时
devaluation *n.* 贬值
dip *n.* 下跌
feel the pinch 感到手头有点紧
flip side 反面；对应面
go bust 破产
nervy *adj.* 紧张的

Questions

1. Why did the pound suffer huge devaluation during this period?
2. Who benefits more when the pound is devalued?
3. Who is responsible for stabilising the pound?

Gap-filling

ASAD: So, the pound has ________________ a two-year low against the dollar and the ________________ against the euro, ________________, that's not much better. Holiday-makers ________________ are feeling the pinch, but on the ________________, tourists coming to London are deciding to spend, spend, spend. But it's not good news for ________________, as Tolu Adeoye found out.

TOLU: There is ________________ and drink from all over Europe here at Borough ________________. With the pound ________________ to a two-year low against the euro and the dollar yesterday, ________________ who rely on imports are ________________.

MAN: In the last two ________________, due to the ________________ of the pound, we are definitely under a lot of ________________.

Dictation

What needs to happen … a more attractive destination.

Translation

1. Holiday-makers heading abroad are feeling the pinch.
2. Many could go bust if no plan is in place come Brexit day in October.

Post-class task

Discussion: Do you wish a weaker or stronger pound if you plan to study in the UK? Why?

19. Right Direction

LOUISE: Sir David Attenborough, what an absolute pleasure to be able to speak to you. Thank you so much. Where are we with the planet right now? How would you summarise, how would you assess it?

DAVID: Since I made the first television programme, there's three times as many people on the planet as it was then. And we have overrun it. And now we are realising what appalling damage we've done.

LOUISE: You seem to have, and there is a particular moment in the film, where we can really get a sense of your feeling of grief. But you don't despair, do you? Why not?

DAVID: I don't despair because what would you go and do? Just go and hide in a corner, crying in a corner, and forgetting it all and giving up? I mean, we have a responsibility. And if there is a fragment of hope left, you have the responsibility to do something about it, which is why we are here.

LOUISE: In the face of, you know, huge countries like China or Brazil or the United States doing something entirely different, it seems irrelevant, sometimes.

DAVID: Well, we have to do what's in our power. We can't take that sort of excuse for doing nothing. We must do everything that all of us can do and must do. And China is taking very big steps, you know, in very many directions. It is a huge country with an immense population and they are starting doing things about sorting out their climate and their weather which have caused them such problems. So China is moving in the right direction. I agree that the present administration in America is, from a natural(ist) ... from a conservationist point of view, disastrous. But there we are. I mean, that is who's been elected and we have to go through it.

LOUISE: If there is one choice to make today, what choice would you like people to make?

DAVID: Don't waste. Don't waste anything. Don't waste electricity. Don't waste food. Don't waste power. Just treat the natural world as though it's precious, which it is, and don't squander those bits of it that we have control of. (*BBC-20201003*)

Notes

Sir David Attenborough: 大卫·爱登堡爵士,英国自然博物学家、探险家,54年间与BBC的制作团队一起实地探索过地球上已知的所有生态环境,拍摄了30多部电视系列片,被誉为"世界自然纪录片之父",1985年被授封为爵士。2020年10月的纪录片 *David Attenborough: A Life on Our Planet* 发行后接受本文记者的专访。

Words and Expressions

appalling *adj.* 令人震惊的;使人惊骇的
conservationist *n.* 环境保护主义者
despair *vi.* 绝望
fragment *n.* 碎片
grief *n.* 悲伤;伤心
irrelevant *adj.* 不相关的
naturalist *n.* 博物学家
overrun *vt.* 超过;肆虐
sort out 解决,处理
squander *vt.* 浪费,挥霍
there we are 别无他法;无计可施;只能这样了

Questions

1. Why doesn't David despair even though he is sad about the present situation?
2. What does David think about China?
3. What does David think about the USA?
4. What is David's advice to the world?

Gap-filling

LOUISE: In the face of, you know, huge countries like China or ________________ or the United States doing something entirely different, it seems ________________, sometimes.

DAVID: Well, we have to do what's in our ________________. We can't take that sort of excuse for doing nothing. We must do everything that ________________ can do and must do. And China is taking very big ________________, you know, in very many directions. It is a huge country with an ________________ population and they are starting doing things about ________________ their climate and their weather which have caused them such ________________. So China is moving in the right direction. I agree that the present __________________ in America is, from a natural(ist) ... from a conservationist point of view, ________________. But there we are. I mean, that is who's been ________________ and we have to ________________ it.

Dictation

You seem to have ... why we are here.

Translation

1. If there is a fragment of hope left, you have the responsibility to do something about it.
2. We have to do what's in our power.
3. Just treat the natural world as though it's precious, which it is.

Post-class task

Watch at least one of the following series of BBC documentaries narrated by Sir David Attenborough, such as *Blue Planet I & II*; *Planet Earth I & II*; *Seven Worlds*, *One Planet*; *Dynasties*; *The Hunt*; *Frozen Planet*; *Africa*; and *Life*.

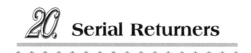

20. Serial Returners

CHARLENE: Online stores are threatening to cancel the M Accounts of customers who routinely over-order or wear clothes before returning them. While free return is the upside for shoppers, there is the downside for sellers like ASOS, who have now changed their policy. Rebecca Barry has more.

REBECCA: It's the UK's biggest independent online fashion site that helps revolutionize the way we shop for clothes. ASOS made it easy to bulk-buy, try on at home, then send back anything unwanted. But now, it's cracking down on so-called "serial returners".

SOPHIE: None of these items are kept. These I didn't keep.

REBECCA: 28-year-old Sophie orders from ASOS once a week. But most of it ends up going back. Now, be honest. Do you sometimes wear an item and return it?

SOPHIE: Yeah, the shoes are definitely. Yeah, I wear them for the day, see if they are comfy, see if I can walk around in them, clean the bottom off the soil, package them up and return them.

REBECCA: Do you feel guilty about that?

SOPHIE: No.

REBECCA: So today, ASOS customers received this email saying, "If we notice an unusual pattern of returns activity ... for example, we suspect someone's actually wearing their purchases and then returning them, we might have to deactivate the account." Recent research suggests almost half of what UK consumers spend online on clothes ends up being refunded. Social media is thought to have contributed to the so-called "snap and send back" culture.

IMOGEN: Oh, yes!

REBECCA: Influencer Imogenation has more than 300,000 subscribers on YouTube, who watch her clothing haul videos.

IMOGEN: I am answering some questions for ITV News.

REBECCA: We asked her to make a vlog for us about the new ASOS's rules.

IMOGEN: I do clothing hauls where I order from multiple websites online and I showcase what I bought to my followers. The thought that maybe we are gonna get our account looked into and banned because other people may have abused the policy—the returns policy in the past, it really does worry me.

REBECCA: ASOS pioneered easy returns. Now that they are changing the rules, others will inevitably follow suit. Rebecca Barry, ITV News. (*ITV-20190405*)

Notes

M Account：维珍理财英国公司(Virgin Money UK)推出的一款现金账户，允许用户在信用差、经济拮据时仍能适量透支提现。

Words and Expressions

abuse *vt.* 滥用
bulk-buy *vt.* 批量购买
comfy = comfortable *adj.* 舒适的
crack down on 严厉打击
deactivate *vt.* 关闭
downside *n.* 缺点
follow suit 仿效
haul *n.* 视频购物分享；直播带货
package *vt.* 将……包装好
pioneer *vt.* 开创，开发；倡导
refund *vt.* 退款
revolutionize *vt.* 彻底改变
routinely *adv.* 惯常地
showcase *vt.* 展示
subscriber *n.* 追随者；粉丝
upside *n.* 优点
vlog = video log *n.* 视频博客

Questions

1. What potential risk do online stores face?
2. Does the serial returner feel she is doing anything wrong?
3. What sort of items are most frequently returned?
4. Does social media have anything to do with the current shopping trend?

Gap-filling

REBECCA: It's the UK's biggest independent online fashion site that helps ________________ the way we shop for clothes. ASOS made it easy to ________________, try on at home, then send back anything ________________. But now, it's cracking down on so-called "________________ returners".

SOPHIE: None of these items are ________________. These I didn't keep.

REBECCA: ________________-year-old Sophie orders from ASOS once a week. But ________________ ends up going back. Now, be honest. Do you sometimes wear ________________ and return it?

SOPHIE: Yeah, the ________________ are definitely. Yeah, I wear them for the day, see if they are ________________, see if I can walk around ________________, clean the bottom off the ________________, package them up and return them.

Dictation

So today … "snap and send back" culture.

Translation

1. Almost half of what UK consumers spend online on clothes ends up being refunded.
2. I showcase what I bought to my followers.
3. Now that they are changing the rules, others will inevitably follow suit.
4. Social media is thought to have contributed to the so-called "snap and send back" culture.

Post-class task

Discussion:

1. Please share your online shopping experience, and give an instance of being refunded.
2. Do you follow a hauler online, or can you be influenced by a clothing haul?
3. Pros and cons of live commerce.

21. Sniffing Out Covid

KYLIE: Scientists have been given half a million pounds to teach sniffer dogs to detect Covid-19 before symptoms even appear. They'll try to teach the canines to use that powerful sense of smell to spot the virus, and it's hoped it can be added to the list of diseases that dogs can already identify, like cancer and Parkinson's. Ivor Bennett explains.

IVOR: Already man's best friend, can they and their noses be its savior too? By harnessing these dogs unique sense of smell, scientists in London and Durham are hoping they can train them to sniff out Coronavirus before symptoms appear, and create an early warning system that could prove vital in stopping the spread of the disease.

JAMES: This is not some sort of old wives' tale. There's, you know, a lot of research for the last 20 years of this being published in scientific journals, scientifically proven that dogs can do this. Most diseases do have a distinctive odour. Covid-19 could be exactly the same.

IVOR: Sniffer dogs like Kiwi are already used in some medical settings. She's been taught to identify prostate cancer while others trained by the charity that filmed these videos can detect malaria and Parkinson's too, even when diluted to the equivalent of one teaspoon of sugar in two Olympic-sized swimming pools. Six dogs, all Labradors and cocker spaniels, will be put through their paces for the Covid trials with odour samples taken from the face masks and nylon stockings of NHS staff in London.

JAMES: Yeah, I think this could be profoundly impactful on the spread of the disease. You know, being able to diagnose people and detect people who are infected before they have any symptoms is extremely important. And that's what we're focusing on.

IVOR: If successful, the dogs could be deployed within months, each one able to screen 250 people per hour.

LINDSAY: For me that the main use would be ports of entry in airports, just in the same way that we use dogs now for detecting explosives or people carrying drugs. You'd have the dogs there as the first line of defense.

IVOR: Defenses that still need all the help they can get. Ivor Bennett, ITV News. (*ITV-20200516*)

Notes

NHS：即 National Health Service，（英国）国家医疗服务体系。

Words and Expressions

canine *n.* 犬
cocker spaniel 长耳猎犬；可卡犬
deploy *vt.* 部署；利用
dilute *vt.* 稀释
distinctive *adj.* 独特的；特别的
explosive *n.* 爆炸物
harness *vt.* 利用
impactful *adj.* 有效的；有影响力的
Labrador *n.* 拉布拉多猎犬（常用于导盲）
malaria *n.* 疟疾
nylon *n.* 尼龙
odour *n.* 气味
old wives' tale 无稽之谈；迷信
Parkinson's（disease）帕金森病
port of entry 入境口岸
prostate *n.* 前列腺
savior *n.* 拯救者；救星
sniffer dog （训练来嗅查毒品或炸药的）嗅探犬
symptom *n.* 症状

Questions

1. What kind of disease can sniffer dogs already detect?
2. How powerful can some dogs be in detecting diseases?
3. How many dogs are being trained to sniff out Covid-19?
4. Where might be the most needed place for such dogs to be deployed?

Gap-filling

IVOR: Already man's best friend, can they and their ________ be its ________ too? By ________ these dogs unique sense of smell, scientists in ________ and Durham are hoping they can ________ them to sniff out Coronavirus before ________ appear, and create an early warning system that could prove ________ in stopping the ________ of the disease.

JAMES: This is not some sort of old wives' ________. There's, you know, a lot of research for the last 20 years of this being published in scientific ________, scientifically proven that dogs can do this. Most diseases do have a distinctive ________. Covid-19 could be exactly the same.

Dictation

Sniffer dogs like Kiwi ... NHS staff in London.

Translation

1. This is not some sort of old wives' tale.
2. Most diseases do have a distinctive odour.
3. The dogs can detect malaria and Parkinson's, even when diluted to the equivalent of one teaspoon of sugar in two Olympic-sized swimming pools.

Post-class task

Discussion: Are you a dog lover? Why (not)?

22. Top Tourist Attractions

ALICE: Many of the country's top tourist attractions, like the British Museum, Tate Modern and the National Portrait Gallery, are here in London. And new figures show just how popular they are. Sonja Jessup has the details.

SONJA: From students taking time out in the Turbine Hall to art lovers admiring the aerial sculptures, Tate Modern is drawing more of us through its doors, crowned today as the UK's top visitor attraction.

VISITOR 1: It's value for money, I think, as well. And there's so much space, you can bring little kids.

VISITOR 2: I work with theatre, so I'm constantly here trying to find details that I can steal for myself.

VISITOR 3: It's very easy just to wander in and out of somewhere for a couple of hours and take my kids.

SONJA: Tate Modern attracted almost 5.9 million visitors last year, a rise of 3% on the year before and knocking the British Museum into second spot. It had 5.8 million visits, down by 1%. The National Gallery came in third place. It had 5.7 million visits, up 9%.

BERNARD: I think we've just been reminded of the amazing cultural assets that we have on our doorstep, and Brits in particular have just fallen back in love with holidaying

in Britain and in London again.

SONJA: Some outdoor attractions did take a hit last year, blamed on the extreme weather. At RHS Garden Wisley, visitor numbers dropped by more than 70,000, while, unsurprisingly, big blockbusters like Picasso at Tate Modern, proved popular.

FRANCES: One of the marvellous things about the blockbusters is that they are trust-builders. If you take an artist who's well known, then high on name recognition, there're very enticing shows to bring people in to demonstrate they can get great value out of art, but then introduce them to some other maybe more challenging things.

SONJA: But what about next year? Will tourists continue to flock here post-Brexit? There's concern that continued uncertainty over travel plans could put them off. Oversea visitor numbers are already down. It's hoped that Londoners and people from other parts of the UK will continue to come, perhaps holiday at home and explore what's on their doorstep. Sonja Jessup, BBC London News. (*BBC-20190327*)

Words and Expressions

asset *n.* 资产
crown *vt.* 给予荣誉;授予称号
enticing *adj.* 诱人的
holiday *vi.* 度假
on one's doorstep 离……很近
put off 使反感;使疏远
sculpture *n.* 雕塑
take a hit 受到严重影响
value for money 物有所值

Questions

1. Can you name UK's top three tourist attractions?
2. What are the common reasons for tourists to enjoy visiting Tate Modern?
3. How can a museum keep its constant attraction?
4. Which sector of tourism became less visited and why?

Gap-filling

SONJA: From students taking time out in the ________ Hall to art lovers admiring the ________ sculptures, Tate Modern is ________ more of us through its doors, ________ today as the UK's top visitor attraction.

VISITOR 1: It's ________ for money, I think, as well. And there's so much

__________, you can bring little kids.

VISITOR 2: I work with __________, so I'm constantly here trying to find details that I can __________ for myself.

VISITOR 3: It's very easy just to __________ in and out of somewhere for a couple of hours and take my kids.

Dictation

I think we've just ... proved popular.

Translation

1. Tate Modern is crowned today as the UK's top visitor attraction.
2. Some outdoor attractions did take a hit last year, blamed on the extreme weather.
3. Uncertainty over travel plans could put tourists off.

Post-class task

Discussion: What are the top tourist attractions in your local city?

23. Toxic London

VICTORIA: Three-quarters of patients in London have been found to be registered at GP surgeries where the air outside is "toxic", according to a study by campaigners. Lambeth and Newham fared worst, where every doctor's surgery is situated in streets where pollution levels are breaching guidelines. Here's our environment correspondent Tom Edwards.

PHOEBE: Normally, this is absolutely congested. It is full of traffic, especially at school run time.

TOM: Phoebe has asthma, but to get to her doctor's surgery in Mortlake, she has to walk along the busy South Circular.
Does it worry you, I mean, the levels of pollution, having to walk along here to your GP surgery?

PHOEBE: Yes, it really worries me. I mean, I am already ill, and I am making my health worse.

TOM: And like many other Londoners, her doctor's surgery is also in an area where the pollution is high.

And you mentioned before, you were trying to get to the GP surgery when you were having an asthma attack, so that's …

PHOEBE: Absolutely. I had no idea; it was my first asthma attack. And I arrived at the GP surgery, they immediately put me on a nebulizer. And he said, you know, "I may still yet have to send you to hospital. Let's see how we go." I had to go back every day to see him. Obviously I am going always along the road and through into these high pollution areas.

DOCTOR: Big breath in. Keep going.

TOM: Campaigners say that the latest figures show that 7.5 million patients attend a surgery in areas that breach air pollution limits. The worst boroughs are Lambeth, Newham and Tower Hamlets. The Government says its Clean Air Strategy has new targets and powers for local government, and the Mayor is planning an Ultra Low Emission Zone, where older, more polluting vehicles will have to pay. But campaigners want much more.

POLLY: It's great we are gonna have the Ultra Low Emission Zone, here in London, which will make a significant difference to cleaning up our air, but overall, we need a national framework with strong national laws and strong national investment, in helping us all make a shift to cleaner ways of getting around.

TOM: A summit on Thursday in London will try and find more solutions. Many like Phoebe, though, want much cleaner air where she lives, now. Tom Edwards, BBC London News. (*BBC-20190211*)

Words and Expressions

asthma *n.* 哮喘
borough *n.* 行政区
breach *vt.* 违背;违犯(法规等)
campaigner *n.* 运动倡导者;活动家
congested *adj.* 拥挤的
fare worst 情况最糟糕
get around 出行
GP = general practitioner 全科医生
guideline *n.* 指导原则
nebulizer *n.* 喷雾器
school run 接送学童上学(或放学)的行程
strategy *n.* 策略;行动计划
summit *n.* 峰会
surgery *n.* 诊所
toxic *adj.* 有毒的

Questions

1. What has caused the toxic air quality in London?

2. What health issue is likely to be caused by bad air?
3. What is London's decision to clean up the air?

Gap-filling

VICTORIA: Three-quarters of patients in London have been found to be ________________ at GP surgeries where the air outside is "toxic", according to a study by ________________. Lambeth and Newham ________________, where every doctor's surgery is ________________ in streets where pollution levels are ________________ guidelines. Here's our environment correspondent Tom Edwards.

PHOEBE: Normally, this is absolutely ________________. It is full of traffic, ________________ at school run time.

TOM: Phoebe has ________________, but to get to her doctor's surgery in Mortlake, she has to walk along the busy South Circular.

Dictation

Campaigners say that … ways of getting round.

Translation

1. They immediately put me on a nebulizer.
2. Patients attend a surgery in areas that breach air pollution limits.
3. The framework can help us all make a shift to cleaner ways of getting around.

Post-class task

Discussion: The feasible ways to clean up the air.

24. Treasure Trove

SOPHIE: A couple using a metal detector in Somerset have uncovered thousands of silver coins dating back to 1066 in the Battle of Hastings. It's the second largest find of Norman coins ever uncovered in the UK. Here's Jon Kay.

(*Oh my God. There's pennies everywhere.*)

JON: In a muddy Somerset field, the discovery of a lifetime. This was the moment metal detectorists found more than 2,000 silver coins. (*There's another one. Lovely.*) Today, looking like lottery winners, Lisa Grace and her partner Adam Staples, came to inspect their jackpot.

LISA: They're in fantastic condition.

JON: Now, all cleaned up and catalogued at the British Museum in London.

LISA: Just a fantastic find and I don't think we'll ever find anything like it again.

ADAM: No, it's a dream come true.

EXPERT: I think it's King Harold.

JON: Experts say the hoard is hugely significant. Half the coins are from the reign of King Harold II. The rest were minted when Harold was defeated by William the Conqueror at the Battle of Hastings in 1066. (*There's another one as well.*) Lisa, Adam and their friends couldn't believe it when their metal detectors just kept beeping.

ADAM: It went from two to ten, to 50 to 100, to wow, how many are there? And from then on, it was just crazy.

JON: That's a lot of beeps. (*Yeah.*) I bet you were saying a lot of beeps as well, weren't you, when it happened?

LISA: Oh, yeah. There was a lot of swearing going on.

JON: The precise location where the hoard was found is being kept top secret, but it's somewhere here in the Chew Valley.

If a coroner declares it treasure, then the landowner and the group of metal detectorists could share a reward, possibly millions of pounds.

So what are you going to do with the money when it comes?

LISA: Maybe buy a house, yeah.

ADAM: Maybe more than one.

JON: It's hoped the hoard will go on display in Somerset although at least one private collector also wants to buy it. Jon Kay, BBC News. (*BBC-20190828*)

Notes

Battle of Hastings：黑斯廷斯战役，发生在1066年10月14日，是英格兰国王哈罗德二世的军队与诺曼底公爵征服者威廉的军队在英格兰南部海岸的黑斯廷斯地域进行的一场交战，以征服者威廉获胜告终。此战意义重大，扫清了威廉继承英国王位的所有障碍；此后的300年中英国的贵族语言是法语，从而在英语中增添了大量由法语演变而来的词汇。

Harold II：哈罗德二世，英格兰最后一位盎格鲁-撒克逊国王。1066年，在黑斯廷斯战役中，他的军队被征服者威廉的军队击败,哈罗德战死。

Somerset:萨默塞特郡,位于英格兰西南部。

William the Conqueror:征服者威廉,英格兰的第一位诺尔曼国王,又称"威廉一世";1066年他率军队入侵英国,并在黑斯廷斯战役中打败哈罗德二世。

Words and Expressions

catalogue *vt.* 登记
coroner *n.* 无主珍宝调查官
detectorist *n.* 探测器使用者
hoard *n.* 秘藏
jackpot *n.* 头奖
lottery *n.* 抽彩给奖法
mint *vt.* 铸造
Norman *adj.* 诺曼人的
reign *n.* 君主统治时期
swearing *n.* 脏话
treasure trove 无主宝藏

Questions

1. How many coins were found?
2. How old are the coins?
3. Who will benefit from this discovery?

Gap-filling

JON: Experts say the ________________ is hugely significant. Half the coins are from the ________________ of King Harold II. The rest were ________________ when Harold was defeated by William the ________________ at the Battle of Hastings in ________________. (*There's another one as well.*) Lisa, Adam and their friends couldn't believe it when their ________________ detectors just kept beeping.

ADAM: It went from two to ten, to 50 to ________________, to wow, how many are there? And from then on, it was just ________________.

JON: That's a lot of beeps. (*Yeah.*) I bet you were saying a lot of beeps as well, ________________, when it happened?

LISA: Oh, yeah. There was a lot of ________________ going on.

Dictation

In a muddy … anything like it again.

Translation

1. Half the coins are from the reign of King Harold II.
2. The precise location where the hoard was found is being kept top secret.

Post-class task

Describe a situation where you have discovered something extremely valuable.

25. Young Gamblers

SOPHIE: Well, the number of children classed as problem gamblers has quadrupled to more than 50,000 in just two years according to a study by the Gambling Commission. It also says almost half a million children aged 11 to 16 are betting more regularly than drinking alcohol, smoking or taking drugs. Sima Kotecha reports.

SIMA: Some of society's most vulnerable turning to gambling. Children young as 11 betting with friends in playgrounds, using slot machines and buying scratchcards.

MATT: I got addicted very quickly. And that's a pretty common characteristic of children that get into gambling. It's the parts of the brain that regulate risk unproperly developed. Yeah, I became addicted within weeks of starting gambling.

SIMA: Today's report indicates a worrying rise in the number of young gamblers. Nearly 3,000 people aged 11-16 were surveyed. 1.7% of those were deemed to be problem gamblers. Extrapolating that across England, Scotland and Wales, it would be the equivalent of 55,000 youngsters.

Loot boxes sold on some of the world's most popular video games have come under criticism, with the commission saying almost a million young people were exposed to gambling through them. People pay to see what virtual item is inside the box, and critics say that process can fuel addiction. Campaigners want fewer adverts on prime time television, while others are calling on gambling companies to put money towards helping those worst affected.

LORD: I want 1%, and that would produce £140 million a year, so we could treat people, we could educate people.

SIMA: Ministers say they expect the Gambling Commission to take the strongest action against organisations that don't behave responsibly. Campaigners want today's findings to instigate change, with some warning that without new legislation these children could be at risk of ruining their lives. Sima Kotecha, BBC News. (*BBC-20181121*)

Words and Expressions

advert *n.* 电视广告	loot *n.* 战利品
be exposed to 接触	prime time (广播与电视的)黄金时段
class *vt.* 把……分类	quadruple *vt.* 成四倍;翻两番
commission *n.* 委员会	regulate *vt.* 约束;控制
deem *vt.* 认为	scratchcard *n.* 刮奖卡
extrapolate *vt.* 类推出	slot machine 投币式自动赌博机
fuel *vt.* 增加;刺激	virtual *adj.* 虚拟的
instigate *vt.* 发起	vulnerable *adj.* 脆弱的;易受……伤害的
legislation *n.* 法规	

Questions

1. What might be the cause of young gamblers?
2. What types of gambling do teenagers tend to engage in?
3. Why is gambling easy to be addictive to young people?
4. What measure can be adopted to reduce young gamblers?

Gap-filling

SOPHIE: Well, the number of children ________________ problem gamblers has ________________ to more than 50,000 in just two years according to a study by the Gambling ________________. It also says almost half a million children aged 11 to 16 are ________________ more regularly than drinking ________________, smoking or taking drugs. Sima Kotecha reports.

SIMA: Some of society's most ________________ turning to gambling. Children young as 11 betting with friends in playgrounds, using ________________ machines and buying scratchcards.

MATT: I got ________________ very quickly. And that's a pretty common characteristic of children that get into gambling. It's the parts of the brain that ________________ risk unproperly ________________. Yeah, I became addicted within weeks, starting gambling.

Dictation

Loot boxes sold … those worst affected.

Translation

1. It's the parts of the brain that regulate risk unproperly developed.
2. Many young people were exposed to gambling through loot boxes.
3. The process of paying to see virtual items can fuel addiction.
4. Campaigners want today's findings to instigate change.

Post-class task

Discussion:

1. Do you know of anybody who is addicted to something unhealthy or illegal? What happened to him/her?
2. How to prevent addition?

Part II

扫码看视频

扫码填空

扫码听写

26. Armistice Day

NINA: The scale of Armistice Day commemorations may have been reduced by virus restrictions, but the simpler ceremonies lacked nothing of the enduring gratitude felt for the country's war dead. The bravery and sacrifice will be remembered as ... the same as they always are around the UK, and in London there was a particular poignancy with the 100th anniversary of the tomb of the Unknown Warrior in Westminster Abbey.

CHRIS: The annual pause at 11 o'clock on Armistice Day this year looked so very different. Different too for the Prince of Wales and Duchess of Cornwall, they arrived with masks at Westminster Abbey. The planned service here for 2,000 people were scaled back to just 80, each spaced apart.

CHARLES: Greater love hath no man than this, that a man lay down his life for his friends.

CHRIS: And this was the reason they had gathered here, the grave of the Unknown Warrior. Exactly a hundred years ago, the body of a soldier, name and rank unknown, was chosen from one of the many World War I battlefields. On November 11, 1920, King George V placed flowers on the coffin, and then unveiled the newly-built Cenotaph for the very first time. The King then followed the coffin on foot to a new grave in Westminster Abbey.

Today, Prince Charles placed a wreath at that spot, a replica of the one his great grandfather laid a century before. After the body of the Unknown Warrior was laid here in his final resting place, onto the coffin King George scattered soil from the Western Front. So many were the grieving widows and grieving mothers at that time, more than a million people filed past this grave in the days which followed.

JOHNSON: There was thousand and thousand of family being in that position and the Unknown Warrior gave them something to grieve over.

CHRIS: And despite the Covid restrictions, people did still fall silent across the country.

And for veterans who normally go to their local British allegiance service every year, this year they held their own at home. It was a different kind of Armistice Day for 2020, but not a reason for failing to remember. Chris Ship, News at Ten, Westminster Abbey. (*ITV-20201111*)

Notes

Armistice Day：第一次世界大战停战纪念日，每年的 11 月 11 日。

Duchess of Cornwall：康沃尔公爵夫人，文中指卡米拉，英国王储查尔斯的夫人。

Prince of Wales：威尔士亲王，文中指英国王储查尔斯。

the Cenotaph：衣冠冢纪念碑，特指伦敦白厅街的一座纪念石碑，是为纪念在两次世界大战中牺牲的战士而建的。

Western Front：西部战线（第一次世界大战期间西欧的战斗区域）。

Westminster Abbey：威斯敏斯特教堂。

Words and Expressions

allegiance *n.* 忠诚；效忠
commemoration *n.* 纪念；纪念仪式
enduring *adj.* 持久的
file *vi.* 排成一行行走
grieving *adj.* 悲痛的；伤心的
poignancy *n.* 哀伤
replica *n.* 复制品；仿制品
scatter *vt.* 撒播
space *vt.* 把……分隔开；以一定间隔排列
wreath *n.* 花圈

Questions

1. Why is London's commemoration particularly poignant this year (2020)?
2. How did the pandemic affect today's service?
3. Who appeared in today's service representing the royal family?
4. How sincere was King George V to the unknown warrior?
5. Why were there so many people visiting the newly-built tomb of an unknown warrior?

Gap-filling

CHRIS: And this was the reason they had ____________________ here, the grave of the Unknown Warrior. Exactly a hundred years ago, the body of a soldier, name and __________________ unknown, was chosen from one of the many World War I ____ _______________. On November 11, 1920, King George V placed flowers on the coffin, and then ___________________ the newly-built Cenotaph for the very first time. The King then followed the coffin ___________________ to a new grave in Westminster Abbey.

Today, Prince Charles placed a(n) __________________ at that spot, a(n) ______ ____________ of the one his great grandfather laid a(n) __________________ before. After the body of the Unknown Warrior was laid here in his final __________ place, onto the coffin King George __________ soil from the Western Front. So many were the grieving __________ and grieving mothers at that time, more than a million people __________ this grave in the days which followed.

Dictation

The scale of Armistice Day ... in Westminster Abbey.

Translation

1. The simpler ceremonies lacked nothing of the enduring gratitude felt for the country's war dead.
2. The planned service here for 2,000 people were scaled back to just 80, each spaced apart.
3. More than a million people filed past this grave in the days which followed.

Post-class task

Discussion: The importance of memorizing our national heroes.

27. Artificial Organ

SOPHIE: Every year hundreds of children are born in the UK with parts missing from their oesophagus, the tube that connects your mouth to your stomach. Repairing it requires complex surgery and causes many of them problems for life. But now scientists in London have managed to grow one that is capable of the muscle contractions needed to move food down into the stomach. Our medical correspondent Fergus Walsh has been talking to the scientists at Great Ormond Street Hospital and the Francis Crick Institute who are behind it.

FERGUS: Suspended in the middle of this glass jar is a laboratory-grown oesophagus. You can see the wave-like contractions of the muscle. The oesophagus is a muscular tube which carries food down into the stomach. In this animal study, scientists stripped a rat oesophagus of its cells, leaving a collagen scaffold. They seeded it with several cell types. These form muscles, nerves and the delicate lining tissue. The ability to contract is essential for moving food through the organ.

The work, published in *Nature Communications*, was led by scientists at Great Ormond Street Hospital and the Crick Institute, who are pioneering regenerative medicine.

PAOLO: I think it's very crucial. This has implication for the oesophagus, first of all, of course, but it has implication for other organs like the gut, the intestine, because the structure is not so different.

FERGUS: A key advantage of the bio-engineered oesophagus is that it can be seeded with a patient's own stem cells, minimising the risk of organ rejection, which is one of the major hurdles in transplantation.

NICOLA: Is that nice? Yeah?

FERGUS: Hudson and Hank are twins and enjoy the same foods, but Hudson was born with part of his oesophagus missing, and needed surgery to pull his stomach up to connect with his throat. An artificial oesophagus could have helped him.

NICOLA: I think we definitely would have picked that option, if it had been there at the time. It would take a lot of pressure off of him, I think, with his eating; it would be more natural; the feeling would have been more normal.

FERGUS: Clinical trials are still at least five years away, but this promising research could ultimately help many children every year. Fergus Walsh, BBC News. (*BBC-20181016*)

Words and Expressions

artificial *adj.* 人工的
bio-engineer *vt.* 生物工程制造
clinical *adj.* 临床的
collagen *n.* 胶原蛋白
for life 终生
gut *n.* 消化道
hurdle *n.* 障碍
intestine *n.* 肠
lining tissue 黏膜组织
muscle contraction 肌肉收缩
muscular *adj.* 肌肉的
oesophagus *n.* 食管
organ rejection 器官排异
promising *adj.* 有前途的
regenerative medicine 再生医学
scaffold *n.* 支架
seed *vt.* 在……播种
stem cell 干细胞
strip ... of ... 剥去
suspend *vt.* 悬挂
transplantation *n.* 移植
ultimately *adv.* 最终

Questions

1. What is the determining factor in the success of the artificial organ?
2. What animal has been used for this study?
3. Can the artificial organ be used in humans yet?
4. What are potential applications of this research?

Gap-filling

SOPHIE: Every year hundreds of children are born in the UK with ________ missing from their oesophagus, the ________ that connects your mouth to your stomach. Repairing it requires complex ________ and causes many of them problems ________. But now scientists in London have ________ ________ to grow one that is capable of the ________ contractions needed to move food ________ the stomach. Our medical correspondent Fergus Walsh has been talking to the scientists ________ Great Ormond Street Hospital and the Francis Crick Institute ________.

FERGUS: Suspended in the middle of this ________ is a laboratory-grown oesophagus. You can see the ________ contractions of the muscle. The oesophagus is a(n) ________ tube which carries food down into the stomach. In this animal study, scientists ________ a rat oesophagus of its cells, leaving a collagen scaffold. They ________ it with several cell types. These form muscles, nerves and the ________ lining tissue. The ability to contract is ________ for moving food through the organ.

Dictation

A key advantage ... could have helped him.

Translation

1. The scientists are pioneering regenerative medicine.
2. The bio-engineered oesophagus can be seeded with a patient's own stem cells.
3. Organ rejection is one of the major hurdles in transplantation.

Post-class task

Retell the news story using your own words.

28. Buy Before You Die

MARY: Hello, and welcome back. ITV News has learned that consumers are now paying out billions of pounds on their funerals before they die. New figures show that Britain's prepaid funeral industry's booming, but some bereaved families are calling for great regulation, especially over what they feel of the hidden fees that some companies charge. Our consumer editor Chris Choi reports on the concerns over so-called "buy before you die" plans.

CHRIS: It's Britain's buy-before-you-die funeral boom. Thousands are seeking to avoid rising cost by locking in at today's prices.

Frances Staton believes regulation has failed to keep up. Her sister Katherine paid in almost £700 before she passed away, but not a penny was available for her funeral.

FRANCES: I rang the company of the funeral plan and I was told that she'd paid in about £690 up to that point. But that cost wouldn't cover their marketing costs.

CHRIS: After complaining, she was refunded. But the family believes there is a wider issue. Some customers are surprised the firm selling the plan can take a portion for its overheads of marketing and administering the scheme, and there is no legal obligation to disclose what they retain. New figures showed the scale of the "pay before you go" sector: 1.3 million plans have been sold, 200,000 in the last 12 months; over £4 billion has now been set aside for funerals while the customers are still alive and kicking, and on average the cost is just over £3,000.

JOSEPH: Ross, you're gonna be driving the limousine ...

CHRIS: This industry insider is also calling for greater clarity.

JOSEPH: I had a family coming to see us. Their mother had taken out a prepaid funeral plan and it was with an unscrupulous company, and she paid in over £4,000, and of all that £4,000, £1,500 was taken out of that.

CHRIS: The industry says customers get funerals worth every penny because savings from wholesale cost are passed on. And they carry the financial risk of freezing their prices.

GRAEME: I think funeral plans are a really good way for people to put in place the sort of funeral they want in a controlled and thoughtful way. I think the other benefit is if it's done right, then it allows people to manage the costs.

CHRIS: Government is now considering official regulation. After all, in this industry, customers won't be around to complain if anything does go wrong. Chris Choi, ITV News. (*ITV-20181011*)

Words and Expressions

administer *vt.* 管理
alive and kicking 活蹦乱跳
be around 存在
bereaved *adj.* 丧失亲友的
booming *adj.* 飞速发展的
clarity *n.* 清晰
insider *n.* 知内情者
limousine *n.* 豪华轿车
overheads *n.* 营运费用
prepaid *adj.* 预付费的
unscrupulous *adj.* 无耻的;肆无忌惮的
wholesale *adj.* 批发的
worth every penny 物有所值

Questions

1. Why is UK's buy-before-you-die funeral industry booming?
2. Is every funeral service provider doing business as expected?
3. For what purpose is some money taken away from funeral plans?
4. Why should the government regulate funeral business?

Gap-filling

JOSEPH: I had a(n) __________________ coming to see us. Their mother had taken out a prepaid funeral plan and it was with a(n) __________________ company, and she paid in over £4,000, and __________________ that £4,000, £1,500 was taken out of that.

CHRIS: The industry says customers get funerals __________________ every penny because savings from __________________ cost are passed on. And they __________________ the financial risk of __________________ their prices.

GRAEME: I think funeral plans are a really good way for people to __________________ the sort of funeral they want in a(n) __________________ and thoughtful way. I think the other __________________ is if it's done right, then it allows people to __________________ the costs.

Dictation

After complaining ... £3,000.

Translation

1. The firm selling the plan can take a portion for its overheads of marketing and administering the scheme.
2. Customers get funerals worth every penny because savings from wholesale cost are passed on.
3. After all, in this industry, customers won't be around to complain if anything does go wrong.

Post-class task

Retell the story.

29. Captain Sir Tom Moore

CLIVE: Captain Sir Tom Moore, the centenarian who's raised more than £32 million for NHS charities, was knighted by the Queen today. He received the honour in an outdoor ceremony at Windsor Castle and said chatting with Her Majesty capped "an absolutely outstanding day". Our royal correspondent Sarah Campbell was there.

SARAH: For such an inspiring individual, it seemed appropriate that he should be given a uniquely special investiture. Beneath brilliant blue skies, and adhering to socially-distant guidelines, she used the sword which had belonged to her father, George VI, to knight Captain Sir Thomas Moore.

THOMAS: To me, to meet the Queen was more than anyone could expect. I mean, it was ... Never, ever, ever did I imagine that I should get so close to the Queen and have such a kind message from her. That was really outstanding. It really was truly outstanding.

SARAH: And can you explain the message, what did she say?

THOMAS: No!

SARAH: That's between you and Her Majesty?

THOMAS: That's between the Queen and I, yes. I've been really honoured that this should happen and I'm thrilled that it did happen. And thank you everybody who subscribed to the funds. I really appreciate it, and thank you all very much.

SARAH: It all started with a family challenge to walk 100 lengths of the garden to mark his upcoming 100th birthday. Sir Tom's journey captured the imagination of people around the world. The original target was to raise £1,000 for NHS charities. The final amount topped 32 million. There to support him on his big day, his family.

HANNAH: We've stood by in awe as a family as these amazing things happened to him. And we've been so delighted. We've never wanted the limelight. Him ... It's him. He's the beacon of hope.

GEORGIA: I can't believe we're actually here. We've come and visited sometimes but now it's ... Oh, I'm speechless.

SARAH: This was a ceremony involving two people—one aged 94, the other 100 years old. Both can be said to have helped keep people's spirits up during the darkest of days. Sarah Campbell, BBC News, Windsor Castle. (*BBC 20200717*)

Notes

Windsor Castle: 温莎堡,英国王室住所,也是英国君主主要的行政官邸,位于英格兰东南部伯克郡,最初由“征服者威廉”下令在一处早期要塞原址上建造而成。

Words and Expressions

adhere to 遵守
beacon *n.* 灯塔
cap *vt.* 使达到高潮;使圆满结束
capture the imagination of ... 使……着迷;受……关注
centenarian *n.* 百岁老人
Her Majesty 陛下
in awe 满怀敬畏
investiture *n.* 授衔仪式
knight *vt.* 封(某人)为爵士
limelight *n.* 公众注意的中心
speechless *adj.* (尤指由于震惊或强烈感情而)一时讲不出话的
subscribe (to) 向(某个基金、项目或慈善事业)捐款
thrilled *adj.* 非常激动的

Questions

1. Why and where was Captain Tom knighted?
2. How special is the sword that the Queen used?
3. Did Tom tell the reporter what the Queen had said to him?
4. What do the family members think of today's event?

Gap-filling

CLIVE: Captain Sir Tom Moore, the ________________ who's raised more than £32 million for NHS ________________, was knighted by the Queen today. He received the ________________ in an outdoor ceremony at Windsor ________________ and said chatting with Her Majesty ________________ "an absolutely outstanding day". Our ________________ Correspondent Sarah Campbell was there.

SARAH: For such a(n) ________________ individual, it seemed appropriate that he should be given a(n) ________________ special investiture. ________________ brilliant blue skies, and ________________ socially-distant guidelines, she used the ________________ which had belonged to her father, ________________, to knight Captain Sir Thomas Moore.

Dictation

It all started with ... his family.

Translation

1. Chatting with Her Majesty capped an absolutely outstanding day.
2. We've never wanted the limelight.
3. He's the beacon of hope.
4. Both have helped keep people's spirits up during the darkest of days.

Post-class task

Discussion: Have you ever done something for the charities? Can you describe what you have done?

30. Cardboard Cut-down

JANE: Now how often have you received a product you've bought online delivered in an oversized box? Excess packaging wastes space in delivery vehicles, which means more journeys are taken and lots of unnecessary cardboard is used. So, our business correspondent Emma Simpson has been to look at one solution that might tick all the right boxes.

EMMA: It's the time of year when the online deliveries are coming thick and fast. How many of us have had this, an online purchase in an oversize box?

It drives us mad, and it's bad for the environment. All this wasted space means more delivery vans in our towns and cities, and the bigger the parcel, the bigger the cost for retailers. So what can be done? We've come to France to see a new machine that can produce a box to fit the product.

ALEX: Well, this machine can take a standard sheet of cardboard and can make 10 million different varieties of box, to make sure that we have no wasted space at all around the product that somebody's trying to send in the post to a customer.

EMMA: So let's put it to the test. I've got my Christmas decoration, and a few other items. Stefan, press the button. Cuddly toy. Some toiletries. Clothes.

The item is scanned to take the exact dimensions. Meanwhile, the box is being assembled, the cardboard creased and then folded around the product. It can make and pack up to 1,000 boxes every hour.

Hey! Here it is. Look at that. Not much empty space. Alex, how big a difference can this machine make?

ALEX: It's a game-changer, because already the UK is the biggest e-commerce market in Europe. 18% of what we buy goes online, so imagine if that doubles.

EMMA: There is a mountain of cardboard already. Most is recycled, but campaigners say bigger changes are needed for all this Internet shopping to be sustainable.

JULIET: As well as looking at reducing the amount of packaging, we also need to look towards different systems, different systems of getting products to people, looking at reusable packaging options, and also looking at decarbonising the vehicles which are used to transport the products.

EMMA: This machine isn't in operation just yet, but it is one way our everyday online purchases could eventually be made to fit the box. Emma Simpson, BBC News. (*BBC-20191211*)

Words and Expressions

assemble *vt.* 装配
cardboard *n.* 硬纸板
come thick and fast 铺天盖地而来
crease *vt.* 压褶
cuddly *adj.* (儿童玩具)柔软的;适于拥抱的
decarbonise *vt.* 降低……的碳排放
delivery *n.* 递送
dimension *n.* 大小;尺寸
game-changer *n.* 规则改变者;在很大程度上改变形势的产品(或事件)
oversize *adj.* 过大的
oversized *adj.* 过大的
packaging *n.* 包装材料;外包装
sustainable *adj.* 可持续的
tick all the right boxes 一切如愿;众口皆调(本文一语双关)
toiletry *n.* 洗漱用品

Questions

1. What impact do oversized boxes bring to society?
2. How does the machine save space?
3. What production capacity does the machine have?
4. Why is the machine a game-changer?
5. What other solutions are proposed to ensure online shopping is sustainable?

Gap-filling

ALEX: It's a game-changer, because already the UK is the biggest ________________ market in Europe. 18% of what we buy goes online, so ________________.

EMMA: There is a(n) ________________ of cardboard already. Most is ________________, but campaigners say bigger changes are needed for all this ________________ shopping to be ________________.

JULIET: As well as looking at ________________ the amount of packaging, we also need to look towards different systems, different systems of getting ________________ to people, looking at reusable packaging ________________, and also looking at decarbonising the ________________ which are used to transport the products.

Dictation

It's the time of year … fit the product.

Translation

1. One solution that might tick all the right boxes.
2. It's the time of year when the online deliveries are coming thick and fast.
3. We should look at decarbonising the vehicles which are used to transport the products.

Post-class task

Discussion: What do you usually do with the packaging?

31. Digital Fossils

CLIVE: Now, how do you give fossils a future? Well, you put them online, and that's exactly what London's Natural History Museum and Washington's Smithsonian Institution in the U. S. have set out to do. They're digitally recording millions of fossils in their collections, many of which have been hidden away in drawers for decades. Our science correspondent Victoria Gill has the story.

KATHY: So we're in our brachiopod collection.

VICTORIA: Tucked into thousands of drawers, the entire history of life on earth.

KATHY: There're dozens of things in every box in every ...

VICTORIA: Wow! Yes, yes. There are 40 million fossils stored here at the Smithsonian Museum, and a team is carrying out the mammoth task of digitally recording every single one.

KATHY: We have drawers here in the collection that haven't been opened in decades. The data held within the museum drawers is trapped, and we are bringing that trapped data out into the light. We are mobilising it for research.

VICTORIA: Photographing and logging the details of each specimen in this collection alone will take an estimated 50 years. But it's part of an effort by institutions around the world to create a global digital museum where every piece of the fossil record can be studied online. The devastating fire at Brazil's National Museum this year destroyed knowledge that was amassed over two centuries and was a stark reminder of the need to protect and log such scientifically valuable collections.

This goes way beyond insuring this huge collection. It means that this triceratops skull, for example, could be in dozens of places at once, anywhere in the world for any scientist to study.

And with a very detailed digital scan and a 3D printer, researchers here at Bristol University have been able to bring these dinosaurs into their lab.

EMILY: This model is great because it allows us to look in detail at the anatomy and pick it up and hold it and turn it around.

VICTORIA: Amazing.

EMILY: Now we can actually test ideas about how these animals actually functioned.

VICTORIA: The digital skulls can be given virtual stress tests to work out what the animals ate, how they moved, and so what their environment was like 150 million years ago. Museums have gathered vast amounts of evidence of hundreds of millions of years of evolution. Now the challenge is to make sure it's shared and studied, not hidden away in the dark. Victoria Gill, BBC News in Washington, D. C. (*BBC-20181209*)

Notes

Natural History Museum：(英国)自然历史博物馆,欧洲最大的自然历史博物馆,位于伦敦市中心西南部,馆藏约 7 000 万件标本,原为 1753 年创建的大英博物馆的一部分,1881 年由总馆分出。

Smithsonian Institution：(美国)史密森学会,是唯一由美国政府资助的半官方性质的博物馆机构,由英国科学家 J. 史密森遗赠捐款,于 1846 年创建于首都华盛顿。学会下设 14 所博物馆和 1 所国立动物园。

Words and Expressions

amass *vt.* 积累;积聚
anatomy *n.* 结构
brachiopod *n.* 腕足动物
evolution *n.* 演化
hide away 隐藏
log *vt.* 记录
mammoth *adj.* 极其巨大的
mobilise *vt.* 动员;调用
skull *n.* 颅骨
specimen *n.* 标本
stark *adj.* 明显的
triceratops *n.* 三角龙
tuck *vt.* 收藏;把……藏入
way *adv.* 大大地;远远地

Questions

1. Why do people digitally record fossils?
2. Why is a fire in Brazil mentioned?
3. What can a 3D printer do in the research of fossils?

4. What is the purpose of giving virtual stress tests in the study of fossils?

Gap-filling

VICTORIA: Photographing and logging the details of each ________________ in this collection alone will take a(n) ________________ 50 years. But it's part of ________________ by institutions around the world to ________________ a global digital museum where every piece of the ________________ record can be ________________ online. The devastating fire at ________________ National Museum this year destroyed knowledge that was ________________ over two centuries and was a(n) ________________ reminder of the need to protect and ________________ such scientifically valuable collections.

This goes ________________ this huge collection. It means that this triceratops ________________, for example, could be in dozens of places ________________, anywhere in the world for any scientist to study.

Dictation

There are 40 million fossils … for research.

Translation

1. Many fossils have been hidden away in drawers for decades.
2. This model allows us to look in detail at the anatomy.

Post-class task

Discussion: How often do you go to museums? Why are museums important to a city and a country?

32. Female Conductor

CLIVE: Just one of Britain's leading orchestras has a female principal conductor. But efforts are under way to try redress the imbalance, including at Welsh National Opera, where a new role of Female Conductor in Residence has been specially created. Sian Lloyd went to meet Tianyi Lu, as she began her first week on the job.

SIAN: Taking on one of opera's best-known and best-loved pieces of music in her own way.

TIANYI: I think a rehearsal should be like children playing. Let's try this, let's try this, oh, wow, this works, and sometimes an orchestra or a chorus might give me something that I hadn't thought of.

SIAN: Tianyi Lu is one of only a handful of women to have titled roles, the top jobs among the several hundred conductors on the staff of British orchestras.

TIANYI: Perhaps sometimes, the second beat of the bar go a little bit.

SIAN: As she begins her position as first Female Conductor in Residence with Welsh National Opera, she takes that number to eight.

TIANYI: Even at the very beginning of my career, when I tried conducting for the first time and I loved it, the thought of conducting didn't even cross my mind because I had never seen a woman in a professional context conducting before at that stage. I therefore didn't think it was possible.

SIAN: That shortage of role models is something the opera company is trying to change. With this newly created post, it's one of a growing network of organisations creating opportunities to give women the means and confidence to conduct.

EMMA: I think it's positive action. We are addressing the gender imbalance in the sector at the moment, and if there is an imbalance, then you've got to do something about changing that and giving people opportunities to progress.

SIAN: Already an assistant conductor with the Melbourne Symphony Orchestra, Tianyi was one of more than 50 women who applied for the job in Cardiff. They'd all gained experience in leading an orchestra, but the opportunity to also lead voices in an opera was new to many.

TIANYI: Even the idea of calling yourself a female conductor is unusual. I would love the day when labels are gone, where we just see the person for who they are, and they are creating artwork and we just see the artwork that they are making and the story they are trying to tell.

SIAN: That day is now looking closer, although the pace of change could be quicker for some. Sian Lloyd, BBC News, Cardiff.

CLIVE: Good luck to her. (*BBC-20190816*)

Words and Expressions

address *vt.* (着手)解决;处理	orchestra *n.* 管弦乐队
bar *n.* 乐谱的小节	principal conductor 首席指挥
beat *n.* 节拍	redress *vt.* 纠正
chorus *n.* 合唱团	rehearsal *n.* 排练
cross one's mind (念头)闪现;掠过	role model 模范;榜样
in residence 常驻	symphony orchestra 交响乐团
label *n.* 标签	take on 呈现

Questions

1. What role was Ms. Lu accepted at Welsh National Opera?
2. How does Ms. Lu understand a rehearsal?
3. Is this the first time for Ms. Lu to have become a female conductor in residence?
4. Was Ms. Lu very confident that she would become a successful female conductor at the very beginning of her career? Why (not)?
5. Does Ms. Lu like being called a female conductor? Why (not)?

Gap-filling

CLIVE: Just one of Britain's leading orchestras has a female ____________ conductor. But efforts are under way to try ____________ the imbalance, including at Welsh National Opera, where a new role of Female Conductor in ____________ has been specially ____________. Sian Lloyd went to meet Tianyi Lu, as she began her first week ____________.

SIAN: Taking on ____________ opera's best-known and best-loved pieces of music in her own way.

TIANYI: I think a ____________ should be like children playing. Let's try this, let's try this, oh, wow, ____________, and sometimes an orchestra or ____________ might give me something that I ____________.

Dictation

That shortage of … opportunities to progress.

Translation

1. Efforts are under way to try redress the imbalance.
2. She takes that number to eight.
3. The opportunity to lead voices in an opera was new to many.
4. The thought of conducting didn't even cross my mind.

Post-class task

Discussion: Do you find this story inspiring? Why (not)?

33. Fibre Benefit

SOPHIE: Now most of us do not have enough fibre in our diet—despite the fact it reduces the chance of heart attacks, strokes as well as Type 2 diabetes. Fibre is present in fruit, vegetables, wholegrain bread, pasta and grains like lentils. Researchers advise eating 30 grams a day—but nine out of ten of us are failing to do that, as our medical correspondent, Fergus Walsh, now reports.

FERGUS: It's the super-ingredient most of us don't get enough of, fibre. A landmark study in *The Lancet* journal has confirmed that fibre in fruit, veg, wholegrains, pulses and nuts has major health benefits. Researchers analysed more than 200 studies and found a high-fibre diet significantly cut the risk of heart disease and stroke as well as bowel cancer and Type 2 diabetes. The overall risk of death was reduced by at least 15%. Adults should be aiming to eat 30 grams of fibre a day. The average in the UK is just 18 grams.

WOMAN 1: I don't think we eat as much fibre as we should do, especially whenever we shop and cook and things.

WOMAN 2: I don't really think about fibre, to be honest.

WOMAN 3: I would have no idea how many grams of fibre is in anything. So, yeah, it'd be good to know.

FERGUS: So how do you get your 30 grams of fibre a day? Let's start with breakfast. Two slices of wholemeal toast—6.4 grams of fibre, more than double what you get in white bread. Add to that a banana and you're nearly a third of the way there. Or you could have some porridge plus fruit. At lunchtime, this meal has a whopping

21 grams of fibre: the baked potato with its skin on, some baked beans and a large apple. Well, that's your recommended intake in just two meals. Then, in the evening, you could have some wholewheat pasta, some pulses, like kidney beans, some wholegrain rice. Don't forget the veg. Each of these has three grams of fibre, and then a handful of unsalted nuts and you're getting all the roughage you need.

URSULA: Around 9% of the population hit that 30 grams target. So it's a lot of us that are quite deficient, really. And that's for a variety of reasons. But generally, you know, if we were to all increase our fruit and vegetable intake, fruits and vegetables at every meal and every snack, you know, for most of us that would bump us up really significantly and really help decrease those, you know, those risk factors.

FERGUS: Fibre is crucial for our digestive and overall health. Those on popular low-carb diets may be missing out on this key ingredient. Fergus Walsh, BBC News. (*BBC-20190111*)

Words and Expressions

bowel *n.* 肠
bump up 提升
carb = carbohydrate *n.* 碳水化合物
digestive *adj.* 消化的
kidney bean 菜豆
landmark *adj.* 有重大意义或影响的
lentil *n.* 兵豆
miss out on 遗漏;错过
porridge *n.* 粥
pulse *n.* 豆子
roughage *n.* 粗纤维
unsalted *adj.* 未加盐的
veg = vegetable(s) *n.* 蔬菜
white bread 白面面包;精粉面包
wholegrain *adj.* 含全谷物的
wholegrains *n.* 全谷物;全麦
wholemeal *adj.* (面粉或面包)全麦的
wholewheat *adj.* 全(小)麦的
whopping *adj.* 极大的;异常大的

Questions

1. What benefits does fibre have to our health?
2. How much fibre does an average UK citizen eat?
3. How can people increase their fibre intake significantly?

Gap-filling

FERGUS: ... Well, that's your recommended ________________ in just two meals. Then, in the evening, you could have some wholewheat ________________, some pulses, like kidney beans, some ________________ rice. Don't forget the ________________. Each of these has three grams of fibre, and then a handful of ________________ nuts and you're getting all the ________________ you need.

URSULA: Around ________________ of the population hit that 30 grams target. So it's a lot of us that are quite ________________, really. And that's for a(n) ________________ of reasons. But generally, you know, ________________________________ at every meal and every snack, you know, for most of us that would ________________ really significantly and really help ________________ those, you know, those risk factors.

Dictation

It's the super-ingredient ... 18 grams.

Translation

1. A high-fibre diet significantly cut the risk of heart disease and stroke as well as bowel cancer and Type 2 diabetes.
2. Those on popular low-carb diets may be missing out on this key ingredient.

Post-class task

Discussion: What feasible measures can you offer to make up for fibre deficiency?

34. Football Finances

REETA: The football season gets under way tonight with the first of the Championship fixtures, but it's been a troubling time for League One clubs Bury and Bolton. Bury's opening match has been suspended after the club failed to satisfy the authorities that it has the necessary finances in place and their second fixture is under threat too. Our sports editor Dan Roan reports.

DAN: There's no shortage of cash in the Premier League. Today Manchester United spending £80 million on England and Leicester defender Harry Maguire. But life below the top-flight isn't as easy. Cash-strapped Bolton Wanderers became the first Football League club in six years to enter administration this summer. The crisis saw a food bank set up to help staff and amid relegation from the Championship the players were affected, too.

ANDREW: We'd been paid up until February. Then we've not received anything from the club since. It is hard to deal with the stress and everything else. But I think it is more difficult for our families.

DAN: Like Bolton, Bury have also been docked 12 points before the campaign has even begun for getting into financial trouble, but the situation here is even more dire. Tomorrow, Gigg Lane was meant to host the club's opening game of the season, but in an unprecedented move the Football League has suspended the fixture because they say the club has failed to provide proof of funds.

Bury denied that and have accused the League of working against them. With almost three quarters of the League's 72 clubs ending last season in the red, some fear more turmoil.

JOHN: Bury involved the first of what we think is going to be many instances where clubs will find themselves in deep trouble. When we look at the financial profile of these clubs and football in general in England, it's not a pretty picture.

DAN: As Bolton edges towards a takeover, the League's come under pressure to toughen up scrutiny of club owners, but it suggests too many of its members live beyond their means.

DEBBIE: Player wages are a big chunk of where the turnover goes, and that's something that needs to be considered, and we need to look at the reliance there is on owners. We need to, as a league, look and reflect upon that, and see what we can do, since we need to do ourselves differently.

DAN: With the Premier League richer than ever, some now want the top clubs to do more to help. Expect plenty of intrigue this season, both on and off the pitch. Dan Roan, BBC News. (*BBC-20190802*)

Words and Expressions

beyond one's means 入不敷出
cash-strapped *adj.* 资金短缺的
chunk *n.* 相当大的量
dire *adj.* 极糟的;极差的
dock *vt.* 扣除
edge *vi.* 徐徐移动
enter administration 进入破产管理状态
finances *n.* 财力
in the red 负债;有赤字
intrigue *n.* 吸引力
pitch *n.* 球场
profile *n.* 概况
relegation *n.* 降级
scrutiny *n.* 详细审查
suspend *vt.* 停赛
takeover *n.* 收购;接管
top-flight *adj.* 第一流的
toughen up 加强;强化
turmoil *n.* 动乱;混乱
turnover *n.* 营业额

Notes

The Football League:英格兰和威尔士地区的足球联赛,不包括参加英超联赛(The Premier League)的球队,分为冠军组(The Championship)、一级组(League One)和二级组(League Two)。

Questions

1. How many clubs in UK Football League are experiencing deficit?
2. What consequences will there be if a club fails to prove it is financially strong?
3. What sector consumes most of a football club's revenue?

Gap-filling

JOHN: Bury involved the first of what we think is going to be many ________________ where clubs will find themselves ______________________. When we look at the financial __________________________ of these clubs and football in general in England, it's not a ______________________.

DAN: As Bolton ____________________ towards a takeover, the League's ____________ ________ pressure to toughen up ____________________ of club owners, but it suggests too many of its members live __________________.

DEBBIE: Player wages are a big __________________ of where the turnover goes, and that's something that needs to be considered, and we need to look at the ______________ ____ on owners. We need to, ___________________, look and reflect upon that, and see what we can do, since we need to do ourselves ________________.

Dictation

Like Bolton ... fear more turmoil.

Translation

1. Life below the top-flight isn't as easy.
2. Too many of its members live beyond their means.
3. We need to look at the reliance there's on owners.
4. Expect plenty of intrigue this season, both on and off the pitch.

Post-class task

Discussion: What makes a football club successful?

35. Gross Footage

SOPHIE: Police are questioning six men from South London about footage posted online which shows a group of people laughing as they burnt a cardboard model of Grenfell Tower on a bonfire. The men aged between 19 and 55 handed themselves in last night after the video was widely circulated on social media. They've been arrested on suspicion of intentionally causing harassment, alarm or distress. Our home affairs correspondent June Kelly reports.

JUNE: This afternoon, a house in southeast London became the focus for police gathering possible evidence. 24 hours on from the appearance of the video, the investigation was well under way. This is a still from the video which shows a model of Grenfell Tower on a bonfire. The footage emerged on social media, and today, neighbours near the house being searched joined the chorus of outrage.

DAVIS: How can anybody wake up in the morning and think it's OK to make a box in detail of cutting out windows, cutting out the outlines of people, with their hands up in the air!

JUNE: The men being questioned are being held under the *Public Order Act*, which says that a person is guilty of an offence if, with intent to cause a person harassment, alarm or distress he uses threatening, abusive or insulting words or behaviour, or disorderly behaviour.

NAZIR: The reality is that as grossly offensive as this is, it doesn't necessarily mean that it's a criminal offence. When you post grossly offensive material online, you can be guilty of an offence under the *Communications Act*, for which you can go to prison for about six months.

JUNE: The video has horrified all those affected by the Grenfell tragedy. Like Rukayet Mamudu, who escaped from the tower with her grandson.

RUKAYET: There are still people who have no human feelings, particularly when there are people going through the enquiry now, going through what they went through during the fire, and some other people are making it like a joke, with children at the background.

JUNE: Tonight, Scotland Yard announced a further arrest—a 19-year-old was detained after he went to a police station in south London today. He's now in custody with the five others who handed themselves in last night. June Kelly, BBC News. (*BBC-20181106*)

Notes

Grenfell Tower：格伦费尔大楼，伦敦北部一幢 24 层的住宅大楼，2017 年 6 月 14 日遭遇火灾，导致 72 人死亡。

Words and Expressions

bonfire *n.* 篝火；营火
circulate *vt.* 传播
chorus of 齐声
cut out 剪出
detain *vt.* 拘留
disorderly *adj.* 目无法纪的
footage *n.* 影片片段
hand oneself in 自首
harassment *n.* 骚扰
in custody 在押；被拘留
offence *n.* 违法行为
on suspicion of 涉嫌
Scotland Yard 苏格兰场（英国大伦敦警察局的总部）
still *n.* 定格画面
with intent (to do sth.) 怀有（做某事的）意图

Questions

1. On what charge were the six men arrested?
2. What laws might be related to this offence?

3. What can be the punishment if they are convicted?
4. How did the victims of the Grenfell fire feel when they saw the footage?

Gap-filling

JUNE: The men being questioned are ________________ under the *Public Order Act*, which says that a person is ________________ of an offence if, ________________ to cause a person ________________, ________________ or distress he uses threatening, ________________ or ________________ words or behaviour, or disorderly behaviour.

NAZIR: The reality is that as grossly offensive ________________, it doesn't necessarily mean that it's a(n) ________________ offence. When you post grossly offensive material online, you ________________ guilty of ________________ under the *Communications Act*, for which you can go to prison ________________.

Dictation

This afternoon ... the chorus of outrage.

Translation

1. The video was widely circulated on social media.
2. Neighbours near the house being searched joined the chorus of outrage.
3. A person is guilty of an offence if, with intent to cause a person harassment, alarm or distress he uses threatening, abusive or insulting words or behaviour, or disorderly behaviour.

Post-class task

Discussion:

1. What do you believe are acceptable and unacceptable behaviours on social media?
2. Freedom of speech: a fallacy.

36. HIV Breakthrough

TOM: Now when the world first woke up to the threat of AIDS, the idea that people could be cleared of the disease was really, to be honest, unimaginable, but now a British man has been free of it for 18 months. He doesn't even need antiviral drugs. This new advance involves transplanting stem cells from a donor who has a genetic resistance to the HIV virus. It won't become a standard treatment, but it is a step on the way to eliminating HIV altogether.

CLARKE: HIV was once a death sentence. Now drugs allow those with the virus near normal lives, but there's still no cure. So the case of an anonymous man's HIV being eradicated following cancer treatment here at the Hammersmith Hospital in London is a breakthrough.

IAN: We're very lucky that four years out from transplant, he now remains in remission, but also is undetectable with regards to his HIV. His antiretroviral, HIV therapy's been withdrawn. And with all the techniques that we have available to us in 2019, we can't detect his virus.

CLARKE: The London patient already had HIV when he was diagnosed with a life-threatening blood cancer. His treatment required a risky bone marrow transplant, implanting cancer-free stem cells from a donor. And since HIV also lives in the bone marrow, it gave doctors a unique opportunity to give him new bone marrow cells from a donor with a rare genetic mutation making them naturally resistant to HIV. And now 18 months after the operation, the patient is free of both cancer and HIV.

Until now, this man, Timothy Brown, was the only person known to have been cured of HIV following aggressive cancer treatment. The anonymous London patient proves his case wasn't a fluke. But a bone marrow transplant is far too dangerous a procedure to ever be a treatment for the virus.

What happened to the London patient will never on its own become a cure for HIV, but it's still seen as a landmark case among HIV researchers in labs like this one, because it points very clearly to where future cures may come from.

KATE: Findings like today really mean that people are excited about the possibility of being able to cure HIV. Now we have two patients, we can compare them and we can see what was similar in both cases and what was different, and therefore try and get a better idea of what's important and then hopefully the idea would be to take that and use that information.

CLARKE: Techniques like genetically reprogramming a patient's cells are fast becoming a reality. So after decades of research, the London patient's legacy may well be a cure for HIV. Tom Clarke, News at Ten. (*ITV-20190305*)

Words and Expressions

anonymous *adj.* 匿名的	implant *vt.* 将……植入
antiviral *adj.* 抗病毒的	in remission 康复期;病情好转
eliminate *vt.* 清除;消除	reprogram *vt.* 为……重编程序
eradicate *vt.* 根除;消灭	with regard to 关于

Questions

1. Hong long has the London patient been free of HIV virus?
2. Is the London patient the only person free of HIV virus after treatment?
3. How can it be possible for the London patient to be free of HIV virus after a bone marrow transplant?
4. What is the significance of the London patient's case?

Gap-filling

CLARKE: The London patient already had HIV when he was ________________ with a life-threatening blood cancer. His treatment required a(n) ________________ bone marrow transplant, ________________ cancer-free ________________ from a donor. And since HIV also ________________ the bone marrow, it gave doctors a(n) ________________ opportunity to give him new bone marrow cells from a donor with a(n) ________________________________ making them naturally ________________ to HIV. And now 18 months after the operation, the patient is free ________________ cancer and HIV.

Until now, this man, Timothy Brown, was the only person known ________________ cured of HIV following ________________ cancer treatment. The ________________ London patient proves his case wasn't ________________. But a bone marrow transplant is far too dangerous a procedure ________________ a treatment for the virus.

Dictation

Now when the world … HIV altogether.

Translation

1. The anonymous London patient proves his case wasn't a fluke.
2. Doctors gave him new bone marrow cells from a donor with a rare genetic mutation making them naturally resistant to HIV.
3. A bone marrow transplant is far too dangerous a procedure to ever be a treatment for the virus.

Post-class task

Discussion: What can people do to avoid being infected by HIV virus?

37. Honey and Health

TOM: And finally it was Mary Poppins who famously suggested that a spoonful of sugar helps the medicine go down. Well, now scientists in Oxford have their own theory. They reckon a spoonful of sugar honey, to be specific, can be as good for you as the medicine itself. Long used as a home remedy, researchers now say, they have proof honey really can be a more effective treatment than cough and cold medicines.

ADVERT: There's a wonder product the world can't live without.

REBECCA: The healing powers of honey have long been proclaimed. (*A healthy, grown-up, busy-busy bee.*) For generations it's been used as a home remedy for the common cold.

KOURTNEY: I've been using Manuka Honey for years.

REBECCA: Even celebrities have waxed lyrical about its health benefits, but now scientists from the University of Oxford have confirmed honey is better than over-the-counter medicines for treating coughs and colds.

KATE: They're pretty fascinating. The more you learn, the more you want to learn.

REBECCA: At this urban beekeeping centre in South London, the capacity of these tiny honey-makers comes as no surprise.

KATE: Anti-fungal, antibiotic, different vitamins and minerals in there. But generally, they keep us ticking over. They are one of our biggest pollinators, so they are a great health-giving provider and always have been.

REBECCA: The study found honey was more effective than conventional treatments for coughs, blocked noses and sore throats, reducing the frequency and severity of coughs and speeding up recovery.

As the sniffly autumn months approach, we are more keen than ever to stay fit and healthy, and keep the strain off the NHS. Maybe these little insects can help.

The report also says prescribing honey could prevent the over-prescription of antibiotics.

MAYUR: The common cold is caused by a virus. Antibiotics are only effective for bacteria, so what's not to like about the use of honey for the common cold? You don't need to go to the doctor, and it helps me because it helps doctors reduce the unnecessary prescribing of antibiotics.

REBECCA: Though not suitable for children under one, a spoonful of honey really could be the best medicine. Rebecca Barry, News at Ten.

TOM: I knew it. That's the best news ever. Good night. See you tomorrow. (*ITV-20200819*)

Notes

Manuka Honey:(新西兰)麦卢卡蜂蜜。

Mary Poppins:魔法保姆,英国经典文化符号,作家特拉弗斯(P. L. Travers)笔下儿童故事书中的神奇保姆。她会撑着一把大伞缓缓从空中飘落,让淘气的孩子变得礼貌服帖。

Words and Expressions

antibiotic *n.* 抗生素
adj. 抗菌的
anti-fungal *adj.* 抗真菌的
bacteria *n.* 细菌
conventional *adj.* 传统的
come as no surprise 不足为奇
healing *adj.* 治愈的
keep sth. off sb. 使……远离某人
mineral *n.* 矿物质
over-the-counter *adj.* 非处方的
pollinator *n.* 传粉昆虫
prescribe *vt.* 给……开(药)
proclaim *vt.* 宣告;声明
reckon *vt.* 想;认为
remedy *n.* 疗法;药品
sniffly *adj.* 抽鼻子的
speed up (使)加速
strain *n.* 压力;重负
tick over 维持原状;稳定运行
vitamin *n.* 维生素
wax lyrical 盛赞

Questions

1. What has the Oxford research revealed?
2. What healthy ingredients does honey contain?
3. Why does the reporter say eating honey helps the NHS?
4. Why are antibiotics not suitable for common colds?
5. Is honey good for every person?

Gap-filling

REBECCA: Even celebrities have ____________________ about its health benefits, but now scientists from the University of Oxford have ____________________ honey is better than ____________________ medicines for treating coughs and colds.

KATE: They're pretty ____________________. The more you learn, the more you want to learn.

REBECCA: At this ____________________ beekeeping centre in South London, the ____________________ of these tiny honey-makers comes as no surprise.

KATE: Anti-fungal, antibiotic, different ____________________ and ____________________ in there. But generally, they keep us ____________________ over. They are one of our biggest ____________________, so they are a great health-giving provider and ____________________.

Dictation

And finally it was Mary … cold medicines.

Translation

1. Even celebrities have waxed lyrical about its health benefits.
2. The capacity of bees comes as no surprise.
3. Bees keep us ticking over.
4. As the sniffly autumn months approach, we are more keen than ever to stay fit and healthy, and keep the strain off the NHS.

Post-class task

Discussion: How do you cope with a cold?

38. Intelligent Speed Assistance

GEORGE: Speed kills—that's the warning drummed into motorists from the minute they pass the driving test. But, soon, it may not be up to the driver alone. By 2022, the European Commission wants all new cars to be fitted with devices to automatically stop people breaking the speed limit—although the driver could override it. The Department for Transport here said the measure would apply in the UK. Our Scotland correspondent Lorna Gordon reports.

LORNA: For those with a passion for getting behind the wheel, rural Scotland has winding roads and breathtaking views to enjoy. The vast majority of motorists are responsible and focus on their driving. There are signs to remind us of the legal limits, but speed is still a big killer. Now technology to be fitted in all new cars could make speeding a thing of the past.

MOTORIST 1: I think it's a good thing. It drives people to drive a bit more safely. I'm big on safety.

MOTORIST 2: I can't see that people will take to the idea of having their speed limited when they got the option of buying a second-hand car.

MOTORIST 3: It will make things safer in possibly especially slower areas.

LORNA: Here is how the intelligent speed assistant works. The car gets its position via a GPS satellite along with the current speed limit. Cameras could also read road signs to determine the maximum speed. The car is then limited to whatever the speed restriction is, but with the ability to override it, and that is vital according to motoring organisations.

JACK: When it comes to intelligent speed assistance, what we want to see are those elements where a short temporary burst of speed to get out of a sticky situation like overtaking a tractor, or coming out of a junction where they have misjudged it, that all of that kind of thing is built into the system and makes sure that the whole thing is safe.

(*The lane-keeping assistant* ...)

LORNA: Car companies point out that many vehicles already have sophisticated systems that limit speeds automatically. Once set by the driver the car will brake itself to meet a specific speed. Road safety campaigners say having these devices automatically fitted in every new car will be a big leap forward in making our roads more safe. They hope that with more than 1,700 people killed on the roads every year, the new speed limiting measures will prove life-saving. Lorna Gordon, BBC News, on the roads around Loch Lomond. (*BBC-20190327*)

Notes

Loch Lomond：洛蒙德湖，英国苏格兰最大的湖泊，位于苏格兰高地南部，南端距格拉斯哥27千米，四周被山地环绕，是英国最伟大的自然奇观之一。

Words and Expressions

a thing of the past 成为历史
be big on sth. 非常喜欢
behind the wheel 在驾驶汽车
breathtaking *adj.* 动人心魄的
drum sth. into sb. 向……反复灌输
junction *n.* 交叉路口
override *vt.* 超控
sophisticated *adj.* 复杂的
sticky *adj.* 难办的；棘手的
take to 喜爱
winding *adj.* 蜿蜒的

Questions

1. How does the intelligent speed assistant work?
2. Why is the option to override the intelligent system necessary?
3. How many people are killed by road accidents every year in Britain?

Gap-filling

LORNA: Here is how the intelligent speed ________________ works. The car gets its position ________________ a GPS satellite along with the current speed limit. ________________ could also read road signs to ________________ the maximum speed. The car is then ________________ to whatever the speed ________________ is, but with the ability to ________________ it, and that is vital according to ________________ organisations.

JACK: When it comes to intelligent speed ________________, what we want to see are those elements where a short temporary ________________ of speed to get out of a(n) ________________ situation like ________________ a tractor, or coming out of a(n) ________________ where they have ________________ it, that all of that ________________ is built into the system and makes ________________ that the whole thing is safe.

Dictation

Speed kills … apply in the UK.

Translation

1. The technology could make speeding a thing of the past.
2. I can't see that people will take to the idea of having their speed limited when they got the option of buying a second-hand car.
3. A short temporary burst of speed is sometimes needed to get out of a sticky situation.

Post-class task

Discussion:

1. Are you going to buy this type of car if they are available on the market?
2. Your ideal car.

39. Jetpack for Paramedics

JULIE: And finally, not so long ago, they only existed in the realms of science fiction and Bond movies. It is not so much the hills of the Lake District, but trials have been taking place of a jetpack to propel a paramedic to the scene of hard-to-reach medical emergencies where even a helicopter can't go and hiking will take precious minutes. Saving time could mean saving lives.

DAN: Could this be a glimpse of Britain's new flying squad of emergency services? Now, you're not seeing things. This man really is floating up a mountain powered by a jetpack. This trial was conducted in the Lake District and has been described as a game-changer by local paramedics who think the technology could be used to slash response times.

ANDY: First flight in Cumbria for a jet suit that's going to save lives and ease suffering. So incredible moment, truly, truly incredible moment.

RICHARD: There you go, starting to accelerate.

DAN: The inventor Richard Browning showed me the kerosene-powered machine which has been refined over the last four years.

RICHARD: We're much cheaper than a helicopter. We can get to the casualty much quicker than you can on foot or by vehicle. And actually I think the film speaks for itself. We ended up shaving, you know, 23 minutes off a 25-minute walk.

DAN: This simulation with the Great North Air Ambulance Service gave a sense how the jetpack might be used to rapidly triage hard-to-reach casualties, ensuring that a helicopter is only deployed when absolutely necessary.

LEE: It is the difference between life and death for some people. We cannot at the moment. We're trying to, you know, investigate on the data that we have collected all the time. And we try to look down and see, you know, how many lives we can potentially save. We know we can reduce suffering. That's off the bat, but it's how many lives we can actually save.

DAN: It can even run on diesel. At £340,000, it's not cheap, but he's hoping some emergency services may now lease the jetpacks on a trial basis.

RICHARD: This is great for getting the expert to the paramedic to the ... to the location. It's a bit like a paramedic motorbike in that it gets them very quickly to site. They then call in whatever other resources are required once they stabilise the casualty.

DAN: For those whose lives are saved by them, ambulance crews are already superheroes. If this technology is adopted, it will give them a matching super power, an ability to literally fly to the rescue. Dan Rivers, News at Ten. Salisbury.

JULIE: Just can't watch too much of those pictures. They're amazing. Time for us to fly. We'll see you tomorrow. Night, night. (*TTV-20200929*)

Notes

Bond：邦德，英国电影"007"系列中的男主角，全名为 James Bond。

Cumbria：坎布里亚，英格兰西北部的一个郡。

Words and Expressions

casualty *n.* 伤亡者
jetpack *n.* 飞行背包
kerosee *n.* 煤油
lease *vt.* 租用
off the bat 毫不耽搁
paramedic *n.* 急救医士
propel *vt.* 推动
realm *n.* 领域
refine *vt.* 改进；改善
see things 出现幻觉
shave *vt.* 削减
simulation *n.* 模拟
slash *vt.* 大幅度削减
speak for itself 不言而喻；有目共睹
squad *n.* 小队；特别行动组
triage *vt.* 确定治疗顺序

Questions

1. Why can the jetpack be a game-changer?
2. How is the jetpack powered?
3. How much does one jetpack cost?
4. How long did it take the inventor to upgrade the jetpack to the present condition?

Gap-filling

DAN: It can even run on ________________. At £340,000, it's not ________________, but he's hoping some emergency services may now ________________ the jetpacks on a(n) ________________ basis.

RICHARD: This is great for getting the expert to the paramedic to the ... to the location. It's a bit like a paramedic ________________ in that it gets them very quickly to ________________. They then call in whatever other ________________ required once they ________________ the casualty.

DAN: For those whose lives are saved by them, ________________ are already superheroes. If this technology is ________________, it will give them a(n) ________________ super power, an ability to ________________ fly to the rescue.

Dictation

And finally, not so long ago, ... mean saving lives.

Translation

1. They only existed in the realms of science fiction and Bond movies.
2. You're seeing things.
3. The film speaks for itself.
4. The jetpack might be used to rapidly triage hard-to-reach casualties.
5. They then call in whatever other resources are required once they stabilise the casualty.

Post-class task

Retell the story of jetpack.

40. New Green Initiative

RANVIR: Welcome back. Green number plates could seem the issue to electric vehicles under government plans to boost sales. It's also hoped it will encourage councils to introduce measures such as free parking and access to bus lanes for zero-emission vehicles. This year alone there have been 25,000 new registrations of electric cars. That's already more than for 2018, but they still only make up a fraction of the 32.5 million cars on UK roads. That's a long way off the government's target to make most new car sales low emission by 2030. Here's our consumer affairs editor Chris Choi on the new green initiative.

CHRIS: Nottingham is plugging into the future. Here the number of electric vehicles has doubled since 2017.

ROB: Once you take off your running cars, it's actually significantly cheaper.

CHRIS: Rob Cooling does 20,000 miles a year in his.

ROB: I don't think anyone's gonna really buy an electric car just to have a green mark on their number plate, but I do think the awareness of realizing "Well, if everyone else is doing it, if my neighbour is doing it, if my friends are doing it, then maybe it might work for my lifestyle as well".

CHRIS: The government is consulting on these three designs for electric car registration plates. It says they could make incentives like free parking and access to bus lanes easier and boost public awareness of growing electric vehicle use.

This bus lane in Nottingham is the first of its kind in the UK. What's different is that electric car drivers are already allowed to use it.

It's hoped that green plates would spark a range of similar perks but it will be up to councils to pay for any incentives. And that could be a problem. This Nottingham councilor is enthusiastic about electric cars but doubts they can afford to fund more perks.

SALLY: The council at the moment is in a very difficult financial position.

CHRIS: So, no free parking even if you got an electric vehicle.

SALLY: Not in Nottingham at the moment, no. The government need to help people. We could do with a scrappage scheme so that people driving the most dirty vehicles can afford to make the change.

MEL: And this is a typical EV engine.

CHRIS: Mel Creedy too wants new money, not new ideas, from government. She helps run an electric car lease firm in Nottingham.

MEL: I do think the government could support the manufacturers in bringing the price down and also put a little bit money, more money, into research for the batteries to hopefully bring the price down.

CHRIS: The message is clear: it's not the number plate on electric cars that's the issue, it's the price tag. Chris Choi, ITV News, Nottingham. (*ITV-20191022*)

Words and Expressions

bus lane 公共汽车专用道
enthusiastic *adj.* 热心的;热衷的
EV = electric vehicle 电动车
fraction *n.* 小部分;少量
incentive *n.* 刺激;激励
initiative *n.* 倡议;新方案
lease firm 租赁公司
number plate (汽车)牌照
perk *n.* 额外待遇;特权
scrappage *n.* 为报废旧车提供金钱补偿
spark *vt.* 引发;激励
zero-emission *adj.* 零排放的;无污染的

Questions

1. How many cars are on UK roads?
2. What is the UK government's plan about car sales by 2030?
3. What incentives does the government plan to offer to those using electric cars?
4. What problem do the local councils have against the government's initiative?
5. How can the price of electric cars be lowered?

Gap-filling

ROB: I don't think anyone's gonna really buy an electric car just to have a(n) ________________ on their number plate, but I do think the ________________ of realizing "Well, if everyone else is doing it, if my ________________ is doing it, if my friends are doing it, then maybe it might work for my ________________ as well".

CHRIS: The government is ________________ on these three designs for electric car ________________ plates. It says they could make ________________ like free parking and access to ________________ easier and ________________ public awareness of ________________ electric vehicle use.

Dictation

Welcome back ... low emission by 2030.

Translation

1. The measures include free parking and access to bus lanes for zero-emission vehicles.
2. It's hoped that green plates would spark a range of similar perks.
3. She helps run an electric car lease firm in Nottingham.
4. It's not the number plate on electric cars that's the issue, it's the price tag.

Post-class task

Do a research about Chinese electric car production and sales in recent years and predict the future of electric cars. Write a report of your research in 200 words.

41. Roadside Eyesight Test

MARY: Drivers stopped by police in parts of England will lose their licences on the spot, if they fail an eyesight test. Three forces are trialling a new scheme in a bid to reduce road deaths. Road safety charity Brake says there are around 3,000 casualties every year in the UK caused by drivers with defective eyesight. The latest figure showed almost 6,000 drivers had their licences revoked in a single year, for failing to meet the minimum standard. Here's Richard Paulo on the new crackdown.

RICHARD: On board a police car in Surrey this weekend, on a one-way slip road. To the right, an 87-year-old at the wheel does not spot the "No Entry" sign and almost crashes head-on. When officers checked, it turned out he could only see a third of the legally required distance. The pensioner who killed Cassie McCord had also failed an eyesight test, but after refusing to surrender his licence, he drove again. Three days later and moments after this footage, he would fatally hit the 16-year-old. As a result, *Cassie's Law* was introduced, permitting police to instantly strip drivers of their right to the roads.

JACKIE: I carry her ashes with me.

RICHARD: But for her mother Cassie (Jackie) current regulations are still not strong enough.

JACKIE: To find out that actually there's nothing unless you've got a registered medical condition. Then you can drive until you can no longer sign the form to say you're fit to drive.

RICHARD: And if there had been one, then Cassie would still be alive.

JACKIE: Colin wouldn't have been on the road; she would be here, yeah.

RICHARD: Under existing rules, a learned driver must be able to read a number plate 20 metres away when they're taking their test. From then on they must assess their own vision and inform the authorities if they have a problem. Now three police forces will check the eyesight of everyone they stop and immediately withdraw their licence should they fail.

You've got no idea what the eyesight is like on any of these drivers.

SAMUEL: Absolutely not. None of them have ever been officially tested over in reading a number plate from 20 metres. That's why Brake ... we're calling for a mandatory eye test every 10 years when you have to renew your photocard licence.

RICHARD: So we're changing the law?

SAMUEL: Absolutely. That's what we want a change in the law.

RICHARD: Whether drivers with failing vision will be the ones watching such adverts is debatable, but campaigners will this autumn press MPs for tougher regulation and penalties to prevent more avoidable deaths on the roads. Richard Paulo, ITV News. (*ITV-20180903*)

Notes

Three police forces: 文中特指英国泰晤士河谷(Thames Valley)、汉普郡(Hampshire)和西米德兰兹郡(West Midlands)三个警察局的警员。

Words and Expressions

at the wheel 在驾驶汽车
crackdown *n.* 严厉打击
defective *adj.* 有缺陷的
head-on *adv.* 正面地
in a bid to 试图
mandatory *adj.* 强制的
on the spot 当场
pensioner *n.* 领取养老金的人
photocard licence 含驾驶人照片和签名的塑封卡片式驾驶证
renew *vt.* 使继续有效
revoke *vt.* 撤销;吊销
slip road 匝道
strip ... of ... 剥夺
surrender *vt.* 交出

Questions

1. What will the police do if a driver fails an eyesight test?
2. How many UK drivers lose their licences in a year because of defective eyesight?
3. What is the background of the introduction of *Cassie's Law*?
4. What does Cassie's mother propose to do to impose stronger regulations?
5. What does Brake propose for a change in the law?

Gap-filling

RICHARD: Under existing rules, a(n) ________________ driver must be able to read a number plate 20 metres away when they're taking their test. ________________ they must assess their own vision and ________________ the authorities if they have a problem. Now three police forces will ________________ the eyesight of everyone they stop and immediately withdraw their licence ________________. You've got no idea what the eyesight ________________ on any of these drivers.

SAMUEL: Absolutely not. None of them have ever been ________________ tested over in reading a(n) ________________ from 20 metres. That's why Brake ... we're calling for a(n) ________________ eye test every 10 years when you have to ________________ your photocard licence.

Dictation

On board ... to the roads.

Translation

1. An 87-year-old at the wheel does not spot the "No Entry" sign and almost crashes head-on.
2. He could only see a third of the legally required distance.
3. The police will check the eyesight of everyone they stop and immediately withdraw their licence should they fail.

Post-class task

Do a research and write a report about road accidents in China in recent years.

42. Spina Bifida Repair

SOPHIE: For the first time in the UK, surgeons have operated on two unborn babies to correct the birth defect spina bifida that can lead to paralysis. The team at University College Hospital in London repaired the babies' spinal cords when their mothers were six months pregnant. Our medical correspondent Fergus Walsh reports.

(OK, I might not go too much deeper ... we might need membranes in a second ...)

FERGUS: This is remarkable surgery. Opening the womb to correct a birth defect. This complex procedure was done in Belgium. Among the vast team, a British surgeon who's now operated on two pregnant women in London. The mothers and their babies are doing well.

(Thank you very much indeed ...)

Spina bifida develops during pregnancy, when the bones of the spine don't form properly. This can cause a bulge from which spinal fluid leaks out. The condition can cause a range of lifelong health issues, such as paralysis, bladder and bowel problems and affect brain development. The delicate surgery happens at around 26 weeks' pregnancy. The womb is opened and the baby's nerve tissues are pushed back into the spinal cord, which is then closed. The pregnancy continues for another three months.

Until now, surgery to correct spina bifida was done after birth, but the team at London's University College Hospital say doing it in the womb has the potential to lead to better outcomes.

ANNA: We anticipate that we will be treating about 10 to 20 babies per year in the UK that have spina bifida. And the benefits are a reduced need to put drains in the baby's brain, improved neural development and improved motor function, and also improved bladder and bowel function.

SURGEON: So this must be my baby! Hello!

FERGUS: This is baby Ayesha from Belgium meeting the British surgeon who corrected her spina bifida when she was in the womb. Doctors expect she will walk normally.

MUM: From hearing that she was going to be paralysed from the waist down, that's like amazing. She is my daughter. She is not only a diagnosis, she is not only spina

bifida. She is what she is and she is perfect the way she is.

FERGUS: The surgery carries risks but Ayesha's mother says it is worth it for the chance of a healthy baby. Fergus Walsh, BBC News. (*BBC-20181024*)

Words and Expressions

anticipate *vt.* 预期
birth defect 先天缺陷
bladder *n.* 膀胱
bulge *n.* 凸起
drain *n.* 导管
membrane *n.* 膜
motor function 运动神经功能
neural *adj.* 神经的
nerve tissue 神经组织
paralysis *n.* 瘫痪
spina bifida 脊柱裂
spinal cord 脊髓
spinal fluid 脊椎液
womb *n.* 子宫

Questions

1. What could be the consequence if spina bifida is not treated in time?
2. How can spina bifida happen?
3. When is the best time to repair this birth defect before the baby is born?
4. Why not treat the baby after it is born?

Gap-filling

FERGUS: ... Until now, surgery ______________ spina bifida was done after birth, but the ______________ at London's University College Hospital say doing it in the ______________ has the potential to ______________ better outcomes.

ANNA: We ______________ that we will be treating about 10 to 20 babies ________ ________ year in the UK that have spina bifida. And the benefits are a(n) ______________ need to put ______________ in the baby's brain, improved ______________ development and improved ______________ function, and also improved bladder and ______________ function.

Dictation

Spina bifida develops … three months.

Translation

1. The mothers and their babies are doing well.
2. The benefits are a reduced need to put drains in the baby's brain, improved neural development and improved motor function, and also improved bladder and bowel function.

Post-class task

Retell the story.

43. Stonehenge Puzzle Solved

HUW: New research that's been published tonight has revealed the origin of Stonehenge's giant upright stones. Scientists have long been confident that the smaller blue horizontal stones were brought from west Wales, but the origin of the vertical stones has been something of a mystery until now. Findings were published in the journal *Science*, and our correspondent, Duncan Kennedy, picks up the story.

DUNCAN: It's stood here for nearly 5,000 years, but where did the stones of Stonehenge come from? We've known the small blue stones here came from Wales, but what about the other 52 massive sarsen stones? Well, now, finally, we have the answer. It's 15 miles away from Stonehenge, at a place called West Woods in Wiltshire. Sarsen stones can still be seen scattered around. Experts say it's here the builders of Stonehenge came.

KATY: It's really exciting to know that West Woods is the source of the sarsens for Stonehenge, because, first of all, it gives us that focus, it gives us that answer, but secondly, it also means we can do some more work. We know where to come now.

DUNCAN: This story starts in 1958, and an engineer called Robert Phillips, on the left, here. He was given a stone rod from a sarsen during repairs, which he then took to Florida, where he started a new life. Two years ago, aged 89, he decided to give the rod back to Stonehenge. That allowed chemical tests to be carried out and pinpointed where the stones came from.

LEWIS: I think he would have been delighted to know that, through his husbandry of this important artefact, that it's been able to be used to make this great discovery and pinpoint the location of where these stones have come from.

DUNCAN: Finding the source of the sarsens has been a goal of archaeologists for centuries. Until now, it was thought that the sarsens of Stonehenge could have come from anywhere between Devon and Norfolk. The fact they've now pinpointed it to this one location in Wiltshire is a major scientific and archaeological achievement.

SUSAN: When I was told the news, I was really, really excited, kind of shaking. You know, it's one of those moments where you know something that people have been asking questions about for so long, and we finally got an answer.

DUNCAN: An answer thanks to a stone rod kept as an office souvenir has now rewritten our knowledge of this pre-eminent, prehistoric monument. Duncan Kennedy, BBC News, Stonehenge. (*BBC-20200729*)

Words and Expressions

archaeologist *n.* 考古学家
artefact *n.* 历史文物
horizontal *adj.* 横的;水平的
husbandry *n.* 保护
pinpoint *vt.* 明确指出;确定(位置或时间)
pre-eminent *adj.* 超凡的;卓越的
prehistoric *adj.* 史前的
sarsen *n.* 砂岩
souvenir *n.* 纪念品
vertical *adj.* 竖的;直立的

Questions

1. Where did the horizontal stones come from?
2. Where did the vertical stones come from?
3. When was Stonehenge built?
4. Why are scientists so excited about the discovery?
5. Can you tell the process of this new discovery?

Gap-filling

DUNCAN: This story starts in 1958, and a(n) ________________ called Robert Phillips, on the left, here. He was given a stone rod from a sarsen during ________________, which he then took to ________________, where he started a new life. Two years ago, ________________, he decided to give the rod back to Stonehenge. That allowed ________________ tests to be carried out and pinpointed where the stones came from.

LEWIS: I think he would __________ delighted to know that, through his __________ of this important __________, that it's been able to be used to make this great __________ and pinpoint the location of where these stones have come from.

Dictation

It's stood here for … of Stonehenge came.

Translation

1. Sarsen stones can still be seen scattered around.
2. His husbandry of this important artefact helps to make this great discovery.
3. An answer thanks to a stone rod kept as an office souvenir has now rewritten our knowledge of this pre-eminent, prehistoric monument.

Post-class task

Do a research on Stonehenge and write a short report in about 200 words.

44. Sugar Warning

MARY: Hello then, welcome back. New figures today revealed the shocking amount of sugar that some children are still eating. It's now got so bad that Public Health England said a pudding tax should be considered, if manufacturers won't cooperate voluntarily to reduce the amount in their products. Rebecca Barry reports.

REBECCA: A new year and families are being told they need to take up new habits as it's revealed children in the UK have eaten more sugar than is recommended for an adult by the time they are 10.

MOM 1: It's quite difficult to avoid it and lots of things. And we can see now I try and get my daughter just to drink water normally, but if you're hanging about and people are having juice, it's quite hard to have the outcome.

MOM 2: They often put all of the sugary things at front so the kids automatically will know this.

MOM 3: You've got to be willing to stand up to them and say "No".

REBECCA: UK children are consuming 13 cubes of sugar every day, that's eight more than they should be, the equivalent of around 2,800 excess sugar cubes every year, which means children have already exceeded the maximum recommended sugar intake for an 18-year-old by the time they reach their 10th birthday.

KIDS: We love sugary things.

REBECCA: With childhood obesity at an all-time high, now parents are being told to change the way they shop. (*So make a swap when you next shop.*) Parents are being encouraged to swap everyday products, for example, switching from a sugary drink like this to a no-added sugar drink like this, and making similar choices for things like yogurts and breakfast cereals. They could reduce their child's daily sugar intake by half.

And health officials are considering going even further, pushing for a so-called "pudding tax" on cakes and biscuits, backed by some celebrity chefs.

CHEF: Yes, I think tax could work. Your taste buds get used to what you get used to, so if you have a less sugary drink, for example, you get to like it in the end. If you eat enough sprouts, you get to like them.

REBECCA: Excess sugar can set children on a slippery slope towards obesity, Type 2 diabetes and tooth decay. But the ways to fight it remain contentious, with one senior cabinet minister today rejecting a new tax as it would hit low-income families. Rebecca Barry, ITV News. (*ITV-20190102*)

Notes

Public Health England: 英格兰公共卫生署。

Words and Expressions

back *vt.* 支持
cereal *n.* 谷类食物
contentious *adj.* 有争议的
cube *n.* 立方块
equivalent *n.* 等量
exceed *vt.* 超过
excess *adj.* 过度的
hang about 闲荡
obesity *n.* 肥胖症
sprout *n.* 球芽甘蓝
stand up to 勇敢反对
swap *vt.* & *n.* 换掉
taste bud 味蕾
voluntarily *adv.* 自愿地
yogurt *n.* 酸奶

Questions

1. How many cubes of sugar at most are acceptable for UK children every day?
2. Why is it very hard to avoid eating too much sugar?
3. What are potential risks if one takes too much sugar?
4. What can parents do to limit children's sugar intake?
5. Why do some chefs support "pudding tax"?

Gap-filling

REBECCA: ... And health ________________ are considering going even further, ________________ for a so-called "pudding tax" on cakes and biscuits, ________________ by some celebrity chefs.

CHEF: Yes, I think tax could work. Your ________________ get used to what you get used to, so if you have a less ________________ drink, for example, you get to like it ________________. If you eat enough ________________, you get to like them.

REBECCA: Excess sugar can set children on a ________________ slope towards obesity, Type 2 ________________ and tooth decay. But the ways to fight it remain ________________, with one senior ________________ minister today rejecting a new tax ________________ would hit low-income families. Rebecca Barry, ITV News.

Dictation

UK children ... 10th birthday.

Translation

1. Children have already exceeded the maximum recommended sugar intake for an eighteen-year-old by the time they reach their 10th birthday.
2. Health officials are pushing for a so-called "pudding tax" on cakes and biscuits, backed by some celebrity chefs.
3. Your taste buds get used to what you get used to.
4. Excess sugar can set children on a slippery slope towards obesity, Type 2 diabetes and tooth decay.

Post-class task

Discussion: Exchange your dieting habit with your classmates and report the best you think.

45. The Scream

JULIE: Now after *The Mona Lisa*, *The Scream* is often said to be the second most famous painting in the world. Edvard Munch's haunting picture sends a chill through anyone who looks at it, and some might say it has a special resonance in the times that we are living through currently. But a new exhibition which includes a black-and-white print of the image suggests it isn't Munch screaming but listening to nature screaming all around him.

NINA: It has long been seen as an image of man's universal anguish, a figure screaming on a bridge under an angry sky. (*And there we have it.*) But now the British Museum says we may have got that wrong; and it's all down to the words on a rare black-and-white print of *The Scream* made by Edvard Munch in 1895.

GIULIA: So here we have the title "Geschrei" in large letters "Scream". Underneath it says "Ich fühlfe das grosge Geschrei durch die Natur"—"I felt a huge scream through nature". And he is blocking off the sound of that noise with his hands over his ears.

NINA: In other words, the figure is not screaming at all. It's nature around him.

GIULIA: The figure is holding the hands to the ears as though blocking off the noise of the scream. The fact that his mouth is in the shape of an "O" or an "ah" sound doesn't necessarily mean at all that he's actually screaming. It's what he's hearing and it's kind of shaking his whole body. You don't see that rather, you know, squiggly line underneath. It's not boldly inscribed in a way that will capture your attention. What captures your attention is the design.

NINA: A design that's been wildly copied. So if you have got the wrong end of the stick, you are not alone. Here's Homer Simpson having a go, Macaulay Culkin paying his own tribute, political cartoonist lampooning the Prime Minister, have found *The Scream* irresistible and there's even an official scream emoji.

GIULIA: Do you think it would have bothered him that so many people down the years have had their own interpretation of that as a man screaming?

GIULIA: The fact that it is known all over the world. He would have, he would have been pleased that his image had that amount of impact, yes.

NINA: The museum hopes to set the record straight with its exhibition of Munch's work opening next month. He may have been misunderstood. If so, it's a mistake that has only made his artwork more iconic. Nina Nannar, News at Ten. (*TFV-20190321*)

Notes

Edvard Munch：爱德华·蒙克(1863—1944)，挪威表现主义画家。
Homer Simpson：霍默·辛普森，美国电视动画《辛普森一家》中的父亲。
Macaulay Culkin：麦考利·卡尔金，系列影片“小鬼当家”(*Home Alone*)中的凯文。

Words and Expressions

anguish *n.* 极度痛苦
cartoonist *n.* 漫画家
chill *n.* 凉意
down the years 这些年
emoji *n.* 表情符号
get the wrong end of the stick 完全误解
haunting *adj.* 使人难忘的
have a go 尝试
inscribe *vt.* 书写
irresistible *adj.* 富有诱惑力的
lampoon *vt.* 嘲讽
line *n.* 一行字
resonance *n.* 共鸣
set the record straight 澄清事实；纠正误解
squiggly *adj.* 弯弯曲曲的
tribute *n.* 致敬
underneath *adv.* 在……下面

Questions

1. How do people normally interpret *The Scream*?
2. What's the British Museum's interpretation of the painting?
3. How does this painting inspire later artists?

Gap-filling

NINA: In other words, the figure is not screaming ________________. It's nature around him.

GIULIA: The figure is holding the hands to the ears ________________ blocking off the ________________ of the scream. ________________ that his mouth is in the ________________ of an "O" or an "ah" ________________ doesn't necessarily mean at all that he's ________________ screaming. It's what he's ________________ and it's kind of shaking his whole body. You don't see that rather, you know, squiggly line ________________. It's not boldly ________________ in a way that will capture your attention. What captures your attention is the ________________.

Dictation

Now after ... all around him.

Translation

1. The haunting picture sends a chill through anyone who looks at it.
2. If you have got the wrong end of the stick, you are not alone.
3. The museum hopes to set the record straight.

Post-class task

Discussion: Tell the class the most remarkable painting you like and why.

46. Titanic Wreckage

REETA: The first team in 15 years to dive down to the wreck of the Titanic say it is deteriorating, partly because it's being eaten by bacteria. Using a specially-built submersible vehicle, an international group of explorers have surveyed it and say that some parts of it are disappearing. Our science correspondent Rebecca Morelle reports.

REBECCA: At the bottom of the Atlantic, nearly 4,000 metres down, the most famous wreck of all time. This is the bow of the Titanic, still recognisable more than 100 years after she sank. It's the first time people have been down to see it for themselves for nearly 15 years. But while some of the wreck is intact, other parts have disappeared altogether.

PARKS: Probably the most shocking area of deterioration was the starboard side of the officers' quarters, where the captain's quarters are. The captain's bathtub is a favourite image among Titanic enthusiasts, and that's now gone. That whole deckhouse on that side is collapsing.

REBECCA: Microbes are eating away at the metal, creating stalactites of rust that dangle from the ship. Amazingly, though, the glass in the portholes is still in place, giving a tantalising glimpse into the Titanic's past.

It was the biggest ship of its time, setting sail from Southampton in 1912 on its maiden voyage, heading to New York. But it never made it. It sank after hitting an iceberg. 1,500 people lost their lives.

These incredibly ornate slippers belong to one of the Titanic's first class passengers, Edith Rosenbaum, a fashion buyer who was on her way to New York. She was one of the lucky ones. She survived, and she brought with her this musical toy pig that she played to soothe the children on the overcrowded lifeboat. Every one of the precious artefacts at the National Maritime Museum tells a story. But exploring the Titanic is also crucial.

ROBERT: I think it's still important to go down and visit the wreck because of course the wreck itself is now the only witness we've got of the Titanic disaster. All of the survivors have now passed away, so I think it's important to use the wreck whilst the wreck still has something to say.

REBECCA: The team are now analysing the footage they have captured to assess how long before the Titanic is lost to the sea. Rebecca Morelle, BBC News. (*BBC-20190821*)

Notes

National Maritime Museum:(英国)国家海事博物馆,位于英国伦敦格林尼治区,由三座相连的馆址组成(海事陈列馆、皇家天文台和皇后之屋)。

Southampton:南安普顿,英格兰南部海岸城市,英国最重要的港口之一。

Words and Expressions

bathtub *n.* 浴缸
bow *n.* 船头
dangle *vi.* 悬垂
deckhouse *n.* 甲板室
deteriorate *vi.* 恶化
eat away at sth. 侵蚀;逐渐毁掉
enthusiast *n.* 爱好者
iceberg *n.* 冰山
intact *adj.* 完好无损的
maiden voyage 处女航
microbe *n.* 微生物
ornate *adj.* 华美的;豪华的
porthole *n.* 舷窗
quarters *n.* 住处;宿舍
rust *n.* 锈
set sail 起航
slipper *n.* 拖鞋
soothe *vt.* 安慰
stalactite *n.* 钟乳石
starboard *n.* 右舷
submersible *adj.* 水下使用的
wreck *n.* 沉船

Questions

1. How many people died in the Titanic disaster?
2. Why is the wreck of the Titanic worsening?
3. Which part of the wreck may still reveal the grand past of the Titanic?
4. Why is it important to use the wreck today?

Gap-filling

REBECCA: ... These incredibly ________________ slippers belong to one of the Titanic's first class passengers, Edith Rosenbaum, a(n) ________________ buyer who was on her way to New York. She was one of the ________________ ones. She survived, and she brought with her this ________________ toy pig that she played to ________________ the children on the overcrowded lifeboat. Every one of the precious ________________ at the National Maritime Museum tell a story. But exploring the Titanic is also ________________.

ROBERT: I think it's still important to go down and visit the ________________ because of course the wreck itself is now the only ________________ we've got of the Titanic disaster. All of the survivors have now ________________, so I think it's important to use the wreck ________________ the wreck still has something to say.

Dictation

Microbes are ... their lives.

Translation

1. Microbes are eating away at the metal, creating stalactites of rust that dangle from the ship.
2. The glass in the portholes is still in place, giving a tantalising glimpse into the Titanic's past.
3. It's important to use the wreck whilst the wreck still has something to say.

Post-class task

Write a report about the present condition of the Titanic in about 150 words.

47. Wet Wood Ban

CLIVE: From next year, owners in England of wood burners, stoves or an open fire will no longer be able to buy wet wood or coal to use. The ban will be rolled out as part of the government's efforts to cut air pollution. Ministers want the public to use cleaner alternatives. Here's Katy Austin.

KATY: Cosy and relaxing. The fire in Ted's front room here in Buckinghamshire heats most of his cottage.

TED: It's the only heating we've got, really.

KATY: If you had a gas boiler or something, you think it would be more ...

TED: I think it would be more expensive that way, yeah.

KATY: He uses smokeless coal and dried-out, seasoned wood—the less polluting options. But burning wood and coal in the UK's 1.5 million open fires and stoves contributes 38% of harmful fine particle emissions. For example, a wood burner churns out 6.7 grams per hour. By comparison, a modern HGV emits just 0.5 grams and a modern diesel car even less, 0.17 grams. The wood on this pub fire is dry and seasoned so it should be a bit better for the environment, but it is the most polluting types of fuel the government is going to ban in England, the wet wood that's often found in bundles, a bit cheaper that you can find in a petrol forecourt or garden centre. Selling traditional house coal will also be phased out with local authorities in charge of enforcement.

WILLIAM: So the estimates have been that we can achieve about a 50% reduction in emissions if we switch from wet wood, which can have up to a pint of water per kilogram of wood, into properly dried and seasoned wood for domestic combustion.

KATY: This is where Ted and the pub get their dry wood from. Log supplier Keith supports the upcoming ban, but doesn't believe everyone will comply.

KEITH: This pile here is ready to be cut now, because it's well seasoned. It's been here nearly two years.

KATY: And do you think the problem will be solved with this ban?

KEITH: Not immediately. Not immediately because they've got nobody to enforce it. While people are offering cheap wood, people will buy it. You know, this is the trouble.

KATY: Concerns have been raised about the impact on rural communities and stretched

local authorities say they need enough funding for the extra responsibilities, but the government insists the move is necessary to address the burning issue of air quality. Katy Austin, BBC News. (*BBC-20200221*)

Words and Expressions

a burning issue 当务之急;亟待解决的问题
alternative *n.* 替代物
bundle *n.* 捆
churn out 大量生产
combustion *n.* 燃烧
comply *vt.* 遵从;服从
cosy *adj.* 小而温暖舒适的
cottage *n.* 小屋
domestic *adj.* 家用的;家庭的
enforce *vt.* 执行
enforcement *n.* 执行
fine *adj.* 很细的
garden centre 园艺品店;花卉市场
gas boiler 燃气锅炉
HGV = heavy goods vehicle 重型货车
log *n.* 原木;木材
particle *n.* 颗粒;微粒
petrol forecourt 加油区
phase out 逐步淘汰
pint *n.* 品脱(容量单位,约0.568升)
roll out 推出(新产品、服务等);实行(新制度)
seasoned *adj.* (木材)风干的,晾干的
stretched *adj.* 手头紧的
wood burner 烧木柴的炉子

Questions

1. Why doesn't Ted use a gas boiler?
2. How many UK people have open fires and stoves? And how much pollution does this contribute?
3. Where do UK people usually buy wood?
4. Why is wet wood banned?
5. Is it going to be easy to execute the ban?

Gap-filling

KATY: He uses ________________ coal and dried-out, seasoned wood—the less polluting ________________. But burning wood and coal in the UK's 1.5 million open fires and ________________ contributes 38% of harmful ________________ emissions. For example, a wood burner ________________ out 6.7 grams per hour. By comparison, a modern HGV ________________ just 0.5 grams and a modern ________________ car even less, 0.17 grams. The wood on this pub fire is dry and seasoned so it should be a bit better for the environment, but it is the most polluting types of __________ the government is going to ban in England, the wet wood that's often found in __________, a bit cheaper that you can find in a petrol __________ or garden centre. Selling traditional house coal will also be __________ with local authorities in charge of __________.

Dictation

From next year, owners ... most of his cottage.

Translation

1. The wet wood is often found in bundles in a petrol forecourt or garden centre.
2. Selling traditional house coal will also be phased out.
3. Stretched local authorities say they need enough funding for the extra responsibilities.
4. The ban is necessary to address the burning issue of air quality.

Post-class task

Retell the story.

48. Wildlife Photographer of the Year

MARY: And finally, wildlife photography often requires immense patience to get that perfect shot. For Russian photographer Sergey Gorshkov, it took almost 11 long months, but it was worth the wait. Not only did he capture a remarkable image of a Siberian tiger, his picture has now won him the title—Wildlife Photographer of the Year. Dan Rivers has the story.

DAN: An image so beautiful, it could have been a painting. This year's winner of Wildlife Photographer of the Year is all the more remarkable because it was captured on a camera trap. The composition and moment that a tiger rubs the tree to mark her territory was partly fate, partly the good planning of winner Sergey Gorshkov who spent years deep in the forests of Siberia, trying to capture images of the rare Amur or Siberian tiger which number only a few hundred. The announcement was made by the Duchess of Cambridge in an online ceremony.

KATE: The skill and creativity of this year's images provide a moving and fascinating insight into the beauty and vulnerability of life on our planet. So it's with great pleasure that I can announce this year's Wildlife Photographer of the Year is Sergey Gorshkov for his image, "The Embrace".

DAN: Sergey's victory clearly a moment to savour, after leaving the camera trap in place for 10 months.

SERGEY: Really I am happy and a big surprise for me. Thank you very much.

DAN: One of the judges told me why they felt this image was the overwhelming winner.

TIM: The one image that we all settled on was a vision of hope, I suppose, and this is an animal that is clearly under threat. The photographer had taken remarkable time and put an enormous amount of effort into getting this image, this intimate image between the Amur tiger and the tree that it's leaving its scent on.

DAN: Other commended images include this one of a monkey in chains, a poignant commentary on the plight of many wild animals in 2020. But although the finalists were all breathtaking glimpses into the animal worlds we rarely see, this tiger burning bright in the forests of Siberia is a compelling and uplifting winner, a portrait of an animal clinging to life, coming back from the edge of extinction. Dan Rivers, ITV News. (*ITV-20201014*)

Notes

Amur or Siberian tiger: 阿穆尔虎,或称西伯利亚虎,我国称"东北虎"。

Words and Expressions

all the more 更加;格外
burn bright 火烧得正旺(本文喻指东北虎极为耀眼)
cling (to) 紧握(本文指"顽强地活下来")
commend *vt.* 赞扬;称赞
commentary *n.* 评注;实况报道
composition *n.* 创作
compelling *adj.* 引人入胜的
embrace *n.* 拥抱
finalist *n.* 入围决赛者
insight *n.* 深刻见解;洞悉
intimate *adj.* 温馨的
overwhelming *adj.* 压倒性的;难以辩驳的
plight *n.* 苦难;困境
poignant *adj.* 悲惨的;酸楚的
savour *vt.* 享受
scent *n.* 气味
settle on 选定
territory *n.* 领地
uplifting *adj.* 鼓舞人心的

Questions

1. How long did it take Sergey to capture this image?
2. What are the reasons that this image became the best of the year?
3. How many such tigers still remain in the world?

Gap-filling

TIM: The one image that we all settled on was a(n) ____________ of hope, I suppose, and this is an animal that is clearly under ____________. The photographer had taken remarkable time and put an enormous ____________ into getting this image, this ____________ image between the Amur tiger and the tree that it's leaving its ____________.

DAN: Other ____________ images include this one of a monkey in ____________, a(n) ____________ commentary on the ____________ of many wild animals in 2020. But although the ____________ were all breathtaking glimpses into the animal worlds we rarely see, this tiger ____________ bright in the forests of Siberia is a(n) ____________ and ____________ winner, a portrait of an animal ____________ to life, coming back from the edge of ____________.

Dictation

An image so beautiful … in an online ceremony.

Translation

1. The skill and creativity of this year's images provide a moving and fascinating insight into the beauty and vulnerability of life on our planet.
2. This tiger burning bright in the forests of Siberia is a compelling and uplifting winner.
3. The image of a monkey in chains is a poignant commentary on the plight of many wild animals in 2020.

Post-class task

Write a report about this winning photograph in about 150 words.

49. Without Pain

SOPHIE: Now, imagine a world in which you feel no pain. That's what it's like for 71-year-old Jo Cameron. That's all she knows. The pensioner from Inverness has a genetic mutation which means she feels virtually no pain—and never feels anxious or afraid. She didn't realise she was different until doctors were astonished that she didn't need painkillers following a serious operation. Our medical correspondent Fergus Walsh reports.

FERGUS: She's had teeth knocked out, broken her arm, suffered serious burns, and felt nothing, because Jo Cameron simply doesn't sense pain.

JO: I put my arm on something and only realise it's burning when I can smell flesh burning. So, it's not clumsiness. The normal reaction is, you cut yourself or burn yourself, once, maybe twice, then you avoid that because your brain says, "Don't do that." My brain doesn't say "Don't do that".

FERGUS: As for giving birth to her two children, again, painless.

JO: Before I realised it, I'd had the children, so it wasn't a case of "I'm a martyr. I don't feel pain". It was, I'm prepared to take anything because they tell me it's going to be awful. I felt things, I felt my body stretching, I felt peculiar feelings, but no ... nothing to make me ... No pain.
(*Want a chilli challenge. OK? All right. One, two, three ...*)

FERGUS: And this is Jo with her husband and doctor eating superhot chillies—a breeze for her. Scientists at University College London have analysed her DNA and found she has two gene mutations. One shuts down the pain pathway from the brain.

JOHN: What we hope is to be able to exploit the mechanism to manipulate pain thresholds in people that have chronic pain, and there's a vast problem of around about 6% or 7% of the population who have ongoing excruciating pain, so we really do need some new therapies.

RESEARCHER: We have our pinprick box.

FERGUS: The team showed me some of the instruments they tested on Jo. No matter how hard the needle was pushed, it didn't hurt her.
Yeah.

RESEARCHER: Yeah?

JO: I cannot stop being happy and I do forget things.

FERGUS: Jo's gene mutation also boosts her mood, and she's never anxious, but it also affects her memory, and she often loses things. However, it's her inability to feel pain which may ultimately help others. Fergus Walsh, BBC News. (*BBC-20190328*)

Words and Expressions

astonished *adj.* 感到震惊的
boost *vt.* 改善;提高
breeze *n.* 轻而易举的事
chilli *n.* 辣椒
chronic *adj.* 长期的;慢性的
clumsiness *n.* 笨拙
excruciating *adj.* 极痛苦的
manipulate *vt.* 操纵;控制
martyr *n.* 殉道者
mechanism *n.* 机制
pain threshold 痛觉阈
painkiller *n.* 止痛药
pinprick *n.* 针刺

Questions

1. What is the reason that Jo does not feel pain?
2. How was this painless phenomenon discovered?
3. What is potential benefit of the finding by UCL scientists?
4. Does Jo's special physical condition cause any disadvantage?

Gap-filling

FERGUS: And this is Jo with her husband and __________ eating superhot chillies—a(n) __________ for her. Scientists at University College London have __________ her DNA and found she has two __________. One shuts down the pain __________ from the brain.

JOHN: What we hope is to be able to exploit the __________ to manipulate pain __________ in people that have __________ pain, and there's a(n) __________ problem of around about 6% or 7% of the population who have ongoing __________ pain, so we really do need some new __________.

Dictation

Now, imagine a world … doesn't sense pain.

Translation

1. Eating superhot chillies is a breeze for her.
2. One gene mutation shuts down the pain pathway from the brain.
3. We hope to exploit the mechanism to manipulate pain thresholds in people that have chronic pain.

Post-class task

Do some research and write a report about a person, except the disabled, who is physically different from normal people.

50. Womb Transplant

TOM: Now, asking any parent, the birth of a baby is indeed a precious gift. Well, how much more so when new life comes from a transplanted womb of a dead donor? There have been womb transplants before 40, in fact, which have led to 11 successful pregnancies and births, but they all involved live donors, relatives or friends who accepted the risk to their own health. Now for the first time, a baby has been born to a woman who had a womb transplanted from someone who had died.

EMILY: They say life is a miracle but when a life has been born from death, it perhaps takes on more meaning. This baby girl in Brazil is the first to have been born using a womb transplanted from a dead woman. She may be unaware of her significance but the medical world is not.

ANDREW: Technically, this is a game-changer because it's something that has never been achieved before. And what is very exciting is that pregnancy is completely normal, so the womb, having been through this transplant and having had the necessary treatments during the pregnancy, has still resulted in what appears to be a very healthy normal pregnancy.

EMILY: The mother of the baby was born without a womb, but unlike similar procedures in the past the uterus came from someone who had died. The donor womb was transplanted in a ten and a half hour operation. The surgery involved connecting dozens of veins, arteries and ligaments. Seven months later, a single IVF embryo was implanted. The pregnancy was normal and the healthy baby was delivered by caesarean section at 35 weeks. Eleven children have already been born from transplanted wombs that were taken from living donors. The first, Vincent, was delivered in Sweden four years ago, but the procedure is risky and controversial.

There are always ethical issues surrounding transplants, but like IVF 40 years ago, doctors say, they hope a uterus transplant could become mainstream even here in the UK.

That's something Lydia Brain thought would never happen. Womb cancer meant she had to have a hysterectomy last year.

LYDIA: I immediately kind of tweeted, like "give me, give me, I want one". It had never been something I thought might happen in my lifetime really. In the news over the last year it's got more and more promising. And the fact that, you know, by the time I may be a bit older and thinking about children, it might be kind of valid option for me.

EMILY: This tiny baby now gives Lydia along with thousands of other women hope that that could become a reality. Emily Morgan, News at Ten. (*ITV-20181205*)

Words and Expressions

artery *n.* 动脉
caesarean section 剖宫产
controversial *adj.* 有争议的
deliver *vt.* 分娩
embryo *n.* 胚胎
hysterectomy *n.* 子宫切除术
IVF = in vitro fertilization 体外受精
ligament *n.* 韧带
mainstream *n.* 主流
uterus *n.* 子宫
valid *adj.* 有效的
vein *n.* 静脉

Questions

1. What is the normal age limit for womb transplant?
2. How many children were successfully born from mums with transplanted wombs before this report?
3. Was the new baby born from natural pregnancy?
4. Who will possibly benefit from this new technology?

Gap-filling

EMILY: The mother of the baby was born without a womb, but unlike similar ____________

______ in the past the __________________ came from someone who had died. The __________________ womb was transplanted in a ten and a half hour operation. The surgery __________________ connecting dozens of __________________, ________ __________ and ligaments. Seven months later, a single IVF __________________ was implanted. The pregnancy was normal and the healthy baby was delivered by caesarean __________________ at 35 weeks. Eleven children have already been ____ ____________ from transplanted wombs that were taken from ________________ donors. The first, Vincent, was delivered in __________________ four years ago, but the procedure is __________________ and controversial.

There are always __________________ issues surrounding transplants, but like IVF 40 years ago, doctors say, they hope a uterus transplant could become ____________ ______ even here in the UK.

Dictation

Now, asking … who had died.

Translation

1. She may be unaware of her significance but the medical world is not.
2. The surgery involved connecting dozens of veins, arteries and ligaments.
3. The healthy baby was delivered by caesarean section at 35 weeks.
4. There are always ethical issues surrounding transplants.

Post-class task

Retell this story.

Part III

扫码看视频

扫码填空

扫码听写

51. Aston Martin Bulldog

KYLIE: And finally for this evening, it was among the fastest vehicles ever made in Britain. Only one Bulldog was ever built—a concept car to show what Aston Martin was capable of. Now, a new owner has rekindled the original designer's dream of seeing it travel at speeds of over 200 miles per hour. Paul Davis visited the workshop hoping to make that dream a reality.

PAUL: Like a creature from another time being brought back to life, a car with a unique place in British motoring history is once again taking shape. Panel by panel, part by part, the only Aston Martin Bulldog ever built is being restored to its former glory.

MAN: As you'll imagine, the performance is absolutely shattering.

PAUL: Designed in the 70s as a new breed of supercar, the Bulldog fell victim to an earlier recession.

RICHARD: So the headlights was William Towns' vision of how a headlight should be for a high-speed vehicle like this.

PAUL: Richard Gauntlett, whose father Victor, as Aston Martin chairman, was forced to sell the only model produced, admits it became a lifetime obsession to find that prototype and restore it.

RICHARD: It's just always been deeply ingrained into my brain, that image, which I still have on my wall, of the car with its doors up and bonnet down showing its five headlights. It's just ... It's just burned into the back of my eyes.

PAUL: These images were filmed shortly before a cash-strapped Aston Martin sold the only Bulldog to a Saudi Prince. Richard Gauntlett traced it to America where it's spent most of intervening decades in storage. Now a specialist company in Shropshire is putting the supercar status back.

For the technically-minded, a 5.3 liter V8 engine sits down there directly behind the driver's seat. It can power this from a standing start to 100 miles an hour in 10 seconds. It was the fastest in the world in its day. Then it clocked 190 miles an hour. The target now faster still.

NIGEL: We are aiming for 200 miles an hour. That's our magic number. If you look at the dynamics of the car, you could discern the power output of the car. We feel confident we can achieve it.

PAUL: Doing that safely involves stripping and checking every individual part, a process that will take another year before the Bulldog returns to the road. Paul Davis, ITV News, Shropshire.

KYLIE: And that's it from the team for now. The weather forecast is coming up next that's followed by the news. Where you are, I will be back with late news that's just after ten o'clock this evening. Until then, whatever you're doing, enjoy your evening. Bye for now. (*ITV-20201011*)

Words and Expressions

bonnet *n.* 引擎盖
bulldog *n.* 斗牛犬
clock *vt.* 达到(某速度)
discern *vt.* 觉察出
dynamics *n.* 动力
fall victim to 成为牺牲品
headlight *n.* (车辆的)前灯
ingrain *vt.* 使……深深印在脑中
intervening decades 几十年间
obsession *n.* 痴迷
panel *n.* 金属板
prototype *n.* 原型
recession *n.* 经济衰退
rekindle *vt.* 重新激起;重新唤起
shattering *adj.* 令人震惊的
specialist *adj.* 专业的;专门的
strip *vt.* 拆卸
take shape 形成

Questions

1. When was the first Bulldog designed?
2. Why and to whom did Richard's father sell the first Bulldog?
3. What kind of image left Richard an enduring memory?
4. How fast was the first Bulldog?
5. How fast will the second Bulldog be?

Gap-filling

PAUL: Designed in the 70s as a new ________________ of supercar, the Bulldog fell ________________ to an earlier ________________.

RICHARD: So the headlights was William Towns' ________________ of how a headlight should be for a high-speed ________________ like this.

PAUL: Richard Gauntlett, ____________________ father Victor, as Aston Martin chairman, was forced to sell the only model produced, ________________ it became a lifetime obsession to find that ________________ and restore it.

RICHARD: It's just always been deeply ________________ into my brain, that image, which I still have on my wall, of the car with its doors up and ________________ down showing its five headlights. It's just … It's just ________________ into the back of my eyes.

Dictation

These images were filmed … in its day.

Translation

1. The Bulldog fell victim to an earlier recession.
2. That image has just always been deeply ingrained into my brain.
3. The car spent most of intervening decades in storage.
4. It can power this from a standing start to 100 miles an hour in 10 seconds.

Post-class task

Discussion:

1. Do you have a dream of owning a supercar?
2. Describe some supercars you know.

52. Blackout Report

CLIVE: A week on from Britain's biggest power blackout in a decade, the National Grid, which manages the network, has delivered its first report to the energy regulator, explaining more about what happened. Our business correspondent Katy Austin is at Little Barford near Bedford, where one of the power stations went down last week. Katy.

KATY: That's right. The report that National Grid has sent to Ofgem this evening is just the first stage of an urgent review the energy regulator told it to carry out, explaining the chain of events that led to nearly 1 million people losing their power supply temporarily, and to extended transport disruption one week ago today.

How did it happen? Trains stopped on the tracks, passengers stranded. Major railway stations in chaos. National Grid says the incident was exceptional. We already know what triggered it—a power station near Bedford and a wind farm off the Yorkshire coast both went off-line in short succession. A drop in supply can have serious knock-on effects, so part of the network had to be cut off to contain the situation. It didn't take long to restore electricity, but critical parts of our infrastructure, such as railways and hospitals, ended up feeling the impact.

DAVID: Even recognising it as being a very rare event, and there are lessons to be learned and we need to look at great flexibility, also the resilience of the response in terms of critical infrastructure that was disconnected.

KATY: It's not only National Grid facing questions. Govia Thameslink and Siemens Mobility are looking into how some trains couldn't be turned back on without a technician. There are questions too about how a back-up generator at Ipswich Hospital failed. Today's report is unlikely to provide comprehensive answers. A full report is due in September.

Well, the overriding question that remains is, could the scale of disruption have been avoided, however rare this event was? Was the necessary resilience in the system there? Well, National Grid's report could potentially mention the role of local distribution networks. It's their job to take power from the National Grid to people's homes, and it's their job to decide when the supply gets switched on or off at a local level, so there could be questions for them in the report that National Grid is submitting. Meanwhile, a government investigation is now under way into what happened, and it will be looking at things including what could be done to prevent the impact being so severe on the public and public services if a future event like this happens again.

CLIVE: OK, Katy, thank you for that. Katy Austin reports for us there. (*BBC-20190816*)

Notes

Govia Thameslink: 高维亚·泰晤士连线铁路，英国最大的铁路经营许可机构。

Ofgem: Office of Gas and Electricity Markets，英国能源监管机构。

Siemens Mobility: 德国西门子轨道交通设备制造商。

Words and Expressions

blackout *n.* 断电；停电
contain *vt.* 控制
disruption *n.* 中断；混乱；扰乱
flexibility *n.* 灵活性
infrastructure *n.* 基础设施
in succession 连续地
knock-on effect 连锁反应
National Grid （英国）国家电网
overriding *adj.* 最重要的
regulator *n.* 监管机构
resilience *n.* 快速恢复的能力；适应力
stranded *adj.* （人或交通工具）被滞留的
submit *vt.* 提交
wind farm 风力发电场

Questions

1. What caused the blackout?
2. What serious impacts did the blackout bring about?
3. What lessons should be learned from this event?
4. Who submitted this report to whom?
5. What role does local distribution networks perform in electricity?

Gap-filling

KATY: That's right. The report that National Grid ________________ to Ofgem this evening is just the first stage of ______________ the energy ______________ told it to carry out, explaining ______________ events that led to nearly 1 million people losing power supply ______________, and to extended transport ______________ one week ago today.

How did it happen? Trains stopped on the tracks, passengers ______________. Major railway stations ______________. National Grid says the incident was ______________. We already know what ______________ it—a power station near Bedford and a(n) ______________ off the Yorkshire ______________ both went off-line in ______________. A drop in supply can have serious ______________ effects, so part of the network had to be cut off to ______________ the situation. It didn't take long to ______________ electricity, but ______________ parts of our ______________, such as railways and hospitals, ______________ feeling the impact.

Dictation

Well, the overriding question … happens again.

Translation

1. A power station near Bedford and a wind farm off the Yorkshire coast both went off-line in short succession.
2. Part of the network had to be cut off to contain the situation.
3. Critical parts of our infrastructure, such as railways and hospitals, ended up feeling the impact.
4. We need to look at great flexibility, also the resilience of the response in terms of critical infrastructure that was disconnected.

Post-class task

Discussion: Have you ever experienced a blackout? What was your reaction then?

53. Breastfeeding Support

RIZ: Now, coming to terms with breastfeeding can be one of the major challenges for new mums. One organisation believes the lack of support in some parts of the capital is contributing to London having one of the lowest breastfeeding rates in the world. It's now calling for better services to help parents through a difficult time, as Victoria Hollins has been finding out.

(*#My legs are long and strong ... #*)

VICTORIA: This is about as quiet as a roomful of babies gets. Baby massage is the secret. But this is primarily a breastfeeding support group run by Tower Hamlets Baby Feeding Service.

JOY: Well, we are everywhere where the mums are. We are there. So whether in hospital, or at home or in these groups, the mums know they are going to get really good support with their breastfeeding.

VICTORIA: That support means there are breastfeeding experts on hand as soon as a baby is born. It's in addition to the usual midwife and health visitor service, but the most crucial aspect of a home visit from an expert.

MUM 1: The breastfeeding support was completely out of the blue and was really lovely, someone coming to see you and spend a good 45 minutes to an hour with you, working with you and your baby and really sort of focusing on you and getting you off to the best possible start.

MUM 2: I mean, I think I would probably have given up on breastfeeding a lot quicker. You know, I don't think I'm the kind of person who would have felt I'd failed or anything, but I think I just wouldn't have continued.

VICTORIA: Research by the campaign group Better Breastfeeding says most areas of London aren't offering this support, and more than a third of boroughs have cut their breastfeeding support services, leaving mums isolated.

HANNAH: When he wasn't sleeping, he was just screaming.

VICTORIA: That was Hannah's experience. She lives in Redbridge, where home visits are no longer offered. She struggled to feed baby Thomas, and he started to lose weight.

HANNAH: The midwife, when she came round, didn't have much time to help me with it. She suggested some breastfeeding cafes that I didn't feel I could get to. It all felt a bit too much, trying to get there a couple of days after giving birth.

VICTORIA: Redbridge says it runs 25 baby clinics a month and ten breastfeeding cafes a week, but councils across London have difficult decisions to make. Almost all face cuts to the public health grants they get from government.

AYALA: For every pound you invest in breastfeeding support, you get ten times over in the health savings that you'll make. So it has an impact on all kinds of childhood illnesses, childhood obesity. It also has a real impact on maternal diseases as well.

VICTORIA: UK breastfeeding rates have recently fallen again. In Tower Hamlets, though, they have risen, and many here seem to be enjoying the efforts. Victoria Hollins, BBC London News. (*BBC-20181122*)

Words and Expressions

as … as … gets 最……;极……

come to terms with 接受(令人不快的事物);适应(困难的处境)

massage *n.* 按摩

maternal *adj.* 产妇的

midwife *n.* 助产士

on hand 在场

out of the blue 出乎意料

Questions

1. What might be the reason for London to be the lowest in breastfeeding rates?
2. Why are breastfeeding experts still necessary when there is already midwife and health visitor service?
3. What are the breastfeeding mums' responses to such support?
4. How much of London is now offering breastfeeding support?
5. Why is the investment on breastfeeding support worthwhile?

Gap-filling

VICTORIA: Redbridge says it runs 25 baby ____________________ a month and ten breastfeeding cafes a week, but ____________________ across London have difficult decisions to make. Almost all face cuts to the public health __________

________ they get from government.

AYALA: For every pound you ________ in breastfeeding support, you get ten times over in the health ________ that you'll make. So it has a(n) ________ on all kinds of childhood illnesses, childhood ________ ________. It also has a real impact on ________ diseases as well.

VICTORIA: UK breastfeeding rates have recently ________ again. In Tower Hamlets, though, they have ________, and many here seem to be enjoying the ________. Victoria Hollins, BBC London News.

Dictation

This is about as ... from an expert.

Translation

1. Coming to terms with breastfeeding can be one of the major challenges for new mums.
2. This is about as quiet as a roomful of babies gets.
3. The breastfeeding support was completely out of the blue.

Post-class task

Do some research on the benefits of breastfeeding and write a report in no less than 200 words.

54. Brexit Deal Done

SOPHIE: Well, let's go back to our main story tonight and the Brexit trade deal that was finally agreed today—four and a half years after the UK voted to leave the EU. Our diplomatic correspondent James Landale looks back at our relationship with Europe.

JAMES: The story of Britain and Europe can be told by maps, a tale of islands set apart from a continent by geography, leaving Britain, as Churchill said, with Europe but not of Europe.

HILL: Most Brits feel that their culture and political identity is different from that of people in the rest of Europe, and the fact that we're an island, our attitude to the EU was an economic relationship, the rest of Europe saw it as a political exercise that brought peace and security.

JAMES: When the European Economic Community was founded in 1957, Britain stayed out, still focused on empire. (*I have just come from making a full statement ...*) By the time it tried to join in the 1960s, mainly for reasons of trade, President De Gaulle of France said "Non" twice. But Ted Heath finally persuaded France to let Britain join in 1973. Even she was keen, campaigning in 1975 to reaffirm Britain's membership in a referendum. In office, Margaret Thatcher took Britain in deeper through the single market, but enthusiasm soon became antagonism.

THATCHER: No, no, no!

JAMES: John Major opted Britain out of Europe's new currency, but it wasn't enough to satisfy many in his divided party who, along with some newspapers and others, resisted what they saw as excessive interference. Migration added to those concerns. David Cameron eventually felt he could no longer resist, —

CAMERON: It will be an in/out referendum.

JAMES: —but he didn't get the result he wanted.

SPEAKER: The answer is, we're out.

STUART: I would argue that in 50 years' time, we will find the fact that we joined in 1973 more remarkable than that we voted to leave in 2016.

JAMES: Theresa May tried, —

MAY: The Article 50 process is now under way.

JAMES: —but she failed to win the support of her party or Parliament. Her successor called an election with a simple promise, and voters took him at his word.
For more than 50 years, Britain has agonised about joining, staying in and now leaving the EU. It's a relationship shaped, yes, by the geography, but also by history and politics and identity. The physical gulf remains, but tonight the relationship is set to change once again, and it won't be for the last time. James Landale, BBC News. (*BBC-20201224*)

Words and Expressions

agonise (about) 为……伤脑筋	opt out 决定退出
antagonism *n.* 敌意	reaffirm *vt.* 重申
article *n.* (协议、契约的)条款;项	referendum *n.* 全民公投
interference *n.* 干涉	successor *n.* 继任者
non *adv.* (法语)不	take sb. at his/her word 对某人深信不疑

Questions

1. When did Britain join the EU?
2. How long did it take both sides to reach the Brexit deal?
3. How many UK leaders have been mentioned in the report and who are they?
4. How do British people understand differently from the rest of Europe about their relationship with the EU?
5. Why does the reporter say the change won't be the last?

Gap-filling

JAMES: The story of Britain and Europe can be told by maps, a(n) ____________ of islands ____________ from a continent by ____________, leaving Britain, as ____________ said, with Europe but not of Europe.

HILL: Most ____________ feel that their culture and political ____________ is different from that of people in ____________ Europe, and the fact that we're an island, our ____________ to the EU was an economic relationship, the rest of Europe saw it as a political ____________ that brought peace and ____________.

Dictation

Theresa May tried … the last time.

Translation

1. The story of Britain and Europe is a tale of islands set apart from a continent by geography, leaving Britain with Europe but not of Europe.
2. Her successor called an election with a simple promise, and voters took him at his word.
3. It's a relationship shaped by the geography, but also by history and politics and identity.

Post-class task

Do some research and write a short report on the history of Brexit in about 200 words.

55. Congestion Fees

ASAD: Good evening, I'm Asad Ahmad. Minicabs will have to start paying London's congestion charge from April. It's because Transport for London (TfL) wants to improve air quality by almost halving the number of private-hire vehicles in central London. But unions warn the £ 11.50 daily charge could put livelihoods at risk. Here's our transport correspondent, Tom Edwards.

TOM: At St Pancras this morning, black cabs and minicabs have been busy as the Christmas getaway begins. But this industry is about to see big changes. From April, minicabs will have to pay the £ 11.50 congestion charge—unless they are zero-emissions.

DRIVER A: It will make a great difference when we have to pay congestion charge. If we are helping London to move round, we are bringing so much revenue into the country.

DRIVER B: I'll have to change cars to get Euro 6 engine cars. That's the only way you can come here. Otherwise, I'll have to stop coming, because you've got the congestion charge and on top of that you're going to have the emissions charge as well.

TOM: So it will make it harder to make a living, do you think?

DRIVER C: Uh, yeah, definitely.

TOM: City Hall says the rapid rise in the number of minicabs driven by hailing apps like Uber adds to congestion and pollution, particularly in the centre of town, but there's also a consultation on the age limit of black cabs. The plan is to bring it down from 15 to 12 years. Cab drivers think that will slash the value of existing cabs.

STEVE: We've invested £ 50 million in the last year in 1,000 new electric cabs, only limited by the supply of the vehicle. Over the next two years, we would have put another 6,000 to 7,000 on the streets. What the Mayor has done overnight is going to kick that stone dead. It's going to take away members' equity. We just don't know why he's done it. It's madness. It's going to affect us, and it's going to have a detrimental impact on London's air quality.

TOM: Transport for London, though, says these plans are about improving air quality, and at the moment about 18,000 minicabs a day come into town. They want to drop that to 10,000.

ALEX: Pollution is the dominant issue here. London, and central London in particular, has an air quality crisis, and this Mayor is determined to address it. And it's not just black cabs and private hire cabs that need to address this. We are cleaning up the bus fleets. All vehicles coming to central London are expected to be Euro 4 petrol, or Euro 6 for diesel, so everyone has to play their part.

TOM: Unions say minicabs paying the congestion charge will cost jobs. The Mayor's opponents say this is aimed at increasing TfL's revenues. City Hall insists it's all about improving air quality. Tom Edwards, BBC London News. (*BBC-20181219*)

Notes

St Pancras：圣潘克拉斯，伦敦火车站之一，紧靠国王十字车站。
Transport for London：伦敦交通局，简写为 TfL。

Words and Expressions

consultation *n.* 商讨；磋商
detrimental *adj.* 有害的；不利的
equity *n.* 财产价值
getaway *n.* 短假
hailing app 手机招车软件
halve *vt.* 使减半
kick sth. stone dead 完全扼杀
livelihood *n.* 生计
minicab *n.*（须电话预订而不能自由揽客的）出租汽车
on top of 除……之外
opponent *n.* 反对者
private-hire vehicle（须电话预约而不能在街上招停的）私人租用汽车
revenue *n.* 收益

Questions

1. What measures have been adopted by TfL to improve London's air quality?
2. What type of vehicles will be charged for congestion? Why?
3. What other vehicles are in need of improvement according to TfL officials?
4. What do opponents think of congestion charge?

Gap-filling

STEVE: We've ________________ £50 million in the last year in 1,000 new ____________ ______ cabs, only limited by the ________________ of the vehicle. Over the next two years, we ________ put another 6,000 to 7,000 on the streets. What the Mayor has done ________ is going to kick that ________. It's going to take away members' ________. We just don't know why he's done it. It's ________. It's going to affect us, and it's going to have a ________ impact on London's air quality.

TOM: Transport for London, ________, says these plans are about improving air quality, and ________ moment about 18,000 minicabs a day come into ________. They want to ________ that to 10,000.

Dictation

Good evening ... are zero-emissions.

Translation

1. Unions warn the daily charge could put livelihoods at risk.
2. What the Mayor has done overnight is going to kick that stone dead.
3. Unions say minicabs paying the congestion charge will cost jobs.

Post-class task

Discussion: Do you think congestion and emission charges will ultimately bring clean air to your city?

56. Discoverer Discovered

RANVIR: And finally tonight, how the British explorer who named Australia has been discovered six-feet down under Euston Station. For almost 200 years, it was thought the remains of Captain Matthew Flinders had been lost. But they've now been found by archaeologists working on the new HS2 line through London, as Paul Davis reports.

PAUL: For months, an army of archaeologists have been carefully sifting through centuries of history, working against the clock. The site alongside Euston Station will disappear when the new HS2 is built. Hundreds of years ago, this was one of the capital's largest graveyards. And among the thousands of human remains, historians were searching for the lost grave of one of Britain's finest explorers. This lead plate

on which the name "Captain Matthew Flinders" can just be made out meant the mystery had been solved.

HELEN: The discovery of Captain Matthew Flinders is really really amazing for us. We knew that he was buried in this burial ground, although, of course, there's an urban myth that said he was buried under Platform 15 of Euston Station. So now we know that's not true.

PAUL: Captain Flinders has been called "history's forgotten man". Between 1790 and 1810, he was the first explorer to circumnavigate Australia, and he's even credited with giving the country its name.

SUSIE: He is not very well-known in this country.

PAUL: Sisters Rachel and Susie, direct descendants of Captain Flinders' five generations on watched the footage of the excavation with delight and admiration.

SUSIE: The fact that it's Matthew Flinders is wonderful for us, but the fact that they've managed to find and identify anybody, that's been late to us there for 200 years, over 200 years. It's a real, it's a real lucky find. It's very very exciting.

PAUL: Their pride in the captain's exploits is evident.

RACHEL: He actually set off from this particular journey on a really leaky old ship. So he ... it was a miracle really he reached Australia in the end.

PAUL: They were brought up with portraits of their eminent ancestor, even a copy of that famous first map of Australia that he made. But it's been a bit galling the towns, streets and buildings are named after him down under, while in his own country, he's often overlooked.

Your great, great, great grandfather has been described as the man that history forgot. Do you hope that now he'll finally get the recognition he deserves?

SUSIE: I would hope so. It would be wonderful for his name to be remembered by more people.

PAUL: When the archaeologists give way to HS2, the remains of Captain Finders and thousands of others will be reinterred at a location yet to be identified. Paul Davis, ITV News. (*ITV-20190125*)

Words and Expressions

against the clock 争分夺秒
an army of 大群;大批
circumnavigate *vt.* 环绕……航行
descendant *n.* 后裔;后代
down under 在澳大利亚
eminent *adj.* 卓越的
excavation *n.* 发掘
exploit *n.* 英勇的行为(通常用复数)
galling *adj.* (因不公平而)使人恼怒的;使人感到屈辱的
give way to 让位于
lead *n.* 铅
leaky *adj.* 渗漏的
make out 看清;辨认清楚
reinter *vt.* 移葬
remains *n.* 遗体;遗骸
sift through 细查;详查
urban myth 都市传奇(街谈巷议的传闻或趣事)

Questions

1. Why do Australians like to name their towns, streets and buildings after Flinders?
2. What is annoying to the explorer's descendants?
3. How was the discoverer discovered?
4. Is there anything left by the explorer to his descendants?

Gap-filling

PAUL: Sisters Rachel and Susie, direct ________________ of Captain Flinders' five generations on watched the ________________ of the ________________ with delight and ________________.

SUSIE: The fact that it's Matthew Flinders is wonderful ________________, but the fact that they've managed to find and ________________ anybody, that's been late to us there for 200 years, over 200 years. It's a real, it's a real lucky find. It's very very exciting.

PAUL: Their pride in the captain's ________________ is evident.

RACHEL: He actually set off from this particular journey on a really ________________ old ship. So he ... it was a(n) ________________ really he reached Australia in the end.

PAUL: They were brought up with portraits of their ________________ ancestor, even a copy of that famous first map of Australia that he made. But it's been a bit ________________ the towns, streets and buildings are named after him ________________, while in his own country, he's often overlooked.

Dictation

For months, an army of ... mystery had been solved.

Translation

1. For months, an army of archaeologists have been carefully sifting through centuries of history, working against the clock.
2. Their pride in the captain's exploits is evident.
3. They were brought up with portraits of their eminent ancestor.

Post-class task

Retell the story of the discovery.

57. Elizabethan Maps

SIMON: A set of hand-drawn, Elizabethan maps depicting the defeat of the Spanish Armada have been saved for the nation after £ 600,000 was raised to buy them. The 10 maps—believed to have been drawn the year after the famous battle of 1588—were sold to an overseas buyer in July, but the government stepped in and called for a museum or an institution to raise funds to purchase them. Duncan Kennedy reports.

DUNCAN: Inside an archive, inside Portsmouth historic dockyard, inside a box, is the story of how England came of age, a story told through ten unique maps.

DOMINIC: It's astonishing that these things have turned up after 500 years. These are extraordinarily important.

DUNCAN: The maps, by an unknown artist, are believed to be the first visual representations of the Spanish Armada in 1588 and they have never been seen on television before. They've been in private hands for centuries, with historians not even knowing they existed, until a chance reading over the breakfast table.

DOMINIC: I was reading the *Antique Trade Gazette* last year and I saw these things on the front page of the magazine and I thought, "Hello. I've never heard of these. What are they?" I read the article, and I picked up the phone to the team and said, I think we need to try and buy these.

DUNCAN: But the maps had already been sold to a foreign buyer, so the government stepped in and imposed an export ban. That led to a frantic chase to raise the £ 600,000 needed to keep them here. And today, after a public appeal, it's been confirmed, the maps have now been saved for the nation.

ANDREW: I think these maps are really hugely significant for the story of England and by extension, Great Britain and the United Kingdom, and for the origins really of the Royal Navy and broader naval history. So they're really, really significant for the naval story, the story of our country, who we are, where we've come from.

DUNCAN: Until the Armada, Spain had been the dominant European force, believing it could overwhelm England. The mapmaker captures every moment of the campaign. One of the maps, Map No. 7, depicts what happened here, off the Isle of Wight. It shows the English in formation chasing the Spanish Armada. What the English were trying to achieve was stop the Spanish from sailing into the Solent, where they could take shelter, or even mount their invasion. The aim now is to send the maps on a tour of the UK, maps that help give direction to our past and set the bearings for what we became. Duncan Kennedy, BBC News, in Portsmouth. (*BBC-20210127*)

Notes

Antique Trade Gazette:《古董贸易报》。

Isle of Wight: 怀特岛,位于英格兰南海岸附近,1974 年设郡;该岛位于南安普顿海域的入口处,中间隔索伦特海峡和斯彼特海德海峡与英国本土遥遥相望。

Portsmouth: 朴次茅斯,英格兰南海岸的港口城市,皇家海军的主要基地,市内有皇家海军博物馆。

Solent: 索伦特海峡,位于怀特岛西北海岸和英国南部大陆之间的一个海峡。

The Spanish Armada: 西班牙无敌舰队。

Words and Expressions

appeal *n.* 呼吁；吁请
archive *n.* 档案馆；档案室
bearing *n.* 方向
call for 号召；呼吁
chance *adj.* 偶然的
come of age 成熟；发达
dockyard *n.* 船坞
dominant *adj.* 主导的；占优势的
Elizabethan *adj.* 伊丽莎白女王一世时代的（1558—1603）
frantic *adj.* 紧张忙乱的
impose *vt.* 强制实行
in formation 编队；列阵
mount *vt.* 发起
overwhelm *vt.* 击败
take shelter 躲避
turn up 被发现；突然出现

Questions

1. Where and how were many maps found?
2. How did the maps catch the attention of UK public?
3. Why are the maps extraordinarily important?
4. How much money was raised to keep the maps within Britain?
5. Who drew these maps?

Gap-filling

SIMON: A set of ______________, Elizabethan maps ______________ the defeat of the Spanish Armada have been saved ______________ after £ 600,000 was raised to buy them. The 10 maps—______________ the year after the famous ______________ of 1588—were sold to an overseas ______________ in July, but the government ______________ and ______________ a museum or an ______________ to raise funds to ______________. Duncan Kennedy reports.

Dictation

Until the Armada … for what we became.

Translation

1. Inside a box is the story of how England came of age.

2. Historians did not even know they existed, until a chance reading over the breakfast table.
3. The government stepped in and imposed an export ban.
4. They could take shelter, or even mount their invasion.

Post-class task

Retell the story of these Elizabethan maps.

58. Fares to Rise

FIONA: Millions of rail passengers will be paying more for their tickets from January with fares rising by an average of 3.1%. About 40% of fares, including season tickets, will be affected. The rise comes after a year of timetable chaos, strikes and delays on some parts of the network. Sophie Long reports.

SOPHIE: (*... for the cramped conditions on board today ...*) Chaos and cancellations as services were scrapped in the summer. Govia Thameslink had to apologise for the fiasco that followed the introduction of its new timetable. Autumn brought more disruption. Passengers were stranded, after a test train damaged power cables. And yet, as winter arrives, commuters are told their journeys will cost more next year.

So, how will the average rise of just over 3% affect ticket prices? Well, an annual season ticket from Brighton to London will go up by nearly £150. If you're travelling between Manchester and Liverpool, you'll be paying £100 more, while Tweedbank to Edinburgh will be £ 88 more expensive from January 2 next year. The hike didn't go down well with customers on the Buxton to Manchester line. They left notes for Northern Rail, saying overcrowding and cancellations meant services aren't worth the prices they're paying at the moment, let alone more. But the organisation that represents the train companies says the revenue will be invested in the railways.

ROBERT: No one wants to pay extra for their fares, but what do these fare increases cover? The day-to-day running of the railways, which allows billions of extra money to be focused on investment. New stations, new carriages and extra services.

SOPHIE: So, how's that going down with passengers?

PASSENGER A: I think it's already very expensive, so, I'm already trying to control how much I use it.

PASSENGER B: The trains are normally late. The trains are usually dead busy. I never get a seat.

PASSENGER C: It's too much money, isn't it? For a very bad service.

PASSENGER D: If the fares don't go up, you won't get the investment. It's as simple as that, really. The costs go up, and what do you want? You know, do you want a situation where the network just declines gradually?

SOPHIE: The industry is promising a more comfortable and more reliable ride on thousands of new services from 2021. But that's cold comfort for passengers who've called for fares to be frozen, fed up with feeling the pain of paying higher prices before they see the improvements.

Well, Fiona, no one wants to pay more, but everyone can see the current system is under strain. The rail delivery group says there will be 7,000 brand-new comfortable carriages, but not for a couple of years. And that is tricky for people who are already struggling with the cost of their commute now. Remember, though, fares don't go up until the New Year. So it might be worth renewing your season ticket before then.

FIONA: Sophie, thank you. (*BBC-20181130*)

Words and Expressions

carriage *n.* （火车的）客车厢	dead *adv.* 非常；绝对；极度
cold comfort 于事无补的安慰	fiasco *n.* 惨败；彻底搞砸
commuter *n.* 通勤者	hike *n.* （价格、花费等的）大幅度提高；猛增
cramped *adj.* 拥挤的	scrap *vt.* 取消
day-to-day *adj.* 日常的；日复一日的	

Questions

1. Why do UK authorities raise train fares?
2. What has caused chaos and cancellations in UK train service?
3. What are passengers' comments on the current UK rail situation?
4. Will the situation improve?

Gap-filling

ROBERT: No one wants to pay extra for their fares, but ________________ these fare increases cover? The day-to-day running of the railways, which ______ ____________ billions of extra money to be focused on investment. New stations, new ________________ and extra services.

SOPHIE: So, how's that ______________________________ passengers?

PASSENGER A: I think it's already very expensive, so, I'm ________________ trying to control how much I use it.

PASSENGER B: The trains are ____________________________. The trains are usually ________________ busy. I never get a seat.

PASSENGER C: It's too much money, ________________? For a very bad service.

PASSENGER D: If the fares don't go up, you won't get the investment. It's ____________ _______________________, really. The costs go up, and what do you want? You know, do you want a situation where the network just _______ _________ gradually?

Dictation

The industry is promising a ... season ticket before then.

Translation

1. The hike didn't go down well with customers on the Buxton to Manchester line.
2. That's cold comfort for passengers who've called for fares to be frozen.
3. Everyone can see the current system is under strain.

Post-class task

Pair work: Talk with your group members about the transportation condition of your hometown.

59. Floating Home

ASAD: Building on water is a suggestion being made for more homes in London. Some architects believe our rivers and canals could unlock space for not just houses, but floating villages too. But creating them presents its own difficulties, as Caroline Davies has been finding out.

CAROLINE: In a tranquil spot of the Chichester Canal, there is one man hoping to start a quiet revolution on the water. It took Mark 12 years to create his floating home.

MARK: Welcome aboard. You're right in nature. You know, we've got lots ... we've got the swans coming past, all the ducks and everything like that. We've got water voles living in the bank. It's a very tranquil place to be.

CAROLINE: Floating homes could technically be anything from a traditional houseboat to a live-on yacht, but Mark wants to create homes like this, more like floating apartments, built to building regulations. According to the Canal and River Trust, the number of people living on London's waterways has increased by 75% in the last five years. But making the move from land to the water comes with new considerations.

It can all look quite idyllic on a clear evening, but there are costs and considerations when living on the water. There is the upkeep of your boat, the safety certificates that are involved, and the cost of a mooring which, for a permanent one in central London, can be between £10,000 and £12,000 a year.

London has around 100 kilometres of waterways, not including the many hectares of open docks. And Mark isn't the only one with ideas of how to use them. This is one architect's vision of a floating village on the Royal Docks.

RICHARD: We are looking at a cluster of somewhere between 50 and 200 homes, all organised around a "village blue", with shops, pubs, workspaces. And then people could have a floating house, where you've got your own mooring. And this is lovely sort of community that could be developed.

CAROLINE: Across London, the team think more homes could be fitted in, too.

RICHARD: So without sort of interfering too much with the waterborne traffic, we can deliver somewhere in the order of between 7,500 and 10,000 homes, right here in the heart of the city.

CAROLINE: So is it feasible to put more homes on our waterways? There is a worry we might crowd them.

SORWAR: It's almost like a park that runs through the city, a blue green space. So we want everyone to enjoy it, whether they are walking a dog, going for a walk. It contributes to people's natural health and well-being, and we'd like that to be a mixed space where everybody can enjoy that. So while we encourage more boats and we want most people to enjoy the water space, it's very much of getting a balance right between those different uses so that everybody can enjoy that space.

CAROLINE: Using London's waterways differently is complicated and requires new ways of looking at how life could be lived on the water. But with pressure to find more places to house Londoners, in the future, could more of us be living a floating life? Caroline Davies, BBC London News. (*BBC-20190228*)

Words and Expressions

cluster *n.* 群;组	moor *vi.* 系泊
crowd *vt.* 使……拥挤	mooring *n.* 停泊处
feasible *adj.* 可行的	tranquil *adj.* 宁静的
hectare *n.* 公顷	upkeep *n.* 保养费
house *vt.* 给……提供住处	village blue 市民天地
houseboat *n.* 船屋	water vole 水鼠
idyllic *adj.* 田园式的;诗情画意的	waterborne *adj.* 经水路的
in the order of 大约	yacht *n.* 游艇

Questions

1. What could be the benefits of living on boat?
2. What difficulties are there for people in floating villages?
3. How many floating homes can be accepted in central London?

Gap-filling

CAROLINE: … It ________________ look quite ________________ on a clear evening, but there are ________________ and considerations when living on the water. There is the ________________ of your boat, the safety certificates that are ________________, and the cost of a ________________ which, for a(n) ________________ one in central London, can be between £10,000 and £12,000 ________________.

London has around 100 kilometres of ____________________, not including the many hectares of open ___________________. And Mark isn't the only one ____ _______________ how to use them. This is one architect's ___________________ of a floating village on the Royal Docks.

Dictation

Floating homes … considerations.

Translation

1. Without interfering too much with the waterborne traffic, we can deliver somewhere in the order of between 7,500 and 10,000 homes.
2. With pressure to find more places to house Londoners, more of us could be living a floating life.

Post-class task

Write a report about floating homes.

60 Future Houses

RIZ: Now we hear a lot, don't we, about London's housing crisis and what needs to be done to solve one of the biggest challenges facing the capital. But does it need more radical thinking, a different way of looking at the issue? Well, one architect is encouraging just that. His vision? A city in the suburbs, 100 miles long, running the circumference of London, all connected by a monorail, as Caroline Davies explains.

CAROLINE: These are fantasy streets of London, full of homes, shops, schools and businesses, not in the heart of the city, but in the suburbs—the idea of architect Peter Barber.

PETER: This is a linear city which is 100 miles long. It's about 100 yards wide, wrapped into the last 100 metres of suburbia.

CAROLINE: He is not planning to start bulldozing the fields yet. This is a theory to change the way we think about where and what we build: densely packed, further out and all walkable.

PETER: It's like a little piece of Soho or a piece of Covent Garden transported on to the edge of London.

CAROLINE: He's put some of the ideas into practice in a development in Stratford, of tall, thin houses.

PETER: When we first presented it to Newham Council, who were our client, they were a bit surprised because they, I think, were expecting, I know they were expecting, a block of flats. A lot of people equate density with tall buildings, and what this project demonstrates is that you can, with a four-storey building, made of houses, you can get the same number of units you would with probably a block of flats, which was six or seven storeys.

CAROLINE: He's also used an old method: homes which share a back wall, also known as back-to-back. Being so close together he thinks creates a more sociable place to live.

Do you think you might have a bit of a rose-tinted view of what it used to be like to live in some of these blocks?

PETER: This project, this scheme is the fruit of about ten years of research and thinking about a kind of revisiting the back-to-back house type and dealing with the shortcomings of it, but making the best of the benefits it brings.

CAROLINE: So where would these houses be built? Peter's 100 mile tour took us to a motorway.

So, why are we here?

PETER: Well, this is the edge of London. That grass verge is the edge of London, and that's the countryside.

CAROLINE: Surely one of the reasons many people move out, further out of the centre of London is to have green space.

PETER: We are not proposing to build on people's parks or on their gardens, but there's loads and loads of empty space which is really contributing nothing.

CAROLINE: This idea will not be to everyone's liking, but Peter hopes that talking about it will get people thinking.

PETER: We have to ask these question to ourselves, and to dream a little, and to imagine a world that's better than the one that we are in at the moment.

CAROLINE: Caroline Davis, BBC London News. (*BBC-20190205*)

Notes

Covent Garden: 考文特广场,伦敦中心区,英国国家歌剧团和芭蕾舞剧团之家。

Soho: 苏活区,伦敦中部的一个区,因其饭店、剧院和夜总会众多而闻名。

Words and Expressions

back-to-back *adj.* 连栋的
bulldoze *vt.* 推平
circumference *n.* 周围
densely packed 鳞次栉比的
fantasy *adj.* 梦幻的；虚拟的
linear *adj.* 线形的
monorail *n.* 单轨铁路（通常为高架）
motorway *n.* （英国）高速公路
revisit *vt.* 重新考虑；重提
rose-tinted *adj.* 极为乐观的
sociable *adj.* 易于社交的；气氛友好的
suburbia *n.* 郊区
to sb.'s liking 中某人的意

Questions

1. What kind of future house arrangement does the architect propose for London?
2. What are the benefits of such design?
3. Has the architect tried his idea somewhere already?
4. Why does the architect favour back-to-back style?

Gap-filling

PETER: When we first ________________ to Newham Council, who were our ________________, they were a bit surprised because they, I think, were expecting, I know they were expecting, a block of flats. A lot of people ________________ density with tall buildings, and what this project demonstrates is that you can, with a four-storey building, made of houses, you can get the same number of units ________________ probably a block of flats, which was six or seven storeys.

CAROLINE: He's also used an old ________________: homes which share a back wall, also known as back-to-back. ________________ so close together he thinks creates a more ________________ place to live.

Do you think you might have ________________ what it used to be like to live in some of these blocks?

PETER: This project, this scheme is ________________ about ten years of research and thinking about a kind of ________________ the back-to-back house type and dealing with the ________________ of it, but making the best of the benefits ________________.

Dictation

Now we hear a lot, don't we, about ... metres of suburbia.

Translation

1. This is a theory to change the way we think about where and what we build: densely packed, further out and all walkable.
2. Do you think you might have a bit of a rose-tinted view of what it used to be like to live in some of these blocks?
3. This idea will not be to everyone's liking.

Post-class task

Discussion: What do you imagine your future house should be like in your city?

61. Healthy Diet

SOPHIE: We should eat far less red meat—no more than the equivalent of a beefburger a week. We should double the amount of fruit and vegetables we consume and dramatically cut down on sugar and dairy products. That's what a group of scientists has come up with as a way of making us healthier, feeding a growing worldwide population, and protecting our environment. Here's our science editor David Shukman.

DAVID: Around the world every day 7 billion of us are cooking, and some of what we eat—especially a diet rich in meat—can damage the environment. So what's the answer? I join a cookery teacher, Kay Mangoshots. She says the key is flavour, not quantity.

KAY: So you use a small amount of lamb or chicken and you can just get ... the impact is just as tasty.

DAVID: So you get the flavour of the meat—

KAY: Absolutely flavour.

DAVID: —without using too much of it.

KAY: Yeah, and I think six or seven small cubes on your plate is ample.

DAVID: A major new report confirms this, saying these things should make up our daily diet of less meat and more veg.

It's really surprising when you see just how little the report recommends that we eat every day. And here are some of the key suggestions. It says no more than 14 grams of red meat a day, that's this little tiny piece here. No more than 13 grams of egg. That isn't a whole egg, it's just a quarter of one. Now for whole grains it says we should have 232 grams, we've represented that with this rice and these rolls. And for veg, they say 300 grams a day but it's got to be colourful. Red, green and orange. The authors reckon that, if we all stick to this diet, it will be not only good for our health but also good for the planet.

Beef in particular has an impact because when cattle burp they give off the gas methane, which adds to global warming. Growing feed for cattle takes a lot of land and water, and eating too much meat can lead to heart trouble and obesity.

The challenge outlined in the report is how to feed a global population of 10 billion by 2050, and prevent the 11 million premature deaths every year because of bad diet. In North America, for example, people eat six and a half times more meat than is recommended. But switching to the new diet won't be easy.

How practical is this for, let's say, a single parent with a busy life and lots of kids?

ROSALIND: Virtually impossible, I would say, because very often, firstly, this depends on really good home cooking and on planning. If you're feeding your children on instant food, impossible. And it requires you to be organised and to think ahead.

KAY: ... and add our carrots.

DAVID: But the scientists behind the report say we need to understand the implications of what we choose to eat, both for ourselves and for the planet. David Shukman, BBC News. (*BBC-20190117*)

Words and Expressions

ample *adj.* 足够的	cut down on 削减
beefburger *n.* 牛肉汉堡包	instant food 速食食品
cookery *n.* 烹饪	premature *adj.* 过早的;提前的

Questions

1. What are the benefits of a healthy diet?
2. What is the cookery teacher's advice for our daily meal?
3. Why does eating meat have anything to do with the environment?

4. Why is it sometimes very difficult to control food intake?

Gap-filling

DAVID: ... Beef in particular has an impact because when cattle ________ they give off the gas ________, which adds to global warming. Growing ________ for cattle takes a lot of land and water, and eating too much meat can lead to heart trouble and ________. The challenge outlined in the report is how to feed a global population of 10 billion by 2050, and prevent the 11 million ________ deaths every year because of bad diet. In North America, for example, people eat ________ ________ more meat than is recommended. But ________ to the new diet won't be easy.

How practical is this for, ________, a single parent with a busy life and lots of kids?

ROSALIND: ________ impossible, I would say, because very often, firstly, this ________ really good home cooking and on planning. If you're feeding your children on ________ food, impossible. And it requires you to be organised and to ________.

Dictation

It's really surprising ... also good for the planet.

Translation

1. The key is flavour, not quantity.
2. The impact is just as tasty.
3. Six or seven small cubes on your plate is ample.
4. Eating too much meat can lead to heart trouble and obesity.
5. It requires you to be organised and to think ahead.

Post-class task

Discussion: Do you approve of the nation-wide initiative of combating food waste?

62. High Street Decline

HUW: It's been a very challenging year for the high street, prompting renewed concern about the future of many town centres, already struggling with decline. A growing number of local councils have been buying shopping centres to try to revitalise their towns. Since 2016, 26 shopping centres have been bought by local authorities at a total cost of more than £800 million, as our business correspondent Emma Simpson explains.

EMMA: Wigan's Galleries Shopping Centre, once worth £83 million in 2006. But it went for £8 million this year, sold to the local council. There are three shopping centres in Shrewsbury worth £119 million pre-recession. They went for less than half that price, sold to Shropshire Council. And here in Bolton's Crompton Place, once valued at nearly £80 million, it went for £14 million in the summer, sold to the local authority. Sounds like a knock-down price, but no one else would have bought this right now, given the state that retail's in. It's huge, and slap bang in the middle of town, but this shopping centre has seen better days.

ADIA: There is a gradual decline that's taking place and clearly, as a council, we've taken the decision to do something about it.

EMMA: Not half. The council has bought it as part of a big plan to regenerate Bolton.
Do you think this is the best use of £14 million?

ADIA: This £14 million is a temporary investment, and we're very confident that we'll get the money back. This will be a game-changer. It will be transformational.

EMMA: You might be wondering, where has the £14 million come from to buy this? Well, it's not from council tax or existing budgets which have been slashed. Councils can access cheap loans, and over the last few years they've been pouring money into commercial property to generate an income to help fund services.
There are better ways to make money than buying shops. Here in Camberley, the council not only bought this mall, but also the House of Fraser building right next to it, not long before the retailer collapsed. They could have bought it for a lot less now.

MARK: There is risk attached to local authorities intervening, and if they're simply doing it to try and make a quick profit, then that's the wrong motivation, but if it's doing and being done in order to regenerate the towns, then that absolutely is the right thing.

EMMA: Because no one else is going to do it?

MARK: The private sector can't take that long-term view. It's not viable.

EMMA: It used to be so easy attracting people into our town centres. It's a real problem today, though. But Bolton Council's bold purchase is kick-starting crucial private investment to help make this place fit for the future. Emma Simpson, BBC News, Bolton. (*BBC-20181227*)

Words and Expressions

have seen better days 已经衰败;今不如昔
intervene *vi.* 出面;介入;干预
kick-start *vt.* 快速启动
knock-down *adj.* 低廉的
regenerate *vt.* 使振兴;使复兴
revitalise *vt.* 使恢复生机;使复兴
slap bang *adv.* 恰好
viable *adj.* 可实施的;切实可行的

Questions

1. Why do councils buy those declining shopping centers?
2. How can councils have so much money to make the purchases?
3. Why are there no private enterprises wanting to buy them?

Gap-filling

MARK: There is risk attached to local authorities ________________, and if they're simply doing it to try and make a quick profit, then that's the wrong ________________, but if it's doing and being done in order to ________________ the towns, then that absolutely is the right thing.

EMMA: Because ________________ is going to do it?

MARK: The private ________________ can't take that long-term view. It's not ________________.

EMMA: It used to be so easy attracting people into our ________________. It's a real problem today, ________________. But Bolton Council's ________________ purchase is kick-starting ________________ private investment to help make this place ________________ for the future. Emma Simpson, BBC News, Bolton.

Dictation

You might be wondering … for a lot less now.

Translation

1. No one else would have bought this right now, given the state that retail's in.
2. It's huge, and slap bang in the middle of town, but this shopping centre has seen better days.
3. They've been pouring money into commercial property to generate an income to help fund services.
4. There is risk attached to local authorities intervening.

Post-class task

Discussion:

1. What might be the reason for the declining shopping malls?
2. What are feasible measures to regenerate city centers?

63. Incentivising Cycling

HUW: Now the government has announced a series of initiatives to boost the number of people cycling in England, as part of its campaign against obesity and to reduce emissions from vehicles. A significant part of the strategy is to expand cycle lanes. There are plans for doctors to prescribe cycling as part of a health regime. And there'll be £50 vouchers to repair bikes that will be offered on a first-come-first-served basis. But does the strategy have the resources and the ambition to achieve its goals? Our correspondent Sian Lloyd reports now from Birmingham.

SIAN: Gearing up for a busy time. People will soon be able to cash in government vouchers towards the cost of fixing up their old bikes and getting back on the road. And during lockdown, this shop saw a surge in demand for cycling.

ALEX: From March to about June time, we sold loads of bikes. We kept bikes going out the door. But now, we've only got two bikes in the store, and we can't get any more until about September.

SIAN: It's something the Government wants to build on and, today, launched its proposals to encourage people to get out of their cars. Plans include improving infrastructure and making cycling safer. It could lead to more schemes like this one in Birmingham, where cyclists are separated from other road users. But for many, picking through the traffic is the norm. These experienced cyclists are used to the challenges. The Government's task is to convince others to join them.

CYCLIST 1: During lockdown, there was so little traffic on the road, it was great that people felt more confident to go out cycling. Now there's an increase in traffic, it does feel like it's getting a little bit more dangerous.

CYCLIST 2: I think in a city, there's absolutely a need for the cycle lanes, it makes total sense, and I think it will give people that confidence that they can get out on their bikes safely.

CYCLIST 3: A car coming past you within about two feet of you. If you're not used to it, you're not going to cycle very far. It's frightening. So, they've got to put their money where their mouth is.

SIAN: The proposals are being described as ambitious, but there are questions about the level of funding.

DUNCAN: We've heard about two billion being invested for cycling and walking, that's over five years, about 400 million a year. It's only 2% of the transport budget. And for this to be delivered, there needs to be a real rethink of how we prioritise our investment in transport.

SIAN: Transforming the way people travel is part of the Government's target to reduce emissions and improve health, but opponents say months have gone by since plans were initially announced, and the pace of change isn't quick enough. Sian Lloyd, BBC News, Birmingham. (*BBC-20200728*)

Words and Expressions

ambition *n.* 雄心
ambitious *adj.* 雄心勃勃的;(计划、想法等)宏大的,艰巨的
cash in 把……兑为现金
gear up 做好准备
health regime 养生法
lockdown *n.* 封锁
make sense 是明智的;合乎情理;可行
prioritise *vt.* 优先考虑(处理)
put one's money where their mouth is 用行动证明自己的话
rethink *n.* 重新考虑
voucher *n.* 代币券

Questions

1. Why does the UK government incentivise cycling?
2. What will the government do to prompt people to cycle more?

3. Why are cycle lanes absolutely necessary in cities?
4. Will the government's plan be easy to accomplish?

Gap-filling

CYCLIST 1: During ________________, there was so little traffic on the road, it was great that people felt more ________________ to go out cycling. Now there's a(n) ________________ traffic, it does feel like it's getting ________________ more dangerous.

CYCLIST 2: I think in a city, there's absolutely ________________ for the cycle lanes. It makes ________________, and I think it will give people that ________________ that they can get out on their bikes safely.

CYCLIST 3: A car coming ________________ within about two feet of you. If you're not used to it, you're not going to cycle very far. It's ________________. So, they've got to put their money where ________________.

Dictation

It's something the Government ... to join them.

Translation

1. There are plans for doctors to prescribe cycling as part of a health regime.
2. Vouchers will be offered on a first-come-first-served basis.
3. For many, picking through the traffic is the norm.
4. They've got to put their money where their mouth is.

Post-class task

Discussion: Do you cycle very often in your local community? Why (not)?

64. Insects in Decline

HUW: Human activity could drive the earth's entire insect population to extinction within a century, according to a major new scientific study. Insects are vital pollinators, so any decline threatens food production, and there are warnings now that 40% of species could be gone within just a few decades. Pesticides, agriculture and climate change are all being blamed. Our environment correspondent Victoria Gill has more details.

VICTORIA: They are the planet's smallest, most essential workers, producing our food, cleaning up our waste. But changes we are making to the environment threaten the very existence of the earth's insect population. That's according to scientists who analyzed dozens of insects surveys that were carried out all over the world over the last 13 years. It revealed that many species are now sliding towards extinction at a dramatic rate. Overall, 41% of the world's insect species are in decline. And that includes some very familiar creatures. 49% of beetles are declining, 37% of mayflies and 53% of butterflies and moths.

That's one of the groups that's troubled?

PHILIP: Absolutely, moths and bees and beetles are all massively in trouble right now.

VICTORIA: Those losses, scientists say, could jeopardise our way of life.

PHILIP: So much of our atmospheric carbon which is linked to climate change, that's stored in the soil, and that's cycled through the soil by insects. Our food is grown in the soil—that's made by insects—and then our food is then pollinated by insects. Every single step along that has an insect associated with it that's doing an important job. Without that, then we'd just lose the ability to produce food, wouldn't we?

VICTORIA: But as much as we rely on insects, it's primarily our activities and our food production practices that have been driving these declines.

There are three key things that this study highlights as threats to our planet's insect diversity—climate change, invasive species and, critically, how we use our land, the increasing intensification of agriculture. Around the world, suitable habitat is being consumed by farming and urbanisation. And the study says widespread use of synthetic pesticides is a major driver of insect loss. Bug lovers can help by making gardens more pollinator friendly, but researchers say food production will have to change to stop our most important pollinators becoming collateral damage in the battle against pests. Victoria Gill, BBC News. (*BBC-20190211*)

Words and Expressions

as much as 虽然;尽管
collateral damage 附带性破坏;附带损害
extinction *n.* 灭绝;绝种
highlight *vt.* 突出;强调
intensification *n.* 增强
invasive *adj.* 侵入的
jeopardise *vt.* 危害;损害
mayfly *n.* 蜉蝣
moth *n.* 飞蛾
pest *n.* 害虫
pesticide *n.* 杀虫剂
pollinate *vt.* 授粉;传粉
synthetic *adj.* 合成的

Questions

1. Why are insects important to humans?
2. What are common useful insects?
3. What has caused the decline of insects?
4. How alarming is the present situation of insects?
5. What immediate action must be done to increase the population of insects?

Gap-filling

VICTORIA: But ______________ we rely on insects, it is primarily our activities and our food production practices ______________ driving these declines.

There are three key things that ______________ highlights as threats to our planet's insect ______________—climate change, ______________ species and, critically, how we use our land, the increasing ______________ of agriculture. Around the world, suitable ______________ is being ______________ by farming and urbanisation. And the study says widespread use of ______________ is a major driver of insect loss. ______________ lovers can help by making gardens more pollinator ______________, but researchers say food ______________ will have to change to stop our most important pollinators becoming ______________ damage in the battle against ______________. Victoria Gill, BBC News.

Dictation

They are the planet's … butterflies and moths.

Translation

1. Changes we are making to the environment threaten the very existence of the earth's insect population.
2. Those losses could jeopardise our way of life.
3. Widespread use of synthetic pesticides is a major driver of insect loss.

Post-class task

Retell the story in your own words.

65. Lyme Disease

CHARLENE: More of us are getting infected by Lyme disease and the figure may be three times more as first thought. A study of GP records show infections across the UK with Scotland and the South of England having the highest number. If untreated it can cause serious long-term health problems, but it's often very difficult to diagnose. Our health correspondent Emily Morgan has more.

EMILY: Sitting in her garden, unable to stand for long without a walking stick, it's not the image Kirsty ever expected. As she watches her children play, she reflects on her life today.

KIRSTY: There isn't a single aspect of life that hasn't changed.

EMILY: Last year, the mother of two was bitten by a tick. It left a rash, and after flu-like symptoms she was diagnosed with Lyme disease. Despite two courses of antibiotics, she still suffers debilitating effects.

KIRSTY: I have a high level of fatigue. I spend most of my time in the house. There are days I don't go out at all. Most of my time is spent resting. I have more problems with my memory now. I forget people's names, people I've known for a long time. My speech becomes more difficult, so I start to slur a little and I have to talk more slowly.

EMILY: This is the tiny insect that spreads the disease when it burrows into the skin to feed. After analysing the medical records of 8.4 million people in the UK, researchers now think there could be more than 8,000 new cases of Lyme disease this year, much higher than the 2,000 initially predicted. In the UK ticks

are most prevalent in Scotland and the south of England, but can be found anywhere.

Obviously not all ticks that live in this sort of undergrowth carry the bacterial disease, but those that do leave a telltale mark. And despite that rash ring that they leave, symptoms are very hard to diagnose, which is why there are so many more potential cases than we first thought.

JONATHAN: So, this is perfect habitat for ticks. You've got, you know, quite luxuriant vegetation, nice and moist conditions.

EMILY: Jonathan Leadley claims climate change is helping to increase tick populations, and says awareness is crucial in mitigating Lyme disease.

JONATHAN: I don't think we should be worried particularly. It's still quite a rare disease, but we just need to be vigilant. (You) need to be vigilant, take ticks off if you find them. And if you're worried about, you know, if you get any symptoms, go and see your doctor straight away, and mention that this could be linked to a tick bite.

KIRSTY: Goal. Have another goal.

EMILY: Kirsty says she is one of the unlucky ones. Lyme disease has left an indelible mark on her and any plans for the future right now will have to be put on hold. Emily Morgan, ITV News, in York.

CHARLENE: And for more information on symptoms of the disease and how to avoid tick bites in the first place, go to our website. (*ITV-20190731*)

Words and Expressions

bacterial *adj.* 细菌的
burrow *vi.* 钻
course *n.* 疗程
debilitating *adj.* 虚弱的
fatigue *n.* 疲劳
indelible *adj.* 消除不掉的
luxuriant *adj.* 茂盛的;浓密的
mitigate *vt.* 减轻
moist *adj.* 潮湿的
prevalent *adj.* 普遍存在的
put on hold 搁置
rash *n.* 皮疹
ring *n.* 圆形标记;圆环,圆圈
slur *vt.* 含糊地说
telltale *adj.* 泄露秘密的
tick *n.* 蜱
undergrowth *n.* 下层灌木丛
vegetation *n.* 植被
vigilant *adj.* 警惕的

Questions

1. How did Kirsty contract Lyme disease?
2. How was Kirsty treated for the disease?
3. What serious impact has Lyme disease brought to Kirsty's daily life?
4. Where in the UK are more likely to have Lyme disease?
5. Why are there more potential cases than expected?
6. Is there any link between Lyme disease and human activities?

Gap-filling

JONATHAN: So, this is perfect ________________ for ticks. You've got, you know, quite ________________ vegetation, nice and ________________ conditions.

EMILY: Jonathan Leadley claims climate change is ________________ to increase tick populations, and says ________________ is crucial in ________________ Lyme disease.

JONATHAN: I don't think we should be ________________ particularly. It's still quite a (n) ________________ disease, but we just need to be vigilant. (You) need to be vigilant, take ticks off if you find them. And if you're worried about, you know, if you get any ________________, go and see your doctor straight away, and ____________________ that this could be linked to a (n) ________________.

KIRSTY: Goal. Have another goal.

EMILY: Kirsty says she is one of the unlucky ________________. Lyme disease has left a(n) ________________ mark on her and any plans for the future right now will have to be put ________________. Emily Morgan, ITV News, in York.

Dictation

This is the tiny insect … than we first thought.

Translation

1. Despite two courses of antibiotics, she still suffers debilitating effects.
2. This is the tiny insect that spreads the disease when it burrows into the skin to feed.
3. You've got quite luxuriant vegetation, nice and moist conditions.

Post-class task

Retell the story of Lyme disease.

66. Museum of the Year
(St Fagans National Museum of History)

SOPHIE: It's been called a magical place made by the people of Wales. St Fagans National Museum of History has tonight been named the winner of one of the most prestigious museum prizes in the world, the Art Fund Museum of the Year, after beating off four other museums across the UK. Our arts editor Will Gompertz visited all the contenders, and sent this report.

WILL: Five very different cultural destinations who are vying to be the Art Fund Museum of the Year 2019. But there could only be one winner, and it was ... St Fagans National Museum of History near Cardiff. It's a 100-acre visitor attraction, boasting over 40 different Welsh buildings that have been relocated with extraordinary attention to detail to tell the story of the country's past. A major £30 million development has just been completed, which includes the creation of this Iron Age farmstead, made with the help of both visitors and volunteers.

ANNA: Hi, my name's Anna Rochanski. I'm a volunteer at St Fagans and I'm standing in the middle of an Iron Age farmstead called Bryn Eryr, and I helped to lay the floor. It's all about recreating the past. I think we all have that feel inside that's we want to step back in time. Thinking about how people live their lives, I think that's really important.

WILL: To see all the museums on this year's shortlist requires a country-hopping tour taking you from St Fagans in Cardiff to HMS Caroline in Belfast. The ship is the last remaining British World War I light cruiser still afloat, and the sole survivor of the Battle of Jutland. It is now a star attraction in a major dockside renovation which won the judges' approval, for putting education at its heart.

Across the water in Scotland is the V&A Dundee. Its striking architecture caught the judges' eye, while its contents captured the imagination of many in the city.

ALISA: I think the fact that the museum has always had young people at its heart really just allows people to come in and feel comfortable and enjoy and feel like it's their museum that they're coming to.

WILL: 350 miles to the south is Nottingham Contemporary, a gallery celebrating its tenth anniversary with a Museum of the Year nomination for its commitment to contemporary art and diversity.

MICHAELA: You can come here and you can do activities to do with. We speak a lot about LGBTQ things going on, racial things going on. There's always something to do.

WILL: The final finalist was the eclectic, eccentric Pitt Rivers Museum in Oxford. It is a remarkable treasure trove of human history, shortlisted for the enlightening way, its rethinking the presentation of its astonishing collection of over half a million objects that span from prehistory to the present day.

But it was St Fagans in Wales that won the prestigious £100,000 prize for being, the judges said, one of the most welcoming and engaging museums anywhere in the UK. Will Gompertz, BBC News. (*BBC-20190703*)

Notes

Battle of Jutland：日德兰海战，1916 年英德双方在丹麦日德兰半岛附近爆发的一场大海战。此战，英国皇家海军将德国海军封锁在了德国港口，使得后者在战争后期几乎毫无作为，从而取得了战略上的最终胜利。

Words and Expressions

afloat *adj.* 漂浮在水上的
contender *n.* 角逐者
cruiser *n.* 巡洋舰
eclectic *adj.* 不拘一格的
engaging *adj.* 有趣的；令人愉快的；迷人的
farmstead *n.* 农庄
hop *vi.* 快速旅行；冲
LGBTQ 性少数群体
shortlist *n.* 入围名单
vt. 把……列入入围名单
vie *vi.* 争夺

Questions

1. How many museums were nominated for the prize?
2. Which city is the winner in 2019?
3. What makes the winner beat off other candidates?
4. What is special for each of the lost nominees?
5. What is the financial reward to the winner?

Gap-filling

WILL: 350 miles to the south is Nottingham Contemporary, a(n) ____________ celebrating its tenth ____________ with a Museum of the Year ________ ____________ for its ____________ to contemporary art and ________ ____________.

MICHAELA: You can come here and you can do activities to do with. We speak a lot about LGBTQ things going on, ____________ things going on. There's always something to do.

WILL: The final ____________ was the eclectic, ____________ Pitt Rivers Museum in Oxford. It is a remarkable ____________ of human history, shortlisted the enlightening way, its rethinking the presentation of its ____________ collection of over half a million objects that ____________ from prehistory to the present day.

Dictation

To see all the museums ... in the city.

Translation

1. It's a 100-acre visitor attraction, boasting over 40 different Welsh buildings that have been relocated with extraordinary attention to detail to tell the story of the country's past.
2. Nottingham Contemporary is a gallery celebrating its tenth anniversary with a Museum of the Year nomination for its commitment to contemporary art and diversity.
3. St Fagans is one of the most welcoming and engaging museums anywhere in the UK.

Post-class task

Discussion: Tell the class the different types of museums you know and explain why they are important.

67. New Homes over Rails

ALICE: Now, building new homes over railway lines—it is the most recent plan to help solve London's housing crisis, and one architect says the idea could see as many as 250,000 properties created. Caroline Davies has the details.

CAROLINE: Look up from the tunnels, and you might catch a glimpse. Is this the future of London's housing? Royal Mint Gardens was once a car park in between the train tracks.

MARK: It's been very challenging. It's taken years proving ourselves, because this is for all intents and purposes, a new type, a new methodology, of construction.

CAROLINE: When finished, this site will have nearly 300 flats, all supported by a tunnel deep in the bowels of the building.

MARK: You have to precast concrete walls that form the sides of the tunnel. And this is the steelwork that sits on the isolation bearings, 600 tonnes of steelwork, and it supports the building.

CAROLINE: Working directly over operating train tracks comes with its own challenges for construction workers.

MARK: Everything has to be tethered back to them. So they're not allowed mobile phones, any tools have to be tethered—the hats have to be tethered, the glasses; pockets are sealed. We cannot afford to have anything dropping.

CAROLINE: It's not the only safety consideration. This was Gerrards Cross in 2005, when a tunnel being built to hold a Tesco store collapsed.

How do you make sure that even if there was an accident, that this building stays standing and the people who are on the trains below are safe?

MARK: This has been designed to withstand train impact, bomb impact. Subsidence is monitored. So everything that can be done has been done.

CAROLINE: So could London be transformed from a city of winding tracks to something more like this? It's perfectly possible, according to some London architects.

BILL: The first thing we did was to really measure all the rail track and tube track in London, and we said if we could only build on 10% of that land to a height of 12 storeys, that would give us 250,000 homes. We've now got maps of all the London boroughs showing where is a good place to start looking.

CAROLINE: Network Rail are already building homes over their stations. But building over the train tracks is more tricky.

DAVID: We have plenty of land, but it is long thin strips along the railway. And our predecessors, British Rail and Railtrack, have sold off the majority of land around those thin strips. So I think the way forward is to work with like-minded neighbours that want to develop their area and we're really open for business. We want to do this.

CAROLINE: Building this way isn't cheap, but as the hunt for places to put new homes continues, more developers may look above the tracks. Caroline Davies, BBC London News. (*BBC-20190226*)

Notes

Gerrards Cross: 格拉茨·克洛斯,英国白金汉郡的一个小镇。

Tesco: 英国连锁超市。

Words and Expressions

concrete *n.* 混凝土
developer *n.* 开发商
for all intents and purposes 实际上;差不多等于
isolation bearings 独立基础
like-minded *adj.* 想法一致的
precast *vt.* 预制
strip *n.* 狭长地带
steelwork *n.* 钢制品
subsidence *n.* 下沉
tether *vt.* 拴住;系住
the bowels 内部最深处
withstand *vt.* 承受;经受住

Questions

1. How many flats will be offered after this building is finished?
2. What are the challenges for workers during the construction?
3. Did any similar project fail in the past?
4. What is the height limit for such buildings?
5. How many new homes can be provided if all available space of London rails can be developed?

Gap-filling

CAROLINE: When finished, this site will have nearly 300 flats, all ________________ by a tunnel deep in the ________________ of the building.

MARK: You have to precast ________________ walls that form the sides of the tunnel. And this is the steelwork that ____________________ the isolation bearings, 600 _________________ of steelwork, and it supports the building.

CAROLINE: Working directly over _________________ train tracks comes with its own ____ _____________ for construction workers.

MARK: Everything has to be tethered back _________________. So they're not allowed mobile phones, any _________________ have to be tethered—the hats have to be tethered, the glasses; pockets are _________________. We cannot afford to have anything dropping.

Dictation

We have plenty of land ... We want to do this.

Translation

1. You have to precast concrete walls that form the sides of the tunnel.
2. Everything has to be tethered back to them.
3. This has been designed to withstand train impact, bomb impact.

Post-class task

Discussion: Are you willing to live in a flat built on a rail?

68. Record Summer Heat

SOPHIE: This summer was the hottest on record for England, with temperatures beating those seen in the famous heatwave of 1976, though only narrowly. For the UK as a whole, 2018 proved to be the joint-hottest summer. And as our science editor David Shukman reports, the warm weather isn't over yet. A warning, his report does contain flashing images.

DAVID: It was a summer of extreme heat that, for much of the country, rolled on for month after month. From fires raging on the hills of Lancashire, to the stark image of a dried-out reservoir in the Lake District, to the punishing temperatures of city streets. Filmed by a thermal camera, the pavements, depicted in yellow, are radiating heat. For anyone on holiday, it was perfect summer weather. Beaches were packed and seaside businesses have been booming—no need to fly to distant resorts for plenty of sunshine. But for many the heat was tough to endure. This field in Hertfordshire was typical of many across Britain: the only trace of green was a cricket pitch. And for farmers, the long, hot dry spell became a constant source of worry. For Mark Wigs in Devon, the land now looks less parched, but the legacy of the heatwave continues.

MARK: It increases our costs, which has an impact on the profitability of what we're doing. So ... It increases the amount of work and worry and stress.

DAVID: We all knew the summer was hot, but what do the Met Office figures actually tell us? Well, the summer had an average temperature of 15.8 Celsius, and because that's within a fraction of what was seen back in 1976, 2003 and 2006, they're calling it a joint record. At the same time, England set a new summer record with an average temperature of 17.1 Celsius. The key thing was that so many nights were warmer. And another record is that this year has seen 80 days where summer in the UK was above 25 Celsius. So does this mean every year will get hotter? Well, no. But as the climate warms, that is set to become more likely.

AIDAN: Going forward into the future, it's expected that because of greenhouse gas emissions and global warming these kinds of heatwaves will occur more regularly, and when they occur, we'll have higher temperatures as a result.

DAVID: The summer ended with a spectacular bang, a barrage of thunderstorms ...

WOMAN: Oh, my gosh!

DAVID: And a lot of questions about how soon it'll be before the next hot summer sets yet another record. David Shukman, BBC News. (*BBC-20180903*)

Notes

Met Office:(英国)国家气象局,其中 Met = Meteorological。

Words and Expressions

a barrage of 一连串的
Celsius *adj.* 摄氏的
cricket pitch 板球场
packed *adj.* 挤满人的
parched *adj.* 晒焦的
punishing *adj.* 艰难持久的
rage *vi.* 迅速蔓延
reservoir *n.* 水库
resort *n.* 度假胜地
roll on (时间)流逝
spell *n.* 一段时间
thermal camera 热感摄影机
with a bang 有强烈影响地;令人难忘地

Questions

1. What was average temperature in the UK in the past?
2. What is average temperature in the UK today?
3. How many days were there when the temperature reaches 25 Celsius or more this year?
4. What might be the cause of rising temperature?

Gap-filling

DAVID: It was a summer of ________ that, for much of the country, ________ ________ on for month after month. From fires ________ on the hills of Lancashire, to the ________ image of a dried-out ________ in the Lake District, to the ________ temperatures of city streets. Filmed by a(n) ________ camera the pavements, ________ in yellow, are ________ heat. For anyone on holiday, it was perfect summer weather. Beaches were ________ and seaside businesses have been ________ —no need to fly to distant ________ for plenty of sunshine. But for many the heat was tough to ________. This field in Hertfordshire was ________ of many across Britain: the only ________ of green was a cricket ________. And for farmers, the long, hot dry ________ became a constant source of ________. For Mark Wigs in Devon, the land now looks less ________, but the legacy of the heatwave continues.

Dictation

We all knew … more likely.

Translation

1. Filmed by a thermal camera, the pavements are radiating heat.
2. For farmers, the long, hot dry spell became a constant source of worry.
3. The land now looks less parched, but the legacy of the heatwave continues.
4. The summer ended with a spectacular bang, a barrage of thunderstorms.

Post-class task

Discussion: What can an individual do to help control the rising temperature?

69. Running for NHS

MARY: And finally tonight with many of us keen to give something back to our frontline workers, meet a woman who's taken more steps than most. Olivia Strong came up with the idea of run for heroes combining her daily exercise with raising money for medics. Well it's been such a hit she's raised millions and gained the support of Olympic champion Mo Farah. In the latest of our series "In This Together", Olivia told our Scotland correspondent Peter Smith about her runaway success.

PETER: On the uphill stretch of a scenic route through Edinburgh, one runner had an idea: what if we could put our daily state-approved socially-distanced exercise to good use? Olivia Strong came up with the concept during her regular 5k jog. When she got home, she set up a fundraiser for the NHS Covid-19 appeal. She called it "Run For Heroes" and it's gone much much further than she anticipated.

OLIVIA: The idea initially was, you know, run 5k, donate £5, nominate five people and to raise 5k. We smashed the 5k target in four days. Hopefully it goes some way in helping the NHS right now because they are the people who need it the most right now.

PETER: "Run For Heroes" has now raised more than £ 4 million and this "money for miles" is making a difference.

NHS WORKER 1: We've been watching your runs, your donations and your nominations.

NHS WORKER 2: And we're so grateful to see so many of you coming together for such a worthwhile cause.

NHS WORKER 3: Every £5 donated to the NHS charities …

NHS WORKER 4: … goes some way to making our lives a little easier.

PETER: If you add up the total distance covered by everyone who's taken part, it would be enough to reach the moon and back. It also has celebrity endorsement.

OLIVIA: Loads of celebrities have been getting behind it, which is amazing, from people like Ellie Goulding, John Terry, and to DJ Chris Moyles.

CHRIS: I think I need a chair for a lie-down.

PETER: This challenge isn't just for the amateur runners in lockdown.

MO:	People are just getting involved no matter who you are, how big you are, how small you are. It's just good for a good cause.
PETER:	If you're wondering how long it takes Britain's most successful track athlete in modern Olympic history to run 5k, well …
MO:	12'53 is my best.
PETER:	12 minutes 53 seconds and a challenge for his favorite news presenter.
MO:	Hi, Mary Nightingale. I nominate you for my 5k.
PETER:	Olivia just started running to keep active. Now she's found a way for people to get their running shoes on and use the miles to help our medics. Peter Smith, ITV News, Edinburgh.
MARY:	There you go. I can't say "No" to Mo, can you? So as they say, watch the space. And that's it for now. Tom is here at 10, but from me and all the team, stay safe, stay well, stay indoors. Bye-bye. (*ITV-20200420*)

Notes

Chris Moyles: 克里斯·莫耶斯,英国电台与电视节目主持人。

Ellie Goulding: 埃利·古尔丁,英国歌手兼创作人。

John Terry: 约翰·特里,英国职业足球教练,早年作为球员司职中后卫,效力英超俱乐部切尔西,是该队队长,亦曾任英格兰国家足球队队长。

Words and Expressions

amateur *adj.* 业余的
endorsement *n.* 支持
fundraiser *n.* 募捐活动
get behind 支持
go some way to doing sth. 对于做某事很有帮助
hit *n.* 风靡一时;轰动
jog *n.* 慢跑(尤作为锻炼)
loads of 大量;许多
medic *n.* 医护人员
news presenter 新闻主播
runaway *adj.* 轻而易举的(本文有双关意)
smash *vt.* 粉碎;打破
track athlete 田径运动员
watch the space 拭目以待
worthwhile *adj.* 有益的;值得做的

Questions

1. What is Olivia's idea of raising money?
2. How much has this program raised so far?

3. How long is the total distance covered by all participants?
4. What is the fastest record of running 5k for Mo?
5. Whom did Mo challenge after he ran?

Gap-filling

PETER: On the uphill stretch of a(n) ______________ through Edinburgh, one runner had an idea: ______________ we could put our daily state- ______________ socially-distanced exercise ______________? Olivia Strong came up with the ______________ during her regular 5k ______________. When she got home, she set up a ______________ for the NHS Covid-19 ______________. She called it "Run For ______________" and it's gone much much further than she ______________.

OLIVIA: The idea ______________ was, you know, run 5k, ______________ £5, ______________ five people and to raise 5k. We smashed the 5k ______________ in four days. Hopefully it goes ______________ in helping the NHS right now because they are the people who ______________ right now.

Dictation

And finally tonight … her runaway success.

Translation

1. She came up with the concept during her regular 5k jog.
2. We smashed the 5k target in four days.
3. Every £5 donated goes some way to making our lives a little easier.

Post-class task

Discussion: Have you ever been involved in raising money for charities? Or, do you have any good idea that might generate a lot of donations for charities?

70 Saving the Beluga Whales

JULIE: The debate over whether whales, another large mammal, should be held in captivity for our entertainment means increasingly that we are seeing the back of such practices. But what happens to the animals who, now reliant on human help, can't simply be released into the wild? Well, for a pair of beluga whales who have called Sea Life Park in Shanghai home for the last decade, the solution involves a 6,000-mile journey that will see them released into the cooler Atlantic waters of Icelandic bay.

DEBI: This pool in central Shanghai is the only environment Little White and Little Grey have ever known. The two beluga whales were captured by Russian poachers and sold to the Changfeng Aquarium when they were just calves. But these two majestic mammals could be about to change the course of animal captivity. Following heightened criticism and awareness about the use of whales and dolphins for entertainment, Sea Life has created an open water sanctuary for them in Iceland. In the next few weeks, they will make the 6,000-mile journey by road, air and sea to their new home.

MEDGE: We started preparing them for it about a year ago, if not more. And we've had to do things for their physical fitness so ... increase their breathhold so they can hold their breath underwater for longer, doing swims to get their actual physical fitness up ready for the bay.

DEBI: Their daily routine now involves a series of steps to prepare them for their move. As well as monitoring their size, their handlers have been practicing getting them into position to be hoisted out of the water.

Ideally, this would be a project to release Little White and Little Gray back into the wild, but the concern about doing that is not that they wouldn't survive, but because they've got so used to human interaction, there will be a real risk of them being captured and sold all over again.

This Icelandic bay will bring them as close as they can to freedom. And the hope is that these belugas will be the first of many captive whales to be rehabilitated and removed from their role as human entertainers.

ROB: And this is an opportunity to retire them to as natural an environment in the North Atlantic in subarctic Iceland, where they can live and act as wild belugas as wild as

they possibly can.

DEBI: The project is a world-first in marine welfare and its success could improve the fate of hundreds of other sea mammals. Debi Edward, News at Ten, Shanghai. (*TTV-20190328*)

Words and Expressions

aquarium *n.* 水族馆
bay *n.* 湾;海湾
beluga whale 白鲸
breathhold *n.* 屏气潜水
calf *n.* 崽;幼兽
captive *adj.* 被关起来的;被困住的
captivity *n.* 囚禁,关押;圈养
dolphin *n.* 海豚
handler *n.* 驯兽员
heightened *adj.* 增强的
hoist *vt.* 吊起
Icelandic *adj.* 冰岛的
majestic *adj.* 雄伟的;壮丽的
marine *adj.* 海洋的
poacher *n.* 偷猎者
rehabilitate *vt.* 使……恢复正常生活
retire (to) 离开(去另外的地方)
sanctuary *n.* 避难所;庇护所
see the back of 结束
subarctic *adj.* 亚北极的

Questions

1. How did the whales come to Shanghai?
2. Where are the whales going be released?
3. What preparations are being made for moving them to the new home?
4. What do experts still worry about after the whales are released to the wild?
5. What is the significance of the success of this project?

Gap-filling

MEDGE: We started preparing them for it about a year ago, ________________. And we've had to do ________________ for their physical fitness so … ________________ their breathhold so they can hold their breath ________________ for longer, doing swims to get their ________________ physical fitness up ready for ________________.

DEBI: Their daily ________________ now involves a series of steps to prepare them for their move as well as ________________ their size. Their ________________ have been practicing getting them into position to be ________________ out of the water.

__________________, this would be a project to __________________ Little White and Little Gray back into the wild, but the concern about doing that is not that they wouldn't survive, but because they've got __________________ human interaction, there will be a real risk of __________________ captured and sold all over again.

Dictation

The debate over whether ... of Icelandic bay.

Translation

1. Increasingly we are seeing the back of such practices.
2. There will be a real risk of them being captured and sold all over again.
3. This is an opportunity to retire them to as natural an environment in the North Atlantic in subarctic Iceland.

Post-class task

Do some research about the fate of the two beluga whales and write a short report in about 200 words.

71. Screen Time Out

ASAD: As you may have heard, the government has published guidelines on limiting children's time on screens. Well, a school in Wembley has developed its own way of dealing with the issue, by working with pupils to hand in their phones. Well, the pupils reluctantly admit it is working, and so now families are being offered a "smartphone detox", too. See what you think, once you've seen Sarah Harris' report.

SARAH: It's become known as "the iGeneration", teenagers spending hours on their phones rather than engaging in the world around them. It's a concern for parents and teachers alike.

Different schools in London have different policies when it comes to their pupils and their mobile phones. Some insist that they're turned off during class time. Others ban them from the school grounds. But this school have taken it one step further.

BILLY: Miss, can I hand in my phone?

TEACHER: Yes.

SARAH: Here at Michaela Community School in Wembley, they're holding a "Smartphone Amnesty", some agreeing to give up their devices for six months.

TEACHER: Maybe next time we'll think about keeping it until the end of your exams?

BILLY: I believe that although I may have short-term pain, it's for the long-term gain.

CATARINA: It's also allowed me to get better quality sleep and spend more time with my family, because I'm not constantly worried about putting up this perfect image online on the Internet.

SHAZIYA: When you get likes, it will give you a notification, and when you hear that, you will start reflecting on that rather than reflecting on your homework.

SARAH: The school does offer basic phones at a subsidised price to encourage a move away from the 24/7 Internet.

KATHARINE: We sell these phones at school for £ 10. We buy them for £14, we sell them subsidised for £10, and the reason is because parents love the convenience. They don't want their child to give up their phone completely because they want to be able to get in touch with their child. You can text them, you can ring them with a brick phone, but what it doesn't allow your child to do is get involved in the murky and disturbing world of Snapchat and Instagram.

GIRL: These days, children are getting bullied and abused ...

SARAH: These students are leading the way. Now, classes are being offered to parents who want a family iPhone detox, too. Many mental health professionals welcome the time out as a first step.

STEFAN: It's giving those children an experience of not having their phones at their side all the time and they're going to have to get used to that and build up some resilience to be bored sometimes and to feel frustrated sometimes, and not to have that instant gratification that the phone normally offers, so it's a good start. But as time goes on, you'd want to reintroduce that and give them the skills to moderate themselves, to learn to self-regulate.

SARAH: It'll be a hard sell for some teenagers to give up the complex and high-tech world of the Internet on their phones. But these students say it's simply made their lives better. Sarah Harris, BBC London News. (*BBC-20190207*)

Words and Expressions

abuse *vt.* 虐待
amnesty *n.* 赦免
brick phone 砖块手机(早期粗重手机的谐称)
bully *vt.* 霸凌
detox *n.* 戒瘾
disturbing *adj.* 令人不安的
frustrated *adj.* 沮丧的
hard sell 强行推销
instant gratification 即时满足
like *n.* 点赞
moderate *vt.* 节制;克制
murky *adj.* 污浊的;隐晦的
subsidised *adj.* 有补贴的

Questions

1. What does "the iGeneration" mean?
2. Why are smart phones distractive to students?
3. What do the students who have handed in their smart phones think of their decision?
4. What benefit has the school offered to those students who are willing to hand in their smart phones?
5. Psychologically speaking, why is smartphone detox good to students?

Gap-filling

GIRL: These days, children are getting ________________ and abused …

SARAH: These students are ________________ the way. Now, classes are being offered to parents who want a family iPhone ________________, too. Many mental ________________ professionals welcome the time out as a first step.

STEFAN: It's giving those children ________________ of not having their phones ________________ all the time and they're going to have to get used to that and build up some ________________ to be bored sometimes and to feel ________________ sometimes, and not to have that ________________ gratification that the phone normally ________________, so it's a good start. But as time ________________, you'd want to reintroduce that and give them the skills to ________________ themselves, to learn to ________________.

Dictation

We sell these phones … and Instagram.

Translation

1. Although I may have short-term pain, it's for the long-term gain.
2. I'm not constantly worried about putting up this perfect image online on the Internet.
3. What it doesn't allow your child to do is get involved in the murky and disturbing world of Snapchat and Instagram.
4. Children need to build up some resilience to be bored sometimes and to feel frustrated sometimes.

Post-class task

Discussion: Are you willing to join "smartphone detox"? Why (not)?

72. Sir Sean Connery

REETA: The James Bond star Sir Sean Connery has died at the age of 90. He was the first screen actor to play 007, a role that brought him global stardom, and which led to decades as one of Hollywood's leading actors. Our arts editor, Will Gompertz, looks back at his life.

WILL: Sean Connery was the first and, for many, the pre-eminent.

SEAN: Bond. James Bond.

WILL: With the inner snarl of Humphrey Bogart and the outward charm of Cary Grant, Connery created a charismatic screen legend, a ladies' man—

URSULA: Looking for shells?

SEAN: No, I'm just looking.

WILL: —with a killer's instinct. He went from being a jobbing actor in his early 30s to an international movie star, an instantly recognisable global celebrity. The attention and fuss that came with the fame did not sit comfortably with the no-nonsense working class Scot, who'd once been a milkman, a model and, briefly, a coffin buffer.

SEAN: I had no awareness of that scale of the kind of reverence and pressure and what have you. I never had a press representative or anything. And I found it a bit of a nightmare.

WILL: Bond was universally popular, but not with the man playing him. Connery felt trapped in 007's gilded cage. He wanted out, to test his talents with more challenging roles. He won plaudits for *The Man Who Would Be King*, playing alongside his old friend, Michael Caine.

SEAN: We've been all over India, we know her cities, her jungles, her jails and her passes. And we have decided that she isn't big enough for such as we.

WILL: He won an Oscar for *The Untouchables*—

SEAN: Want to get Capone? Here's how you get him. He pulls a knife, you pull a gun. He sends one of yours to the hospital, you send one of his to the morgue. That's the Chicago way.

I suddenly remembered my Charlemagne. Let my armies be the rocks and the trees and the birds in the sky.

WILL: —and won legions more fans in *Indiana Jones*. He was a proud Scot and a committed member of the SNP.

NICOLA: He came from humble beginnings, but through charisma, talent, sheer hard work, became one of the world's greatest actors. And, you know, his achievements are absolutely legendary. And I know that across Scotland today, we are mourning one of our best-loved sons.

SEAN: Tell me, Miss Trench, do you play any other games?

WILL: He will always be remembered for playing 007. But James Bond didn't make Sean Connery. Sean Connery made James Bond.

PUSSY: My name is Pussy Galore.

SEAN: I must be dreaming.

WILL: A movie icon, established by an intelligent, versatile, exceptionally talented actor.

REETA: Sir Sean Connery, who's died at the age of 90. (*BBC-20201031*)

Notes

Capone：卡彭(1899—1947),芝加哥黑帮首领。

Cary Grant：加里·格兰特(1904—1986),英国男演员,以英俊幽默著称,11 次当选好莱坞十大卖座明星。

Charlemagne：查理曼大帝(742—814),曾为法兰克国王,神圣罗马帝国皇帝,亦称查理一世。

Humphrey Bogart：亨弗莱·鲍嘉(1899—1957),美国男演员,好莱坞银幕硬汉的代表。1999 年被美国电影学会选为"百年来最伟大的男演员"第 1 位。

Michael Caine：迈克尔·凯恩(1933—),英国男演员,魅力永恒的英国影坛偶像,至今依然活跃在一线影坛。

SNP：即 Scottish National Party,苏格兰民族党。

Words and Expressions

charisma *n.* 个人魅力；感召力
charismatic *adj.* 有超凡魅力的
coffin buffer 擦亮棺材的人
committed *adj.* 忠于职守的
gilded cage 镀金鸟笼(指豪华但不自由的环境)
humble *adj.* 卑微的
instinct *n.* 本能
jobbing *adj.* 打零工的
ladies' man 爱和女人调情的男子；有女人缘的男人
legion *n.* 大量；大批
morgue *n.* 停尸房
mourn *vt.* 哀悼
nightmare *n.* 噩梦
pass *n.* 关口；关隘
plaudit *n.* 褒扬
reverence *n.* 崇敬
snarl *n.* 咆哮；怒吼
stardom *n.* 明星地位
versatile *adj.* 多才多艺的
what have you 等等

Questions

1. What jobs had Sean done before he became an actor?
2. Is Sean from a wealthy family?
3. Why did Sean stop acting as James Bond which was very popular?
4. What contribution did Sean make to the film industry?

Gap-filling

WILL: He went from being a(n) __________ actor in his early 30s to an international movie star, an instantly recognisable global __________. The attention and __________ that came with the __________ did not sit comfortably with the no-nonsense working class __________, who'd once been a milkman, a(n) __________ and, briefly, a coffin buffer.

SEAN: I had no __________ of that scale of the kind of __________ and pressure and what have you. I never had a __________ representative or anything. And I found it a bit of a __________.

WILL: Bond was universally __________, but not with the man playing him. Connery felt trapped in 007's __________. He wanted out, to test his talents with more challenging roles. He won __________ for *The Man Who Would Be King*, playing alongside his old friend, Michael Caine.

Dictation

He came from humble ... our best-loved sons.

Translation

1. The role of 007 brought him global stardom.
2. Connery created a charismatic screen legend, a ladies' man, with a killer's instinct.
3. James Bond didn't make Sean Connery. Sean Connery made James Bond.

Post-class task

1. Watch at least one movie of Sean Connery's.
2. Do some research about Michael Caine.

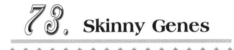

73. Skinny Genes

JULIE: As we're near the end of January and for many the New Year diet is all but forgotten, scientists say there may be good reason to feel envious of those friends who just don't seem to have to bother with all the effort. For many years, we've known about so-called fat genes, which means some people are predisposed to gaining weight, but now researchers from Cambridge University say they've discovered there are others with what you might call "skinny genes".

TOM: Cambridge Rugby Club are all fit fellas, and as you'd expect on a rugby team, men of considerably different sizes. But like the rest of us, they split into two types when it comes to their weight. The most common one, those who have to watch what they eat.

WADE: Yeah, I have to watch what I eat to make sure that I don't put on weight, so I just look at food and I'll tend to get a little chubby.

TOM: You are, you are, you are a professional athlete, is that, is that, is that an issue?

WADE: Yeah. I mean, I have to, I have to train sort of harder than, than the other boys just to maintain sort of weight I'm at.

TOM: And then there is the others and we all know one or two of them, who can eat whatever they want and stay slim.

JAMES: Anything and everything. My sort of calorie quota is around 4,000 calories a day, so that's why I have to sort of get on to, hmm, yeah, get my food right, maintain my body weight.

TOM: You actually have to eat more to keep the weight you need to play?

ATHLETE: Yeah, if I, if I, normally, I'm losing weight, yeah.

TOM: For those effortlessly thin people, the envy of dieters is everywhere, or morally superior—most of them are just lucky. Over at the University, the scientist who discovered the first gene linked to human obesity 20 years ago has now found that thin people have skinny genes.

SADAF: I think the take-home message here, actually, it's all about biology. If you can manage to stay thin, it's because you've been lucky in the genes that you've inherited. And hopefully, that would allow people to be a little bit more sympathetic to people who struggle with their weight.

TOM: They studied 1,500 very thin but healthy people and found that not only do they lack genes known to cause obesity, they have other genes that seem to keep them thin. Some of them could be very important for understanding obesity.

SADAF: For 40% of people, actually they tell us they can eat what they like and they still don't put on weight. Now we're really keen to figure that out. We think some of those people are carrying genes that allow them to burn fat very quickly, to burn calories. And that's how they can stay thin.

TOM: The next step is to understand these mystery skinny genes by expressing them in human cells like this. That could lead to new ways to help people whose biology makes it harder to be thin. Tom Clarke, News at Ten, Cambridge. (*ITV-20190124*)

Words and Expressions

all but 几乎
chubby *adj.* 胖乎乎的
considerably *adv.* 非常
envious *adj.* 羡慕的
fella *n.* 小伙子
predisposed *adj.* 更倾向于;更有可能
put on weight 增加体重
quota *n.* 限额
skinny *adj.* 极瘦的
slim *adj.* 苗条的
sympathetic *adj.* 同情的
take-home message 主要信息,要点;得到的教益
the envy of 忌妒对象;羡慕目标
watch *vt.* 留心;注意

Questions

1. What does the rugby team players' example prove?
2. When did scientists discover "fat genes"?
3. Where could the skinny genes come from?
4. Why should we respect fat people?
5. Why can people with skinny genes stay slim?

Gap-filling

TOM: For those effortlessly thin people, the ________________ of dieters is everywhere, or morally ____________________—most of them are just lucky. Over at the University, the scientist who discovered the first gene linked to human ________________ 20 years ago has now found that thin people have __________________ genes.

SADAF: I think the take-home ________________ here, actually, it's all about ________________. If you can manage to ________________, it's because you've been lucky in the genes that you've ________________. And hopefully, that would allow people to be a little bit more ________________ to people who struggle with their ________________.

Dictation

As we're ... "skinny genes".

Translation

1. For many the New Year diet is all but forgotten.
2. Some people are predisposed to gaining weight.
3. For those effortlessly thin people, the envy of dieters is everywhere, or morally superior.

Post-class task

Discussion:

1. Do you believe there is someone around you who does have skinny genes?
2. How do you keep a slim figure?

74. The Mariana Trench

HUW: An American explorer has carried out the deepest dive ever recorded in a submarine, in one of the most hostile places on Earth. The Mariana Trench lies at the bottom of the Pacific Ocean. At its lowest point, it's nearly 11 km deep—and that is almost seven miles. The explorer Victor Vescovo dived to a depth of 10.9 km, when he reached the seabed. He spent several hours exploring the bottom of the Mariana and discovered four new species. He also found plastic waste, including sweet wrappers—a worrying indication of the impact humans are having even in this kind of remote location. Our science correspondent, Rebecca Morelle, has this report.

VICTOR: OK. Roger that. We'll now go for a release.

REBECCA: The start of an epic journey. In the middle of the Pacific, heading beneath the waves to the deepest place on the planet. A sub with a titanium core, built to withstand the crushing pressure. It takes three and a half hours to plunge 11 km—that's seven miles down. Inside is American explorer Victor Vescovo. Then ... touchdown.

VICTOR: At bottom! It seemed a bit like being on the moon, but a wet version of it. There were small craters here and there. There were slight undulations. There weren't rocks until you get to the southern and northern portions of the Mariana Trench, but it did have some variety. But it was quiet. It was peaceful.

REBECCA: Yet in this most remote of places, life has found a way to thrive. There are eels adapted to live under immense pressures, and a ghostly snail fish—it's the deepest ever found. But signs too of our impact. This pyramid-shaped object to the right looks like a rock, but it's a plastic bag. Scientists say finding out more about the deep is vital.

EMILY: It's such an alien environment and we've got so much to learn. You don't get sunlight penetrating to those depths, so it's important to learn, like, how organisms get their energy and how they survive, and how they interact and rely on each other.

(*Released by the US Navy come these first films of the Bathyscaphe Trieste ...*)

REBECCA: Few have ever set eyes on the Mariana Trench. The first risky descent was in 1960, in a creaking sub that took two explorers down.

VICTOR: Well done, team!

REBECCA: Now, 60 years later, resurfacing after 12 hours underwater, the latest dive has broken records.

VICTOR: Well done.

MAN: You did it, buddy.

REBECCA: And it's part of a wider expedition to visit the deepest spots in all the world's oceans. The hope is the final frontier of exploration is truly open. Rebecca Morelle, BBC News. (*BBC-20190513*)

Words and Expressions

alien *adj.* 陌生的
bathyscaphe *n.* 深海潜水器
crater *n.* 火山口;坑
creaking *adj.* 嘎吱作响的
crushing *adj.* 毁坏性的
eel *n.* 鳗
expedition *n.* 远征;探险
frontier *n.* 前沿;新领域
ghostly *adj.* 幽灵般的;奇异的
hostile *adj.* 恶劣的; 不利的
indication *n.* 暗示;迹象
organism *n.* 有机体;生物
penetrate *vt.* 穿过
plunge *vi.* 骤降
pyramid *n.* 金字塔
resurface *vi.* 再次露出(水面或地面)
snail fish 狮子鱼
submarine *n.* 潜艇(缩写为 sub)
thrive *vi.* 茁壮成长
titanium *n.* 钛
touchdown *n.* 着陆;触底
trench *n.* 海沟
undulation *n.* 起伏

Questions

1. Can human impact reach this deep trench?
2. How long did it take the sub to reach the seabed?
3. How long was the sub under water?
4. When was the first exploration into the trench?

Gap-filling

REBECCA: Yet in this most ________________ of places, life has found a way to ______________. There are eels adapted to live under ______________ pressures, and a ghostly snail fish. It's the deepest ever found. But ______________ too of our impact. This ______________-shaped object to the right

looks like a rock, but it's a(n) ______________ bag. Scientists say finding out more about the deep is ______________.

EMILY: It's such an ______________ environment and we've got so much to learn. You don't get sunlight ______________ to those depths, so it's important to learn, like, how ______________ get their energy and how they ______________, and how they interact and ______________ each other.

Dictation

An American explorer ... has this report.

Translation

1. The plastic waste is a worrying indication of the impact humans are having even in this kind of remote location.
2. It is a sub with a titanium core, built to withstand the crushing pressure.
3. The hope is the final frontier of exploration is truly open.

Post-class task

Write a short report about this new discovery in about 150 words.

75. The New £50 Note

TOM: Now, experience tells us when you ask the British people to name something or suggest faces to appear on it, they don't always take it 100% seriously. Think "Boaty McBoatface". So when it came to choosing who should grace a new £50 note, (*Oh, there goes the keyboard.*) the Bank of England thought it was time to set some rules—it has to be a scientist; he or she has to be dead and it will be the Bank that has the final say.

DARWIN: The Bank of England has asked everyone to nominate who they think should be on the £50 note and, you'll never guess, the theme is?

NEWTON: *Love Island*?

DARWIN: No, not *Love Island*.

NEWTON: Science?

DARWIN: Yes, Isaac. Isn't that great?

REBECCA: Their faces, a part of the very fabric of our society, so the hunt to find the protagonist who'll star alongside the Queen on the new £50 note is no easy task. But the Bank of England has narrowed the search down to a scientist and wants the public to have a say.

SARAH: Science is an area that the UK's made a massive contribution to over the years, from the invention of the steam engine to the discovery of penicillin. There are so many fantastic achievements in the world of science. And a UK banknote is one way that we can celebrate those achievements.

REBECCA: Despite the rise of a cashless society, there are 330 million £50 notes in circulation with a combined value of £16.5 billion. And the favorites for the new starring role—Professor Stephen Hawking, the cosmologist, Alan Turing, the codebreaker, and as no woman's ever featured on the back of a £50 note, Ada Lovelace, the computer programmer. While the granddaughter of the first only British woman to win the Nobel Prize in Chemistry says Dorothy Hodgkin would be a worthy winner.

KATE: Partly, it just says "Look at what women can do in science". She was also very involved as an internationalist, and as a peace's campaigner. She juggled a lot of things and these are things that are still very difficult now for academics, and everyone else, you know, managing children, managing families, managing your career.

REBECCA: The science museum is full of ideas for people you could nominate, but there are a few rules: As well as contributing to the world of science, they must be real, no fictional characters allowed; they must no longer be alive; and most importantly, they must inspire people, not divide them.

So despite a petition signed by thousands, this image of England's World Cup hero Harry Maguire doesn't meet the strict criteria. The public have until mid-December to suggest whose face should be on it. Rebecca Barry, News at Ten.

(*ITV-20181102*)

Notes

Boaty McBoatface：英国南极调查局(BAS)最先进的极地研究船的谐称。2016 年，BAS 邀请公众对这艘价值 2 亿英镑的船只名字进行投票。民意调查结果显示，Boaty McBoatface 以 124 109 票的优势赢得了胜利，但最终是以英国自然纪录片之父的名字，命名为 RRS Sir David Attenborough。

Love Island：《爱情岛》，英国 ITV 婚恋真人秀，2015 年开播。

Words and Expressions

cashless *adj.* 非现金交易的
circulation *n.* 流通
cosmologist *n.* 宇宙学家
criteria *n.* 标准
fabric *n.* 基本结构
fictional *adj.* 虚构的
juggle *vt.* 同时应付
nominate *vt.* 提名
penicillin *n.* 青霉素;盘尼西林
petition *n.* 请愿书
protagonist *n.* 主角
say *n.* 发言权;决策权
star *vi.* 担任主角
starring role 主角
steam engine 蒸汽机

Questions

1. What are rules for naming a new fifty-pound note?
2. What favorable names have been suggested?
3. Why is science recommended for the theme?

Gap-filling

REBECCA: Their faces, a part of the very ________________ of our society, so the hunt to find the ________________ who'll star alongside the Queen on the new £50 note is ________________ task. But the Bank of England has ________________ the search down to a scientist and wants the public to have a say.

SARAH: Science is an area that the UK's made a(n) ________________ contribution to over the years, from the ________________ of the steam engine to the discovery of ________________. There are so many ________________ achievements in the world of science. And a UK banknote is one way that we can ________________ those achievements.

Dictation

Despite the rise … a worthy winner.

Translation

1. It will be the Bank that has the final say.
2. The hunt to find the protagonist who'll star alongside the Queen on the new £50 note is no easy task.

3. They must inspire people, not divide them.

Post-class task

Discussion: List some forgotten Chinese historical persons who you recommend for naming something important and explain why.

Part IV

扫码看视频

扫码填空

扫码听写

76. Admiralty Arch

MISHAL: Finally, for over a century, Admiralty Arch has been one of London's most distinctive landmarks—a gateway to The Mall and Buckingham Palace. After being sold as part of government cost-cutting, it will soon reopen as a luxury hotel. But building work revealed that the Arch includes an entrance to a network of secret tunnels beneath Westminster. Our home editor Mark Easton went to have a look.

MARK: Familiar backdrop to a century of British ceremonial, the secrets of Admiralty Arch are now being unearthed.

We've been granted exclusive access to see what's happening to one of London's most famous landmarks.

Inside, Edwardian opulence and memories of old battles. The ghosts of Navy commanders haunt the corridors, Winston Churchill, Louis Mountbatten, reminders that Admiralty Arch was the residence of the First Sea Lord when Britain ruled the waves. It is also where Ian Fleming, working for naval intelligence, created James Bond, and down in the basement, one discovers a network of secret tunnels stretching beneath Westminster, filmed for the first time. There are strange corridors, bunkers with heavy doors and combination locks. The spirit of the Cold War lives on in this basement. Little is known about who or what happened down here, but we do know about their subterranean billiards room.

From the coronation of George V to the Queen's diamond jubilee, the Arch has spanned the state processional route for a hundred years, but in 2012 it was sold for £60 million as part of Government austerity measures, and not everyone's happy that this significant public building will soon advertise itself as a Waldorf Astoria hotel.

During a debate in the House of Lords, one peer feared security risks, describing the sell-off as privatisation gone mad. Another worried that the White Ensign flown here on state occasions might be replaced by the corporate flag of an American hotel chain.

But the last First Sea Lord to live in the Arch is confident this building's proud heritage will be protected.

JOCK: I think the old and bold who are now no longer with us would be disturbed to think that Admiralty Arch was going to become a hotel. I'm not. I couldn't be more pleased that this building is going to be properly looked after.

MARK: So was that found here?

RAPHAEL: Yeah, we found it here.

MARK: The new owner, Spanish investor Raphael Serrano, tells me he understands he is merely custodian of a much-loved corner of Britain.

RAPHAEL: It is our obligation to make sure that the building looks as it is, a genuine iconic building, and with respect of the British traditions and the location where the building is located.

MARK: So it won't have Waldorf Astoria all over it?

RAPHAEL: Not at all, not at all.

MARK: The Arch is a Grade I listed building and its foundations cannot be touched, so a vast cavern is being dug on the edge of Trafalgar Square to house the essentials of a modern five-star hotel.

MICHELLE: Underneath there will be a ballroom, swimming pool, spa.

MARK: It must be some hole!

MICHELLE: It is, it is. It's a fairly big hole. It will be when we've finished.

MARK: Once, the only people who could access this building were civil servants, sailors and spooks. But now the dusty old corridors are being restored to their former glory as the secrets of Admiralty Arch are revealed at last—including, of course, perhaps London's most splendid view. Mark Easton, BBC News, Admiralty Arch. (*BBC-20190623*)

Notes

Admiralty Arch：海军部拱门，又译“水师提督门”。

First Sea Lord：第一海军军务大臣，英国皇家海军及海军部的最高军职。

The Mall：林荫大道，从西面的白金汉宫，经水师提督门，到东面的特拉法尔加广场，始建于17世纪，专为举行重大仪式而建。

Trafalgar Square：特拉法尔加广场，建于1830年至1841年间，广场上耸立着纳尔逊纪念柱，用以纪念纳尔逊勋爵。

Westminster：威斯敏斯特，伦敦市内的一个区，英国议会和许多政府部门所在地；全名威斯敏斯特城(City of Westminster)。

White Ensign：英国皇家海军旗。

Words and Expressions

austerity *n.* （经济的）紧缩
backdrop *n.* 背景
ballroom *n.* 舞厅
billiards *n.* 台球
bunker *n.* 地堡；掩体
cavern *n.* 大洞穴
ceremonial *n.* 礼仪
combination lock 密码锁
coronation *n.* 加冕典礼
custodian *n.* （建筑物的）管理员；看门人
diamond jubilee 钻石大庆；60 周年庆典
Edwardian *adj.* 英王爱德华七世时代的（1901—1910）
gateway *n.* （通往其他地区的）门户
intelligence *n.* （机密）情报
opulence *n.* 财富
peer *n.* （英国）贵族成员
processional *adj.* 列队行进时用的
spook *n.* 特工
subterranean *adj.* 地下的
the waves 大海

Questions

1. What function did Admiralty Arch perform in the past?
2. Can you name some important ceremonies in relation to Admiralty Arch?
3. What is hidden beneath the building?
4. Why and to whom was Admiralty Arch sold in 2012?
5. What changes will be made to the building by the present owner? And what will be retained?

Gap-filling

MARK: ... From the ________ of George V to the Queen's ________ jubilee, the Arch has ________ the state processional ________ for 100 years, but in 2012 it was sold for £60 million as part of Government ________ measures, and not everyone's happy that this significant public building will soon ________ itself as a Waldorf Astoria hotel.

During a debate in the House of Lords, one ________ feared security risks, describing the sell-off as ________ gone mad. Another worried that the White Ensign flown here on state ________ might be replaced by the ________ flag of an American hotel ________.

But the last First Sea Lord to live in the Arch is ________ this building's proud ________ will be protected.

Dictation

Inside, Edwardian ... billiards room.

Translation

1. Familiar backdrop to a century of British ceremonial, the secrets of Admiralty Arch are now being unearthed.
2. They are reminders that Admiralty Arch was the residence of the First Sea Lord when Britain ruled the waves.
3. The Arch has spanned the state processional route for 100 years.
4. I couldn't be more pleased that this building is going to be properly looked after.

Post-class task

Do a research on Grade I listed buildings in the area of Westminster in London, and report in class 5 most distinguished places you want to visit.

77. AI Eye Diagnosis

REETA: Artificial intelligence can diagnose eye disease as accurately as some of the world's leading experts. Research by Moorfields Eye Hospital in London and the DeepMind, a company linked to Google, found that machine could learn how to read complex eye scans and detect more than 50 types of disease. Our medical correspondent Fergus Walsh reports.

PEARSE: That's quite bright, but ...

FERGUS: On the brink of going blind, Elaine's sight was saved by doctors at Moorfields Hospital. This scan showed she needed urgent treatment.

PEARSE: There's a growth of abnormal blood vessels under the retina ...

FERGUS: Now, artificial intelligence—machines—have learned how to interpret these complex images. A computer analysed a thousand patient scans using a set of rules, an algorithm, and was able to detect over 50 eye conditions and did not miss a single urgent case.

PEARSE: This is a jaw-dropping result and I think that it will make most eye specialists gasp because, you know, we have shown that this algorithm is as good as some of the world's leading experts in interpreting these scans.

FERGUS: Using artificial intelligence to diagnose eye disease could be a game-changer. That's because at present, doctors are swamped by the number of scans they have to read and some patients go blind before they get treated.

ELAINE: I can see the leaves. The detail isn't sharp.

FERGUS: 200 people a day in the UK, like Elaine, develop the blinding form of age-related macular degeneration. She only has vision in her right eye and welcomes the advent of artificial intelligence in health care.

ELAINE: It's extraordinary. It's absolutely brilliant. People will be empowered, because their sight will be saved through this artificial intelligence, this algorithm, and they will be disabled by not having sight at all.

FERGUS: Google's London headquarters is home to its artificial intelligence company DeepMind. They developed the algorithm to read eye scans and are researching AI's use in other health conditions.

KING: We're looking at eye disease, but we're also looking at how you would plan radiotherapy treatment, because it can take a specialist up to eight hours to plan a treatment currently for complex cancers, and also whether we can use artificial intelligence to identify breast cancers more effectively and potentially earlier through mammography screening.

FERGUS: Artificial intelligence is said to have a profound impact in health care, speeding up diagnosis and freeing up clinicians to spend more time with patients. But not everyone will be happy with a tech giant like Google having access to their health data. So the people at DeepMind will need to ensure that patient confidentiality and data protection are embedded in everything they do.

The eye research results, published in the journal *Nature Medicine*, are so promising that artificial intelligence looks likely to play a key role in the NHS within just a few years. Fergus Walsh, BBC News. (*BBC-20180813*)

Words and Expressions

advent *n.* (重要事件、人物、发明等的)出现;到来
algorithm *n.* 算法
clinician *n.* 临床医师
confidentiality *n.* 保密性
empower *vt.* 赋能
jaw-dropping *adj.* 令人惊愕的
macular degeneration 黄斑变性
mammography *n.* 乳房 X 线照相术
profound *adj.* 巨大的;深远的
radiotherapy *n.* 放射疗法
retina *n.* 视网膜
swamped *adj.* 疲于应对的

Questions

1. How accurate is the result of AI eye diagnosis?
2. How many eye conditions can the machine detect?
3. Why can the machine be so intelligent?
4. Why is AI eye diagnosis a game-changer?
5. Where else can this technology be applied?
6. What is the potential risk of AI technology?

Gap-filling

ELAINE: It's ________________. It's absolutely ________________. People will be ________________, because their sight will be saved through this artificial intelligence, this ________________, and they will be disabled by not having sight ________________.

FERGUS: Google's London ________________ is home to its artificial intelligence company DeepMind. They developed the algorithm to read ________________ and are researching AI's use in other ________________ conditions.

KING: We're looking at eye ________________, but we're also looking at how you would plan ________________ treatment, because it can take a(n) ________________ up to eight hours to plan a treatment ________________ for complex cancers, and also whether we can use artificial intelligence to ________________ breast cancers more ________________ and potentially earlier through mammography ________________.

Dictation

Artificial intelligence is said to … just a few years.

Translation

1. This algorithm is as good as some of the world's leading experts in interpreting these scans.
2. Doctors are swamped by the number of scans they have to read.
3. The people will need to ensure that patient confidentiality and data protection are embedded in everything they do.

Post-class task

Discussion: The application of AI in people's daily life and future expectations.

78. Boris Johnson's Journey

FIONA: Throughout his political career Boris Johnson has served as London Mayor, Foreign Secretary and has been credited with securing victory for the Leave campaign in the Brexit referendum. But what else do we know about the man who will enter Downing Street tomorrow? Our chief political correspondent Vicki Young takes a look at the career of our next Prime Minister.

BORIS: Please call me Boris.

ALL: Boris!

VICKI: The celebrity politician who defies the normal rules of politics.

BORIS: The thing I love is being Mayor of London. Say "Brexit"!

ALL: Brexit!

VICKI: And today, Boris Johnson has fulfilled his childhood dream to become Prime Minister.

CONOR: I have seen Boris, over the last few months, become increasingly reflective of the scale of the challenge that he is about to take on and I am absolutely convinced that he is emotionally and intellectually ready for this. He knows the scale of it, and he's up to it.

VICKI: Boris Johnson's path to the top is a well-trodden one—the 20th Prime Minister to be schooled at Eton.

BORIS: The House will proceed to a division.

VICKI: He went on to study Classics at Oxford University. A career in journalism followed with a stint in Brussels for *The Telegraph*, where he relished mocking the European Commission.

BORIS: I didn't want to be totally stitched up here.

VICKI: His profile was boosted by TV appearances. Boris Johnson had set his sights on a political career, and where better than the safe Conservative seat of Henley-upon-Thames?

But even back then, as Boris Johnson tried to become the Conservatives' candidate, the local party was divided over his talents. Some were attracted to this slightly eccentric, larger-than-life personality, but others were concerned about whether he could be taken seriously.

DAVID: What you see is what you get. You get the hand going through the hair, you get the slightly disheveled look. It's appealing to a lot of people. We found that when we were campaigning with Boris and when he was an MP, he would need people behind him to make everything happen. He'd be the person with the charisma, the person who is leading the charge.

VICKI: And that's the approach he took when he was elected Mayor of London in 2008.

BORIS: I'm going to have a pint of bear, please.

WOMAN: Such an honour to have you here, Mr Mayor.

BORIS: Oh, please call me Boris.

VICKI: Mr Johnson was the charismatic frontman, happy to perform for the cameras ... And the mishaps only added to the celebrity status.

BORIS: Release the rings into position ... now!

VICKI: His supporters say his leadership style is all about creating a feel-good factor.

JO: He's very good at bringing people together, actually. Some people consider him to be divisive because of things that he's written and things he's said in the past. However, he's able to go into a room and he's able to get people feeling positive, and feeling like they can achieve some change. He did it in London. Let's hope he can do it for the country.

VICKI: Mr Johnson's two years as Foreign Secretary brought awkward moments, some with serious consequences. He mistakenly told MPs that a British citizen imprisoned in Iran had been training journalists in the country. He suggested Libya had a bright future, if it could only clear the dead bodies away. Colleagues complain that he didn't focus on important details and found it hard to make decisions.

SONIA: There is this real trust deficit so that he hasn't done what he's supposed to have done: he hasn't read his briefs, he hasn't turned up to things, he hasn't put the country first but he's put himself first.

VICKI: But friends insist his unconventional approach can charm even the toughest of audiences.

BORIS: The pasty of independence.

VICKI: Many Conservative MPs are pinning their hopes on Boris Johnson because they believe he's a winner. He drew adoring crowds when he led the Vote Leave campaign, but Brexit has proved to be the most divisive of issues.

BORIS: I like it. It's brilliant!

VICKI: The new Prime Minister will need more than exuberance, charisma and a bit of optimism. Vicki Young, BBC News. (*BBC-20190723*)

Notes

Eton：伊顿公学(Eton College)的简称,英国著名的贵族中学,是一所男生公学,地处白金汉郡泰晤士河河畔，与温莎宫隔岸相望，于1440年由亨利六世创办。

Henley-upon-Thames：泰晤士河畔亨利镇，简称“亨利镇”，位于牛津郡东南部，伦敦西约50千米，泰晤士河从镇中穿过，以举行一年一度的全国性划船比赛闻名。

The Telegraph：(英国)《每日电讯报》。

Words and Expressions

adoring *adj.* 崇拜的
appealing *adj.* 有吸引力的(to)
Classics *n.* 古希腊与古罗马的文化研究
be credited with 归功于
charm *vt.* 取悦
disheveled *adj.* 头发凌乱的
exuberance *n.* 精力充沛
feel-good factor *n.* 快乐感；满足感
frontman *n.* 头面人物
larger-than-life *adj.* 有传奇色彩的
mishap *n.* 小事故
pasty *n.* 肉馅饼
pin one's hopes on 寄希望于
profile *n.* 形象
reflective *adj.* 深思的
relish (doing sth.) *vt.* 喜欢；享受
school *vt.* 教育
set one's sights on 以……为奋斗目标；决心做到
stint *n.* 工作期限
stitch (sb.) up 诬陷
up to sth. 能胜任
well-trodden *adj.* 常有人走的

Questions

1. Can you describe Boris Johnson's leadership style?
2. What do his opponents say against him?
3. In what way is Boris Johnson a controversial figure?
4. Is Boris Johnson's rise from a college student to the Prime Minister very surprising? Why (not)?

Gap-filling

VICKI: His ________________ was boosted by TV appearances. Boris Johnson had set his ________________ on a political career, and where better ________________ the safe Conservative ________________ of Henley-upon-Thames?

But even back ________________, as Boris Johnson tried to become the Conservatives' ________________, the local party was divided over his ________________. Some were attracted to this slightly ________________, larger-than-life ________________, but others were concerned about whether he could be taken seriously.

DAVID: What you see is what you get. You get the hand going through the hair, you get the slightly disheveled look. It's ________________ to a lot of people. We found that when we were campaigning with Boris and when he was an MP, he would need people behind him to make everything happen. He'd be the person with the ________ ________, the person who is leading the charge.

Dictation

He's very good at ... to make decisions.

Translation

1. He relished mocking the European Commission.
2. Boris Johnson had set his sights on a political career.
3. Some were attracted to this slightly eccentric, larger-than-life personality.
4. The new Prime Minister will need more than exuberance, charisma and a bit of optimism.

Post-class task

Do some research on Boris Johnson, and write a report in no less than 200 words.

79. Cancer Treatment

FIONA: A pioneering new machine, which is hoped will transform cancer treatment, has been used for the first time on a patient in the UK. The device, at the Royal Marsden Hospital in South London, allows doctors to see tumours as they administer radiotherapy to them, something that's never before been possible. It's hoped it will lead to more patients being cured of their cancer, with fewer side effects. Our medical correspondent Fergus Walsh was the first to see it.

FERGUS: This is a truly significant moment in cancer treatment, which has taken years of planning and 10 million pounds' investment. Barry Dolling has prostate cancer, and is about to receive radiotherapy in this revolutionary machine, called an MR Linac. For the first time, the body's internal organs can be scanned using MRI while the patient is treated. The machine combines two very different technologies: MRI, which uses magnetic fields, and radiotherapy, which uses X-rays. It had to be specially designed so they'd work together. Tumours can move when patients breathe, so the radiotherapy beam has to be wide enough to ensure all the cancer is treated. Real-time imaging means a narrower dose can be given, with less damage to healthy tissue. Here, Barry's oncologist at the Royal Marsden is drawing the outline of his prostate. Only the area inside the red line will be targeted. Then the radiotherapy beam is delivered, from seven angles, and clinicians can check the prostate position has not moved.

(*How's that? Yeah, very good.*)

Barry will have 20 of these treatments. In future, patients might only need five at higher doses, which could be important in other cancers.

ALISON: In lung cancer, we know we need to give more dose than we can currently do safely to cure the maximum number of cancers, but the lung cancer is often very close to other healthy structures in the chest, and this limits the amount of dose we can give. So with this new technology, we'll be able to see the cancer more clearly, and the healthy tissue, and make sure our radiation goes where it's needed, and not where it can cause harm.

FERGUS: This technology signals the start of a new era in radiotherapy, which should see more cancer patients being cured, with fewer side effects. In the coming months, the Royal Marsden will start to treat patients with cancer of the bladder, rectum, cervix, pancreas, and eventually, lung.

The accuracy of radiotherapy has improved significantly in recent years. Now there could be even fewer side effects for patients like Barry.

BARRY: I feel very privileged, to be perfectly honest, and very excited. I volunteered to go on a trial, and I feel that my treatment will help research for other people that have prostate cancer in the future.

FERGUS: A second MR Linac will start treating patients at the Christie in Manchester, early next year. The NHS will have to prioritise those likely to see the most benefit from this ground-breaking treatment. Fergus Walsh, BBC News. (*BBC-20180924*)

Notes

The Christie(Hospital):(英国)克里斯蒂医院,全欧洲最大的癌症治疗中心。

Words and Expressions

administer *vi.* 施用(to)
beam *n.* 波束
cervix *n.* 子宫颈
dose *n.* 剂量
ground-breaking *adj.* 创新的
magnetic field 磁场
MRI = magnetic resonance imaging 磁共振成像
oncologist *n.* 肿瘤专家
pancreas *n.* 胰腺
pioneering *adj.* 开创性的
rectum *n.* 直肠
side effect 副作用
tumour *n.* 肿瘤

Questions

1. Why is the new therapy groundbreaking?
2. What are the cancers that this new therapy can treat?
3. What does the volunteer think of this therapy?
4. Will the NHS approve of all cancer patients to use this treatment?

Gap-filling

ALISON: In lung cancer, we know we need to give more dose than we can ________________ safely to cure the ________________ number of cancers, but the lung cancer is often very close to other healthy ________________ in the chest, and this limits ________________ dose we can give. So with this new technology, we'll ________________ see the cancer more clearly, and the healthy ________________, and make sure our radiation ________________ it's needed, and not where it can ________________.

FERGUS: This technology signals the start of a new ________________ in radiotherapy, which should see more cancer patients ________________, with fewer ________________. In the coming months, the Royal Marsden will start to treat patients with cancer of the ________________, rectum, cervix, pancreas, and ________________, lung.

Dictation

For the first time … has not moved.

Translation

1. The device allows doctors to see tumours as they administer radiotherapy to them.
2. Real-time imaging means a narrower dose can be given, with less damage to healthy tissue.
3. The NHS will have to prioritise those likely to see the most benefit from this groundbreaking treatment.

Post-class task

Retell the story of this groundbreaking treatment.

80 Chaotic Train Service

SOPHIE: An investigation into the weeks of chaos and thousands of cancellations across the rail network in the summer has concluded that nobody took charge. The report from the Office of Rail and Road found there was a lack of clarity about roles and responsibilities. But the Transport Secretary Chris Grayling has denied any responsibility. Our transport correspondent Tom Burridge reports.

TOM: A big-money upgrade to our railway. Passengers will benefit further down the line. But in May it was the cause of major disruption. The work in Lancashire by publicly-owned Network Rail got way behind schedule and messed up plans for new timetables. Hundreds of trains cancelled on Northern Rail each day meant misery for passengers. It shattered their trust. Liz Peet has now altered her commute.

LIZ: Since a couple of weeks ago, I've had to change my route, so I now get the bus into Stockport and then get the train from Stockport. I just can't rely on the service.

TOM: Today, the rail regulator said the problems on Northern and on Govia Thameslink demonstrated a complete lack of leadership. When things started to go wrong, neither the train companies, nor Network Rail, nor the Government took control.

CHRIS: My job is now to make sure we have a better way going forward.

TOM: Your critics call you "failing Grayling". Given your record, there is some truth in that.

CHRIS: What we've done in the last couple of years is to proceed with an investment programme and in many parts of the country it's making a real difference. It didn't make a difference in areas it was supposed to this summer, on the GTR network and

Northern. We're gonna make sure that doesn't happen again.

TOM: Today the Government also launched a review of the entire rail system, and those who speak for the rail operators say it needs to be bold.

ROBERT: We know we've had a bad summer, we know we've got to improve, we know we've got to change. The industry's got a long-term plan to do that. We're saying to government, "Please work with us. Let's try and do this once-in-a-generation reform to make the system work for passengers and the economy."

TOM: Old infrastructure is being rooted out to modernise the network. The work on this line alone linking Manchester and Preston has taken years and has cost the taxpayer nearly half a billion pounds. But for passengers it will mean that ancient diesel trains can be phased out and replaced by faster, more reliable electric models.

But the work on the Bolton corridor which was the root cause of problems in May shows the dilemma. Britain's rail network needs improving, but if upgrades cause too much disruption, they jeopardise the confidence of passengers. Managing that balance is key.

Sophie, in the wake of all these problems there is an emerging consensus that the rail system we have today isn't fit for purpose. You only have to talk to people arriving at Bedford tonight who know all too well how badly things can go wrong. Industry sources are basically saying this review from the government over the course of the next year needs to be far-reaching and bold. It needs to look at issues like more regional control of the railways, a closer relationship between the management of the track and trains and whether there needs to another body or person overseeing everything to ensure that passengers do get a decent service.

SOPHIE: Tom Burridge, thank you. (*BBC-20180920*)

Words and Expressions

all too 很；极；非常
commute *n.* 通勤
consensus *n.* 共识
corridor *n.* (连接两地，尤指有特色或通往特殊地区的)通道；连接地；走廊；地带
decent *adj.* 体面的
dilemma *n.* 困境
down the line 以后
far-reaching *adj.* 影响深远的；广泛的
in the wake of 随……之后而来；跟随在……后
mess up 弄糟；毁掉
oversee *vt.* 监督
root cause 根本原因
root out 根除
shatter *vt.* 粉碎；破灭

Questions

1. What are the causes to these disruptions?
2. What consequences have these disruptions brought about?
3. What is the dilemma that Britain now faces in rail network?
4. Do the British agree on something with regard to the current rail network?
5. From what aspects can the government's review be far-reaching and bold?

Gap-filling

TOM: Today, the rail ________________ said the problems on Northern and on Govia Thameslink demonstrated a complete lack of ________________. When things started to go wrong, ________________ train companies, nor Network Rail, nor the Government ________________.

CHRIS: My job is now to make sure we have a better way ________________.

TOM: Your ________________ call you "failing Grayling". Given your record, there is ________________.

CHRIS: What we've done in the last couple of years is to ________________ with an investment programme and ________________ of the country it's making a real difference. It didn't make a difference ________________ it was supposed to this summer, on the GTR network and Northern. We're gonna ________________ that doesn't happen again.

Dictation

Sophie, in the wake of … a decent service.

Translation

1. It didn't make a difference in areas it was supposed to this summer.
2. Old infrastructure is being rooted out to modernise the network.
3. In the wake of all these problems there is an emerging consensus that the rail system we have today isn't fit for purpose.
4. This review from the government over the course of the next year needs to be far-reaching and bold.

Post-class task

Discussion: Can China now laugh at Britain for its outdated rail network since our high-speed rail is the most advanced in the world?

81. China Moon Landing

SOPHIE: Good evening, and welcome to the BBC News at Six. China has successfully landed a spacecraft on the far side of the moon—the side that is never seen from earth. It's the first ever such landing and is being seen as a major milestone in space exploration. The probe has already sent back an image of the largest, deepest and oldest crater on the moon's surface. The landing is the latest step for China in its race to catch up with Russia and the United States and become a major space power by 2030. The Chinese are also planning to begin building their own manned space station next year. From Beijing, here's our China correspondent John Sudworth.

JOHN: "Commence landing", the control room says. And then comes the extraordinary sight—the first close-up images of the far side of the moon ever recorded. After a few more tense moments, Chang'e-4 safely touches down inside the moon's largest and deepest crater.

It's all gone according to plan, this scientist tells Chinese state TV. The landing was the most important part. Although the far side of the moon always faces away from Earth, orbiting spacecraft have photographed its surface. But no attempt has been made to land on it until now. This animation shows how the probe's thrusters were fired to slow it, before its sensors guide it gently to the surface, a surface far more rugged and obstacle-strewn than the moon's nearside. Another major challenge has included the need for a relay satellite to carry radio signals from the far side back to Earth.

China plans to follow this mission with another that will bring mineral samples back to Earth and, eventually a reported plan for a lunar base, capable of supporting humans.

WU: If our lunar exploration is a success, we can make bigger contributions to mankind and improve China's ability and technology. So, I don't think our exploration will stop. It will only go deeper, further, and we will invest more.

JOHN: For now, Chang'e-4's lunar explorer will begin examining the surface of its landing spot. The moon's deepest crater is expected to offer important insights into the formation of our solar system. John Sudworth, BBC News, Beijing.

Words and Expressions

animation *n.* 动画
close-up *n.* 特写
go according to plan 按计划进行
lunar *adj.* 月球的
milestone *n.* 里程碑
orbit *n.* 轨道
vt. 沿轨道运行
probe *n.* 航天探测器
relay satellite 中继卫星
rugged *adj.* 崎岖的
solar *adj.* 太阳的
strewn *adj.* 布满……的；……遍地的
thruster *n.* 推进器
touch down 着陆

Questions

1. Why is China's moon landing regarded as a major milestone?
2. Where did Chang'e-4 land on the moon?
3. What is Chang'e-4 expected to find on the moon?
4. What do we know about China's ambition in space exploration?

Gap-filling

JOHN: "________________ landing", the control room says. And then comes the extraordinary ________________—the first ________________ images of the far side of the moon ever recorded. After a few more ________________ moments, Chang'e-4 safely touches down inside the moon's largest and deepest ________________. It's all gone according to ________________, this scientist tells Chinese state TV. The landing was the most important part. Although the far side of the moon always faces away from Earth, ________________ spacecraft have photographed its surface. But no attempt has been made to land on it until now. This ________________ shows how the probe's ________________ were fired to slow it, before its ________________ guide it gently to the surface, a surface far more ________________ and obstacle-________________ than the moon's nearside. Another major challenge has included the need for a ________________ satellite to carry radio signals from the far side back to Earth.

Dictation

Good evening … next year.

Translation

1. After a few more tense moments, Chang'e-4 safely touches down inside the moon's largest and deepest crater.
2. This surface is far more rugged and obstacle-strewn than the moon's nearside.

Post-class task

Discussion: What do you think of BBC's report on China's latest achievement?

82. Commuter Safety

LOUISA: Good evening and welcome to BBC London with me, Louisa Preston. A commuter is still in a critical condition tonight after falling into the path of a tube train during yesterday evening's rush hour. He's believed to have suffered what's been described as "a medical episode" before it happened. The incident, at Oxford Circus, has raised questions over safety on platforms, especially at the busiest times of the day. Sonja Jessop's report does contain some flashing images.

(*Please keep moving!*)

SONJA: Evening rush hour, yesterday, at Oxford Circus, commuters turned away, as emergency services tried to help a man who's fallen in front of a train. Police say he'd suffered a "medical episode". Transport bosses insisted it was not connected to overcrowding, but on Twitter others were concerned. One eyewitness—a former England cricketer—saying, "TfL, this is UNACCEPTABLE that in one of the most sophisticated cities in the world, stations are allowed to get this RAMMED." Tonight, other commuters told us they too worry about safety.

COMMUTER 1: It's not very safe, no. It's literally chock-a-block. It's like a freefall, almost.

COMMUTER 2: Actually, after yesterday's incident, yes. Now, yes. It's kind of scary.

COMMUTER 3: People push, yeah. It's not safe. I mean, I've been living in Republic of Korea before this, and they have like blockades up, but even then, even when it's busy, people don't push.

BRIAN: Our railway is safe. We've put plenty of measures in place to ensure that people can have safe journeys all through London.

(*Base to Vic Gateline. Can we control, please? Control Vic Gateline.*)

SONJA: These are the kind of measures he's talking about—staff monitoring platforms and trains, and holding passengers back if it gets too busy. And here on the Jubilee Line, passengers will be familiar with these sliding platform doors. They're popular in other countries on their metro systems, and some commuters have questioned why we can't have them at all tube stations here.

BRIAN: To put those doors in into a network that's over 150 years old, with many different types of trains, and types of... To retrofit that into the underground, A, the engineering is very, very difficult, and also very, very costly.

SONJA: Recent figures from City Hall revealed cases of overcrowding at stations have risen by almost 50% in one year. That is, incidents where passengers were prevented from accessing platforms. Highbury and Islington had the highest number with 104 cases; Finsbury Park had 49, followed by Oxford Circus with 32.

FLORENCE: One of the things that we are calling for Transport for London to do is making sure there are additional customer security advisers on the platforms. I think the other thing that we definitely want Transport for London to continue to do is investment in other forms of public transport, so improving walking and cycling facility.

SONJA: Tonight, the man hit by the train remains in a critical condition. TfL says the case has been reported to the Rail Accident Investigation Branch. Sonja Jessop, BBC London, Oxford Circus. (*BBC-20191121*)

Words and Expressions

blockade *n.* 屏障
chock-a-block *adj.* 水泄不通的
City Hall 市政厅
costly *adj.* 昂贵的
cricketer *n.* 板球运动员
critical *adj.* 危险的;严重的
episode *n.* 疾病的发作;发病
gateline *n.* 检票通道
metro *n.* 地铁
rammed *adj.* 拥挤的
retrofit *vt.* 翻新
sophisticated *adj.* 先进的
turn away 拒之门外

Questions

1. Why were commuters denied access into the Oxford Circus station?
2. What did commuters say about London tube condition?
3. What measures are already implemented to prevent overcrowding?
4. What do we know about the subway system and people in Republic of Korea?
5. Why can't sliding platform doors be installed in all London tube stations?
6. What other feasible solutions are suggested for commuting in London?

Gap-filling

BRIAN: To put those doors in into a ______________ that's over 150 years old, with many different types of trains, and types of... To ______________ that into the underground, A, the ______________ is very, very difficult, and also very, very ______________.

SONJA: Recent figures from City Hall ______________ cases of overcrowding at stations have ______________ by almost 50% in one year. That is, ______________ where passengers were prevented from ______________ platforms. Highbury and Islington had the highest number with 104 cases; Finsbury Park had 49, ______________ Oxford Circus with 32.

FLORENCE: One of the things that we are ______________ Transport for London to do is making sure there are additional customer ______________ on the platforms. I think the other thing that we definitely want Transport for London to continue to do is ______________ in other forms of public transport, so improving walking and ______________ facility.

Dictation

Evening rush hour ... too worry about safety.

Translation

1. He's believed to have suffered what's been described as "a medical episode".
2. Commuters are turned away as emergency services tried to help a man who's fallen in front of a train.
3. The man hit by the train remains in a critical condition.

Post-class task

Discussion: Do a research about London subway history and report in class.

83. Dirty Streaming

HUW: Well, listening to music and watching films and television programmes by using streaming services is hugely popular, of course, but there are warnings now that this way of enjoying content is harming the environment. To store all the data, there are hundreds of thousands of data centres around the world. Many of them using electricity that is generated by burning fossil fuels. Figures suggest that the needs of IT now create the same volume of carbon emissions as flying. Our environment correspondent Claire Marshall has the story.

CLAIRE: When we post a video or a photo or save something to the cloud it leaves our device and travels through different networks, maybe through cables under the ocean to a building called a data centre, where it's stored. When we want to see it, this data is exploded into thousands of pieces, each one travelling in a different route. When they get to a device, they put themselves back in the right order.

So the Internet, or the cloud, isn't just in the air. It exists in buildings like this one. I'm in London's Docklands, where fruit and veg used to be traded on these streets. Now it's data, huge amounts of it. In this building, thousands of servers and they're capturing and storing and sending all our data.

There are now hundreds of thousands of these energy-hungry data centres. The problem is that many are powered by fossil fuels. This is the US state of Northern Virginia, known as the Internet capital of the world. This is one of the coal-fired power stations supplying it with electricity, belching carbon dioxide, a potent greenhouse gas. It belongs to Dominion Energy, the largest provider, which generates much of its power by burning fossil fuels. Microsoft and Google are here. Amazon has built 55 data centres. We think of Amazon as a giant online supermarket but actually the company makes far more money building and renting data centres.

ALEX: Most of residents are pretty clueless as to what's right here.

CLAIRE: Alex Rough is campaigning for the tech companies to use green energy.

ALEX: We are processing large amounts of data on a daily basis. These data centres are consuming large amounts of energy to process that data to stay operational in a 24/7 environment.

CLAIRE: Dominion Energy told us they were committed to net zero carbon and methane emissions by 2050. Amazon said they were working towards 80% renewable energy by 2024, and 100% by 2030. Technology is adapting quickly. Data centres are more efficient than ever, but there is a whole new challenge, 5G.

IAN: 5G will generate much more traffic and demand much more power, which is not good for climate change. We've all got to change. I think the Internet's got the power to help us control and reduce climate change, but we need to change some of our more frivolous behaviour before we get there.

CLAIRE: Streaming videos in standard definition rather than HD saves four times the emissions and using Wi-Fi rather than 3 or 4G uses a third of the energy. Claire Marshall, BBC News. (*BBC-20200304*)

Words and Expressions

belch *vt.* 喷出;吐出
clueless *adj.* 一无所知的
coal-fired *adj.* 用煤作燃料的
committed *adj.* 坚定的
definition *n.* (图像或声音的)清晰度
fossil fuel 化石能源
frivolous *adj.* 愚蠢的
greenhouse gas 温室气体
methane *n.* 甲烷
potent *adj.* 强烈的
server *n.* 服务器
traffic *n.* 数据流量

Questions

1. How can streaming service be "dirty"?
2. What does it mean to store your data in the "cloud"?
3. What do you know about Amazon now?
4. What lifestyle change is needed according to the report?

Gap-filling

CLAIRE: ... There are now hundreds of thousands of these energy-__________ data centres. The problem is that many are powered by __________. This is the US state of Northern Virginia, known as the internet __________ of the world. This is one of the __________ power stations supplying it with electricity, __________ carbon dioxide, a __________ greenhouse gas. It belongs to Dominion Energy, the largest provider, which __________ much of its power by burning fossil fuels. Microsoft and Google are here. Amazon has built __________ data centres. We think of

Amazon as a(n) __________________ online supermarket but actually the company makes far more money building and __________________ data centres.

Dictation

Well, listening to music … carbon emissions as flying.

Translation

1. These data centres are consuming large amounts of energy to process that data to stay operational in a 24/7 environment.
2. They were committed to net zero carbon and methane emissions by 2050.
3. 5G will generate much more traffic.
4. Streaming videos in standard definition rather than HD saves four times the emissions.

Post-class task

Discussion: What have you done in your daily life to save energy and cut down emissions?

84. Drone Disruption

FIONA: So how can something relatively small like a drone pose such a risk to an aeroplane? And what can be done to stop them? Here's our technology correspondent Rory Cellan-Jones.

RORY: Here is why there is so much concern about what might happen if a drone hit a jet aircraft. This experiment at the University of Dayton shows an extreme and possibly unlikely scenario, but after a number of near misses, airports have to take a safety-first approach. UK regulations mean drones are not allowed within a kilometre of an airport and must not fly above 400 feet. They can fly in this west London Park a few miles from Heathrow as long as they don't enter the restricted zone.

This drone, like most sold in the UK has technology on board which prevents it from even taking off too close to an airport or stops it from entering the restricted zones. It appears those used at Gatwick even didn't have the technology or it was overridden. So what can airports do to get rid of these unwanted intruders?

In the United States the Federal Aviation Authority has tried out a system developed in the UK which cuts off communications between the drone and its operator. British engineers are behind SkyWall which captures the unmanned aircraft in a net and brings it down with a parachute. And the Dutch police have even tried using birds of prey to take down a rogue drone.

What is readily available is equipment to track drones and the people who are flying them.

SCOTT: This is the AeroScope protection system. As you can see here, we've got a live view of an aircraft that's within our vicinity. It's pretty difficult to stop people flying irresponsibly, but what we can do is a better job to help people use a system which we have at the moment. And it gives you the real-time information of where the pilot is flying and also where the drone is flying.

RORY: The police have themselves been using drones for quite a while, but at Gatwick they have struggled to catch up with those who've caused so much disruption.

ANDREW: This is a big wake-up call for counterterrorism police around the world, because this potentially is the first time multiple drones to have been used in a disruptive attack. While they obviously may not have explosives or anything that causes explosions or attacks or injuries, but it's a major disruption to the economy of the UK.

RORY: For many, flying a drone is a great hobby. From late next year, all users will have to be registered and take an online safety test. But that will not make airports safe from those determined to break the rules and reap havoc. Rory Cellan Jones, BBC News.

FIONA: Let's talk to our transport correspondent Tom Burridge. Tom, there have been warnings about drones and near misses for some time, I mean, for years. So how has it come to this? Could more have been done to prevent all this?

TOM: Yes, Fiona. This is a huge wake-up call. Every time there is a near miss between a drone and a plane, it's recorded. In 2014 there were no incidents; this year there've been well over 100. For example, in June, a Virgin Atlantic Dreamliner came within ten foot of a drone. The plane had 250 people on board, flying over South London. Yes, the regulations were tightened earlier this year on drones, but the pilots union BALPA has been calling for months for much tougher regulations. For example, it wants that exclusion zone around airports for drones increased from one kilometre to five. The government also has a consultation open on this and is looking at what action to take already: possibly more powers for the police, more counter-drone technology for the police, possibly on-the-spot fines for more minor offences. I think, you know, this incident at Gatwick will sharpen minds, there is no doubt about that. I think the only saving grace tonight is that we are talking about major disruption for lots of passengers—our hearts go out to them, but it's better than the other type of scenario, more tragic scenario which could be on the cards, of a drone potentially colliding with an aeroplane, possibly causing it to crash.

FIONA: OK, Tom. Thank you. (*BBC-20181220*)

Notes

BALPA: 即 British Air Line Pilots Association,英国民航驾驶员协会。

Gatwick (Airport): (英国)盖特威克机场,英国第二大民用机场,位于伦敦以南 47 千米。2018 年 12 月 19 日至 21 日,该机场持续受到无人机干扰而被迫关闭,致使十余万名旅客出行计划受到影响。这是英国机场首次因无人机而关闭数日。

Words and Expressions

bird of prey 猛禽(捕食其他动物的鸟,如鹰、隼和猫头鹰)
counterterrorism *n.* 反恐怖主义
disruptive *adj.* 扰乱性的;破坏性的
havoc *n.* 灾祸
intruder *n.* 闯入者
near miss (尤指两架飞机)侥幸避开的相撞
on the cards 可能发生的
parachute *n.* 降落伞
rogue *adj.* 反常的;胡作非为的
saving grace 可取之处
vicinity *n.* 周围地区;邻近地区;附近

Questions

1. What are the current UK regulations to a drone?
2. What measures have been taken by different countries to prevent drones from entering restricted zones?
3. What other regulations are proposed by the pilots union?
4. What is the worst scenario of a disruptive drone?

Gap-filling

SCOTT: This is the AeroScope ________________ system. As you can see here, we've got a live view of an aircraft that's within our ________________. It is pretty difficult to stop people flying ________________, but what we can do is a better job to help people use a system which we have ________________. And it gives you the real-time ________________ of where the pilot is flying and also where the drone is flying.

RORY: The police have __________ been using drones for quite ______ ______, but at Gatwick they have struggled to catch up with those who've ______ ______ so much disruption.

ANDREW: This is a big __________ for counterterrorism police around the world, because this __________ is the first time multiple drones to ______ ______ used in a disruptive attack. While they obviously may not have ______ ______ or anything that causes __________ or attacks or injuries, but it's a major disruption to the __________ of the UK.

Dictation

The government also has a consultation ... possibly causing it to crash.

Translation

1. After a number of near misses, airports have to take a safety first approach.
2. The Dutch police have even tried using birds of prey to take down a rogue drone.
3. That will not make airports safe from those determined to break the rules and reap havoc.

Post-class task

Discussion: The justified uses of drones.

85. Easier Recycling

SOPHIE: Good evening and welcome to the BBC News at Six. The government has set out its plans to tackle household waste across England and make recycling less confusing. Under the proposals the government hopes to introduce mandatory food waste collections in England and bring in a consistent labelling system so that consumers know what they can recycle. Companies that produce the materials would also have to pay the full costs of disposing or recycling their packaging. At the moment they pay just 10% of the cost. The plans, set out in the government's waste strategy, have been cautiously welcomed by campaign groups. Our correspondent Jeremy Cooke reports.

JEREMY: The throwaway society in full effect. Mountains of waste, millions of tonnes of household rubbish sent to landfill every year in England. Now, the government's launching a new, radical plan to tackle a festering national problem. It plans how to extend the lives of electrical items like dishwashers, recycle plastics like bottles, deal with methane-producing food waste and old batteries. In Ipswich, Jess Allen is determined to do her bit. But for so many of us, recycling can be complicated.

JESS: It says the bottle is and the cap is, but the label isn't, so I'll have to take that off before it goes in the bin.

JEREMY: Jess welcomes the idea of a new, uniform collection system across England and clear labels on which bin for which waste.

JESS: The supermarket labelling, it tells you it's recyclable, but often you think, "Is that in my local area or is it just generically recyclable if it was to go to the right place?" So I think with the reassurance you are doing the right thing as much as you can will be really helpful.

JEREMY: This recycling plant does plastic. 1.4 billion cartons and bottles, 46,000 tonnes every year. But recycling rates in England are stalled at about 45%, plenty of room for improvement.

The whole process is to convert something which is useless into something of real value. But all of this, of course, takes major financial investment.

Money then is key. Yes, the recycled plastic flakes here are sold to make new products, but we need more capacity. And it's hoped that the government announcement will mean more recycling.

SARAH: To build a plant like this one costs around £40 million. We are not investing for this government or the next government or even the one after that. We are investing for 20 or 30 years. And we need to know that that is going to be a good business for future.

JEREMY: Radically, the government is now saying that manufacturers of packaging should pay the cost of disposal, potentially good news for local councils.

MARTIN: Local government has argued for a long time that the manufacturers who actually produced all the waste, the packaging, material like that, they should pick up the cost rather than council taxpayers.

JEREMY: The government wants to extend food waste collections across England to stop methane, a powerful greenhouse gas, and to roll out a deposit and return scheme like this one in Norway for plastic bottles and cans. There is plenty of detail to thrash out but environmental groups hope this could be a game-changer in the fight against waste. Jeremy Cooke, BBC News. (*BBC-20181218*)

Words and Expressions

carton *n.* 硬纸盒
cautiously *adv.* 谨慎地
consistent *adj.* 前后一致的;一贯的
deposit *n.* 存放
dispose *vt.* 丢弃;处理
do one's bit 做贡献;尽力
festering *adj.* 愈益恶化的
flake *n.* 碎片
generically *adv.* 一般地;通用地
landfill *n.* 废物填埋
pick up 付账
reassurance *n.* 令人安心的保证;清除疑虑
recyclable *adj.* 可回收利用的
stalled *adj.* 停滞的
thrash out 反复讨论
throwaway *adj.* 用后丢弃的;一次性使用的
uniform *adj.* 一致的;统一的

Questions

1. What is British government's plan to tackle household waste?
2. Why is the plan in urgent need?
3. What do common citizens wish the government to do to make recycling easier?
4. Why is building new recycling plants still necessary even though the cost is high?

Gap-filling

JEREMY: ... Money then is key. Yes, the recycled plastic ____________________ here are sold to make new products, but we need more ____________________. And it's hoped the government announcement will mean more recycling.

SARAH: To ____________________ like this one costs around £40 million. We are not investing for this government or the next government or even ____________________. We are investing for 20 or 30 years. And we need to know that that is going to be a good business for future.

JEREMY: ____________________, the government is now saying that manufacturers of packaging should pay the cost of ____________________, potentially good news for local ____________________.

MARTIN: Local government has ____________________ for a long time that the manufacturers who ____________________ produced all the waste, the packaging, material like that, they should ____________________ the cost rather than council ____________________.

Dictation

Good evening and welcome to ... Jeremy Cooke reports.

Translation

1. The government's launching a new, radical plan to tackle a festering national problem.
2. Recycling rates in England are stalled at about 45%, plenty of room for improvement.
3. Yes, the recycled plastic flakes here are sold to make new products, but we need more capacity.
4. The manufacturers who actually produced all the waste should pick up the cost rather than council taxpayers.

Post-class task

Discussion: What do you propose your local government and people to do to promote recycling?

86. Fake Products

MISHAL: The UK is being inundated with fake designer goods are on a scale never seen before—that's according to the trade body, the Anti-Counterfeiting Group. An undercover investigation by the BBC has discovered vast quantities of fake or replica clothing, trainers, perfumes and electrical goods are being sold from living rooms, car parks and even high street shops across the UK. Trading Standards says it is linked to serious organised crime and is costing the Treasury millions in unpaid taxes every year. Our special correspondent Colin Campbell has the story.

COLLIN: Black market Britain is booming.

MAN: We've got two left.

COLLIN: They're fake, are they?

WOMAN: Everything's fake, mate.

COLLIN: I'm in Manchester, where replica designer goods are being sold from shops on an industrial scale.

They're not real?

MAN: Nothing is real, man.

COLLIN: Through this doorway, an Aladdin's cave of fakes spread out over three levels. Belts, bags, coats, jumpers. There's all forms of fake, counterfeit goods in here. Brazenly breaking the law, the area is known as Britain's counterfeit capital. It's estimated that between 50 and 100 shops are involved. Yves Saint Laurent. Michael Kors. Chanel. It's just endless. Outside, amongst the hordes of Christmas shoppers, an army of lookouts to spot police. There are regular raids, but it's not enough.

MAN: They can't stop it. They can't do much about it. They can if they want but they've got better … more other things to do.

COLLIN: We showed our footage to the Anti-Counterfeiting Group, which represents over 3,000 brands.

PHIL: 4% of all imports into the UK are now fake. They're destroying jobs. They're destroying the high street. They're crippling our industries and we seem to be allowing it to happen.

COLLIN: From the north of England to the south, we found scores of dealers knowingly selling fake goods, many openly advertising on social media.
Can you get into trouble for it, then?

MAN: You can, yeah. Because you've got to prove where you got them from and obviously where we get them from, there's no receipts available.

COLLIN: In a Bradford car park, replica Nike trainers.

MAN: They're all er … replicas yeah. I just got these new in today.

COLLIN: From a living room in Hull, a catalogue of fake, phony designer gear.

MAN: Silver, didn't you?

COLLIN: Yeah, please. Yeah. How much are they again?

MAN: 25.

COLLIN: 25.
In Stoke, imitation Beats headphones.

MAN: The thing that lets them down is the tagging. It's fact they've only got the one tag, whereas generally they've got two.

COLLIN: In Bristol, fake North Face hoodies and jackets.
They're replica ones, but they're all right, are they …?

MAN: Yeah, yeah.

COLLIN: In Southampton, another digital Del Boy selling replica perfumes and cosmetics.

MIKE: The sale of counterfeit products is linked to serious and organised crime, terrorism, people trafficking, arms sales. And this is obviously a significant problem that people perhaps don't realise they're funding that level of criminal activity.

COLLIN: Britain is awash with counterfeit designer goods. Everywhere we went, we were able to source fake or replica products. And the stuff is being peddled from towns and cities across the UK.

Manchester City Council says it's doing more work than ever to tackle the problem, but with cuts to funding across the UK, enforcement authorities are, it seems, struggling to cope with the flourishing counterfeit industry. Colin Campbell, BBC News. (*BBC-20181223*)

Notes

Del Boy：德尔男孩，英国喜剧《只有傻瓜和马》(*Only Fools and Horses*)中卖假货的人物德里克·特罗特(Derek Edward Trotter)的绰号，现通指"售假者"。

Words and Expressions

a catalogue of 一系列；一连串(坏事情)
Aladdin's cave 阿拉丁的藏宝洞；宝库
awash *adj.* 充斥的；泛滥的(with)
be inundated with 泛滥
brazenly *adv.* 厚颜无耻地
cosmetics *n.* 化妆品
counterfeit *adj.* 假冒的
vt. 制假
cripple *vt.* 严重毁坏(或损害)
designer *adj.* 名牌的
flourishing *adj.* 繁荣；蓬勃发展
gear *n.* 设备；用具
hoodie *n.* 带帽夹克
hordes of 一群群
jumper *n.* 针织套衫；毛线上衣
lookout *n.* 望风者
peddle *vt.* 兜售
perfume *n.* 香水
phony *adj.* 假的
raid *n.* (警察的)突击搜查
scores of 大量
source *vt.* 找出……的来源
the Treasury (英国)财政部
trafficking *n.* 非法买卖；贩卖
trainer *n.* 运动鞋
undercover *adj.* 暗中进行的；秘密干的

Questions

1. What is the percentage of fake products imported into the UK?
2. What impact do fake products bring to UK economy?
3. If people buy fake products, they are actually funding criminals. Why?
4. Why is counterfeit industry so hard to crack down?

Gap-filling

COLLIN: In Southampton, another digital Del Boy selling replica __________________ and __________________.

MIKE: The sale of counterfeit products is linked to serious and __________________ crime, terrorism, people ____________________, arms sales. And this is obviously a significant __________________ that people perhaps don't realise they're ________ _________ that level of criminal activity.

COLLIN: Britain is __________________ with counterfeit designer goods. Everywhere we went, we were able to __________________ fake or replica products. And the stuff is being __________________ from towns and cities across the UK.

Manchester City Council says it's doing more work than ever to _______________ the problem, but with cuts to funding across the UK, ____________________ authorities are, it seems, struggling to cope with the ____________________ counterfeit industry.

Dictation

The UK is being inundated with ... in unpaid taxes every year.

Translation

1. The UK is being inundated with fake designer goods on a scale never seen before.
2. The sale of counterfeit products is linked to serious and organised crime, terrorism, people trafficking, arms sales.
3. Everywhere we went, we were able to source fake or replica products.

Post-class task

Discussion: Have you intentionally bought any fake product? Explain the situation.

87. Fake Takeaway

SOPHIE: The food delivery company Uber Eats has tightened the way restaurants sign up to its service after BBC News successfully registered a fake takeaway on the site and began processing orders. The company says it's deeply concerned by the incident and is now carrying out an audit of all food outlets currently on the platform. The revelations follow a report last night, on the number of restaurants with low hygiene ratings on delivery apps. Angus Crawford reports.

ANGUS: Fancy a burger from London's newest takeaway? Time to make it official by signing up to the delivery platform Uber Eats. Within days, instructions and equipment delivered by courier. I've told them I don't yet have a hygiene rating but promised to get one. So the Best Burger Corporation, or BBC, is open for business. No checks, no proof of ID and, crucially, (*Ooh ... Never mind.*) no hygiene inspection. But still, I'm up and frying in my front garden. And there's an order on the way ...

MARK: The Best Burger ...

ANGUS: ... from food safety expert Mark McGlynn, who's just down the road.

MARK: Order's been taken. That's really shocking. That's quite shocking.

ANGUS: OK, so that's one plain burger, a little bit of garnish ... Within minutes my very first order is picked up. (*Thank you very much.*) And moments later, delivered.

MARK: Uber Eats. Great, thank you very much.

ANGUS: What do you think about what happened today?

MARK: I could not be more shocked. I am astonished by what I saw, but also very, very alarmed. It's not warm, it's rather cold. We're in desperate times, it seems to me, if very, very large food delivery platforms can be operating in this way.

ANGUS: What do you think of that?

HEATHER: I am almost speechless with horror about that. And aside from wanting to comment on your own hygiene practices, that driver appeared, looked at where you produced that food, took it and went. That's just horrifying.

ANGUS: Uber Eats told us "We are deeply concerned by this breach of our food safety policy". The company says it will update sign-up requirements, and carry out an audit of all restaurants on the app. "We are working hard to ensure this does not happen again."

So how can you know if a takeaway is clean or not? In Wales, hygiene ratings have to be displayed in the shop window, but that law doesn't apply online. The Welsh government says it should across the UK.

I just bought this today from a takeaway with a hygiene rating of just one.

VAUGHAN: So when you're going in to order food on any one of those apps, I want to make sure that as a consumer you have that choice, you have that information in front of you.

ANGUS: So if the big food delivery companies won't change, you'll make them change?

VAUGHAN: Yes.

ANGUS: Deliveroo and Uber Eats don't show individual hygiene ratings, but say they hope to in the future. Following our investigation last year, Just Eat did start a trial, showing ratings for a small number of outlets and says that will go nationwide next month.

Companies making billions from meals they don't cook, in takeaways they don't own. Is it time they were made responsible for the kitchens where that food, and their profits, are made? Angus Crawford, BBC News. (*BBC-20190627*)

Words and Expressions

audit *n.* 审计	hygiene *n.* 卫生
courier *n.* 快递员	outlet *n.* 专营店;经销店
crucially *adv.* 关键是	revelation *n.* 内幕揭秘
desperate *adj.* 极严重的;极危险的	sign up 签约;加盟
garnish *n.* (食物上的)装饰菜	takeaway *n.* 外卖餐馆

Questions

1. What is the normal procedure to register into a food delivery platform in the UK?
2. Why is the reporter's footage shocking to the two experts?
3. What changes does the reporter hope to happen in the online food delivery industry?

Gap-filling

ANGUS: What do you think about what ________________ today?

MARK: I could not be more shocked. I am ________________ by what I saw, but also very, very ________________. It's not warm, it's rather cold. We're in ____ ________________ times, it seems to me, if very, very large food delivery platforms can be ________________ in this way.

ANGUS: What do you __________________?

HEATHER: I am almost speechless __________________ about that. And aside from wanting to comment on your own __________________ practices, that driver appeared, looked at where you __________________ that food, took it and went. That's just __________________.

Dictation

The food delivery company Uber Eats ... on delivery apps.

Translation

1. BBC News successfully registered a fake takeaway on the site and began processing orders.
2. The revelations follow a report last night, on the number of restaurants with low hygiene ratings on delivery apps.
3. Companies make billions from meals they don't cook, in takeaways they don't own.

Post-class task

Discussion: Do you go to a restaurant according to online ratings? And do you find the ratings accurate?

55. Focus on Farming

REETA: How should the British countryside be managed? It's an ongoing debate between environmentalists and farmers. Some say nature should be allowed to take its course, leaving the land so that wildlife can flourish, a practice known as "rewilding". Others say the land should be used mainly for food production. In the latest of our series "Focus on Farming", our environment correspondent Claire Marshall has been to one of the most ambitious rewilding projects in Britain, the Knepp Estate.

CLAIRE: This is a typical slice of British farmland, well designed to produce food for humans and livestock but where wildlife is pushed to the very edges. Look at what happens when you abandon intensive farming and put the natural world first. We have come to look at the largest rewilding project in England, a 3,500-acre estate

in West Sussex.

ISABELLA: This would have been a conventional arable field. It would have been as flat monoculture as far as the eye can see.

CLAIRE: Isabella Tree and her husband gave up traditional farming 20 years ago. They have tried to recreate an ancient landscape where different animals graze freely alongside each other. Tamworth pigs act as ploughs. Old English longhorn cattle and deer help to fertilise the land and spread seeds.

ISABELLA: It's a miracle, when the habitat returns and you have this dynamism, just the species find you. I mean, how, I don't know, but we now have turtle doves. We are about the only place in Britain where turtle dove numbers are actually rising. That's our most likely bird to go extinct from Britain within the next 10 to 15 years. We are a hotspot for nightingales, we have woodlark, we have peregrine falcons, we have purple emperor butterflies. I mean, we have all these species that have found us because there is now the opportunity for them here.

CLAIRE: However, many farmers such as Robin Milton, who farms on the edge of Exmoor, believe you can produce food and care for wildlife at the same time.

ROBIN: We've got quite a selection of habitats that the value, that are of huge value for biodiversity. But alongside that, we are producing beef and lamb of probably the finest quality with one of the lowest environmental footprints you can find.

CLAIRE: We are losing our wildlife in the UK at a dramatic rate. Take skylarks. Their numbers dropped by half in the 1990s and they are still dropping. And bees and hover flies, our key pollinators, a third of their species are in decline. And hedgehogs, we've lost a half in the last 20 years.

There are many reasons for this, but intensive farming methods including the use of pesticides are seen as a key driver. However, the industry says chemicals are essential to food security.

SARAH: There are thousands of pests that are literally after your lunch. If we can make sure the fields are as productive as possible, then we have to use some sort of crop protection.

CLAIRE: But the facts won't disappear—the richness of life in the countryside is fading. Claire Marshall, BBC News, West Sussex. (*BBC-20190821*)

Notes

Tamworth pig: 塔姆沃思猪，英国的一种体态修长、皮毛呈红棕色的猪，其肉主要用于制作培根。塔姆沃思是英格兰中部城镇。

Words and Expressions

arable *adj.* 可耕的
biodiversity *n.* 生态多样性
dynamism *n.* 活力
fertilise *vt.* 给(土壤、土地)施肥
footprint *n.* 足迹(指个人或机构活动对环境的影响)
hedgehog *n.* 刺猬
hover fly 食蚜虻
monoculture *n.* 单种栽培
nightingale *n.* 夜莺
peregrine falcon 游隼
plough *n.* 犁
purple emperor butterfly 紫蛱蝶
skylark *n.* 云雀
take its course 任其发展;听其自然
turtle dove 斑鸠
woodlark *n.* 森林云雀

Questions

1. Why is wildlife important to farming?
2. What are the reasons leading to the decline of wildlife?
3. What is the dilemma that farmers now are facing?

Gap-filling

ROBIN: We've got quite a selection of ________________ that the value, that are of huge value for ________________. But alongside that, we are producing beef and lamb of probably the ________________ quality with one of the lowest environmental ________________ you can find.

CLAIRE: We are losing our wildlife in the UK at a dramatic rate. Take skylarks. Their numbers dropped by half in the 1990s and they are still dropping. And ________________ and hover flies, our key ________________, a third of their species are in decline. And hedgehogs, we've lost a half in the last 20 years.

There are many reasons for this, but ________________ farming methods including the use of ________________ are seen as a key ________________. However, the industry says chemicals are ________________ to food security.

SARAH: There are thousands of pests that are ________________ after your lunch. If we can make sure the fields are as ________________ as possible, then we have to use some sort of ________________ protection.

Dictation

It's a miracle, when ... opportunity for them here.

Translation

1. Nature should be allowed to take its course.
2. Look at what happens when you abandon intensive farming and put the natural world first.
3. We've got quite a selection of habitats that are of huge value for biodiversity.
4. There are thousands of pests that are literally after your lunch.

Post-class task

Discussion: Are you worried, even a little, about the decline of wildlife in our country?

89. Food Safety

SOPHIE: Just Eat—it is a company that allows you to order takeaway food from thousands of outlets all over the UK. And it's become a huge global business valued at more than £4 billion. But Just Eat is facing questions tonight over hygiene standards at some of the takeaways you can choose from on its website. An investigation by BBC News has found that some have been given the lowest possible rating from the Food Standards Agency. Just Eat insists it takes food safety very seriously and works with providers to improve standards. Angus Crawford reports.

ANGUS: They arrive without warning.

HELEN: I'm here to do your food hygiene inspection.

ANGUS: Environmental health officers.

HELEN: The rice, when did you take that out of the fridge? Absolutely filthy. I would again suggest throwing that away.

ANGUS: Food for the table ends up in the bin. There are rat and mouse droppings too. And that's not just a worry for people eating in. Customers can also get a takeaway through the website Just Eat.

The smell in the kitchen was really unpleasant and in the backroom, the storage room, it was almost overpowering at times. As far as the local council is concerned, this gets a zero hygiene rating, but on Just Eat, it gets four stars.

HELEN: That food, potentially, had it been served to a consumer, could have caused some harm. So, yeah, I mean, it's not great.

ANGUS: Would you eat in there?

HELEN: No. Absolutely no.

ANGUS: And it happens a lot. Zero-rated takeaways, the Food Standards Agency says, are in urgent need of improvement, on Just Eat but with great customer reviews. Our research found 20 out of the 31 zero-rated takeaways in Birmingham are on Just Eat. 9 of the 13 takeaways with a zero rating in Liverpool are listed there. And in Manchester, Bristol and London, half of the takeaways with a zero rating are on the platform. Places like this in east London, closed for three weeks in April when inspectors found a mouse infestation. The owners say it's been completely refurbished and is now pest-free. Or this one in York, shut down in June because of cockroaches. It's back open now under new management. They told us the kitchen has been thoroughly cleaned and inspected; the infestation has gone. And Zeera in Swindon, fined £5,000. The judge said the food here could have killed someone. All on Just Eat when the inspectors called.

CHRIS: There's one there, the second one there, three, four ...

ANGUS: But what is the customer to make of it? Consumer rights campaigner Chris Emmins believes the business has got to change.

CHRIS: There is a duty of all businesses to safeguard their customers and it's no good saying you're just an agent. The reality is that Just Eat is making huge amounts of money. They receive the money, they supply the goods. If that was a standard, traditional business—a supermarket or a travel agent—they would be hauled over the coals considerably for a failure for that sort of lack of due diligence.

ANGUS: Just Eat, now a FTSE 100 company worth billions, says it takes food safety extremely seriously, but no one was available for interview. Instead, the company told us, "We actively work to raise standards and now offer free accredited food hygiene training to any restaurant that signs up to our platform." And in case of food safety issues, "our restaurant compliance team will review, investigate and liaise with the relevant local authority".

CHRIS: It's easy to fix, and it's not there.

ANGUS: Campaigners want Just Eat to display the actual hygiene rating for each takeaway on the app. The company says it will trial that soon in Northern Ireland.

HELEN: You should be keeping all in the fridge ...

ANGUS: This pub in west London says it is trying hard to fix the problems highlighted by Environmental Health. But for customers of Just Eat, a simple question—how clean is the kitchen your takeaway comes from? Angus Crawford, BBC News. (*BBC-20181017*)

Notes

FTSE 100：英国富时 100 指数，《金融时报》证券交易 100 指数（FTSE = Financial Times Stock Exchange）。这个指数每天报出 100 家英国公司的股价，显示英国金融市场的状况。

Words and Expressions

accredited *adj.* 官方认可的
cockroach *n.* 蟑螂
compliance team 加盟店守法情况检查组
droppings *n.* （鸟、小动物的）粪
due *adj.* 适当的；充分的
filthy *adj.* 肮脏的；污秽的
haul over the coals 严厉训斥某人
infestation *n.* （昆虫、老鼠等）成群侵扰；滋生
liaise （为双方合作而）建立工作关系；联络
make of 理解；看待
overpowering *adj.* 强烈的；令人无法忍受的
refurbish *vt.* 翻修一新
safeguard *vt.* 保护
takeaway *n.* 外卖的饭菜；外卖食物
value *vt.* 估价；定价

Questions

1. What's wrong with Just Eat?
2. What common problems do takeaway restaurants have?
3. What changes need to be made by Just Eat, according to experts and campaigners?

Gap-filling

CHRIS: There is a(n) ____________ of all businesses to safeguard their customers and it's no good saying you're just ____________. The reality is that Just Eat is making huge amounts of money. They receive the money, they supply ____________. If that was a standard, traditional business—a supermarket or a(n) ____________ agent—they would be ____________ over the coals considerably for a failure for that sort of lack of ____________.

ANGUS: Just Eat, now a FTSE 100 company ____________ billions, says it takes food safety extremely seriously, but no one was ____________ for interview. Instead, the company told us, "We actively work to raise standards and now offer free ________________ food hygiene training to any restaurant that ___________ ______ to our platform." And in case of food safety issues, "our restaurant ______ ___________ team will review, investigate and __________________ with the relevant local authority".

Dictation

And it happens a lot ... and is now pest-free.

Translation

1. That food, potentially, had it been served to a consumer, could have caused some harm.
2. If that was a standard, traditional business—a supermarket or a travel agent—they would be hauled over the coals considerably for a failure for that sort of lack of due diligence.
3. We now offer free accredited food hygiene training to any restaurant that signs up to our platform.
4. Our restaurant compliance team will review, investigate and liaise with the relevant local authority.

Post-class task

Discussion: How do you comment on Chinese food delivery platforms, such as *Meituan* and *Eleme*?

90 Genome Sequencing

FIONA: Now, in a world first, scientists in Cambridge have completed the largest gene sequencing project in healthcare. 85,000 people took part—among them, children with rare diseases, their parents and patients with cancer. 100,000 genomes were mapped. The genome contains all a person's DNA, and errors can trigger a vast range of disorders. Many of those who took part in the project have already benefited from a diagnosis, or treatment for their condition. Our medical correspondent, Fergus Walsh, reports.

FERGUS: The faces behind the numbers. These are some of the people who volunteered to have their entire genetic codes sequenced. Visiting the laboratories near Cambridge, where it was done, some are affected by cancer, others by rare diseases.

WOMAN: Sometimes, what we have to do is go back to the DNA sample during the library preparation ...

FERGUS: All are helping to improve our understanding of how genes influence our health from cradle to grave.

Inside, nearly every one of our cells is a copy of our genome, made up of 3 billion pairs of DNA code and 20,000 genes. It is the instruction manual for how our bodies work. Sequencing the first human genome took 13 years. Now, a genome's worth of DNA can be done in 30 minutes. That dramatic acceleration has enabled scientists here to sequence 100,000 genomes of people affected by rare diseases or cancer.

Every genome mapped by these machines yields vast amounts of data. So, how is that helping individuals and society? Karen Carter has contributed two genomes. First, the gene she was born with. Then, the DNA from her breast tumour, containing the faulty genes that triggered her cancer. By comparing her DNA with that of other cancer patients, it may explain why she and several members of her family have developed cancer at a young age.

KAREN: Knowledge is power and we need to find ways forward, because once you've had cancer, the worry is always there.

HANA: Good girl. Mummy's turn.

FERGUS: Six-year-old Tilly has a rare brain and muscle disorder that used to cause seizures, meant she lost the ability to walk, and made her aggressive around other children, like her brother Arlo. It was not until Tilly and mum Hannah joined the 100,000 Genome Project that scientists were able to compare their DNA and finally found the cause of her condition, and an effective medicine.

HANA: She has been treated now since March and the difference is amazing. Her epilepsy is gone. She's developing every day. She's communicating. She's just full of life and she's not violent any more. She can be around her brother without attacking him.

FERGUS: The 100,000 Genomes Project is just the start. The ambition is to sequence a further 1 million genomes over the next five years, as genomics rapidly becomes embedded in the fabric of healthcare.

JOHN: Well, it's transformational, in terms of what it means to society and humanity. The vision is that your health record will eventually have a genomic backbone to it and, therefore, a more accurate diagnosis or more accurate treatment will be available to you.

FERGUS: Olivia is three weeks old. It is her generation that has the most benefit from genomic medicine, as the growth of DNA data gives more insights to enable us all to stay healthier, longer. Fergus Walsh, BBC News, Cambridge. (*BBC-20181205*)

Words and Expressions

aggressive *adj.* 富于攻击性的
backbone *n.* 支柱;基础
disorder *n.* 失调;紊乱;不适;疾病
epilepsy *n.* 癫痫
faulty *adj.* 有缺陷的
from cradle to grave 从生到死;一辈子
gene sequencing 基因测序
genome *n.* 基因组
genomics *n.* 基因组学
instruction manual 指导手册
map *vt.* 绘制
seizure *n.* 发作
transformational *adj.* 彻底改变的;革命性的
yield *vt.* 产生;提供

Questions

1. What are benefits of genome sequencing?
2. Can you describe the human body in terms of genome, DNA, and genes?
3. How long did it take to sequence the first human genome? And how about now?
4. What can we infer about future cancer treatment from this news?

Gap-filling

HANA: She has been ________________ now since March and the difference is ________________. Her epilepsy is gone. She's developing every day, she's communicating. She's just full of life and she's not ________________ any more. She can be ________________ without attacking him.

FERGUS: The 100,000 Genomes Project is just the start. The ________________ is to sequence a further 1 million genomes over the next five years, as ________________ rapidly becomes ________________ in the ________________ of healthcare.

JOHN: Well, it's ________________, in terms of what it means to society and humanity. The ________________ is that your health record will eventually have a genomic ________________ to it and, therefore, a more accurate ________________ or more accurate treatment will be ________________ to you.

Dictation

Now, in a world first … Fergus Walsh, reports.

Translation

1. The genome contains all a person's DNA, and errors can trigger a vast range of disorders.
2. A genome's worth of DNA can be done in 30 minutes.
3. Every genome mapped by these machines yields vast amounts of data.
4. Genomics rapidly becomes embedded in the fabric of healthcare.
5. Your health record will eventually have a genomic backbone to it.

Post-class task

Do research on gene-engineering and write a short report in about 200 words.

91. Gymnastic Abuse

HUW: Now British Gymnastics is conducting an independent review following allegations raised by a number of gymnasts about mistreatment. BBC News has heard from athletes who claimed that the governing body has fostered a "culture of fear" and emotional abuse. Some gymnasts allege they have been "weight-shamed", leading to the development of eating disorders. Our sports correspondent Natalie Pirks has the story.

NICOLE: When you really realise how much it's affected you, from the eating disorders, the chronic pain, waking up, having nightmares every night, never feeling good enough.

NATALIE: At the age of 12, Nicole Pavier was a promising young English gymnast. Five years later she retired, battling bulimia.

NICOLE: I was always worried about food, but the real problems started at 14, just being terrified that you were gonna go over the scales or …

NATALIE: She says she would also skip meals and take laxatives.

CLAIRE: Come on, move those legs! Come on, push! Push!

NATALIE: Claire Barbieri is one of the most high-profile coaches in the sport and is currently the lead national technical adviser for Scottish Gymnastics. She was one of Nicole's coaches. The gymnast alleges she was weighed several times a day.

NICOLE: It got progressively worse. I remember a session where I was doing a full pirouette on bars and blacked out.

NATALIE: Claire Barbieri told the BBC, "I have never to date had any formal complaint raised against me by a gymnast. In line with standard practice at the time, the Club had a system of weighing and measuring the elite gymnasts daily. Following advice from the GB medical team this was reduced to twice a week. I continue to treat the welfare of the gymnasts as my top priority."

Elsewhere, with a different coach, another athlete told us she also suffered an eating disorder because of a culture, she says, British Gymnastics allowed to continue. "They have created this culture of fear, this culture of negative coaching and emotional abuse of coaching. And those coaches are then passing on to future generations of coaches and this kind of vicious cycle is just continuing. If this doesn't change, I'm not sure there's a future for British Gymnastics."

During the course of this investigation, we've heard terrible stories of young children who were too scared to speak out, or who simply weren't listened to. We've also seen detailed evidence from parents from across the country of the abuse their children suffered. It includes being screamed at, being hit with a stick, being banished to a cupboard for hours on end as punishment, and being made to continue to train in extreme pain with broken bones.

In response to numerous concerns raised by athletes, British Gymnastics has now launched an independent investigation. It says it "condemns any behaviour which is harmful to the well-being of our gymnasts. Such behaviours are completely contrary to our standards of safe coaching". It added, "We have worked particularly hard in recent years to ensure that our athlete and coaching culture is transparent, fair and inclusive."

For Nicole, the effects of how she was coached has had a long lasting impact.

NICOLE: It still plagues my everyday life. I still hate the way I look; I still feel like I'm overweight. These coaches see us as numbers and they just don't realise the effect that it's going to have on the rest of your life.

NATALIE: Ultimately, gymnastics will always be a sport where adults work with children and one, it seems, where too often the line between tough coaching and abuse is blurred. Natalie Pirks, BBC News. (*BBC-20200707*)

Words and Expressions

banish *vt.* 赶走
bars *n.* 高低杠
black out 昏厥
blur *vt.* (使)难以区分
bulimia *n.* 贪食症
condemn *vt.* 谴责
cupboard *n.* 储藏室
elite *adj.* 精英的;最优秀的
foster *vt.* 助长;培养
gymnast *n.* 体操运动员
gymnastic *adj.* 体操的
gymnastics *n.* 体操;体操训练
in line with 与……一致
inclusive *adj.* (团体或组织)可以包容各种人的
laxative *n.* 轻泻药
on end 连续地
pirouette *n.* 单脚尖旋转
plague *vt.* 折磨;使受煎熬
progressively *adv.* 日益增加地;逐步
scales *n.* 磅秤
session *n.* (训练活动的)一节
to date 迄今为止
transparent *adj.* 透明的
ultimately *adv.* 根本上;归根结底
vicious cycle 恶性循环

Questions

1. Why did Nicole sometimes have to skip meals?
2. What could happen when a person has an eating disorder?
3. How did the coach abuse her?
4. What kind of coach style was adopted in UK gymnastics?
5. How has the coach's abuse affected Nicole's life today?
6. Is it easy to determine whether the coach abused Nicole or not?

Gap-filling

NATALIE: ... In response to numerous ____________________ raised by athletes, British Gymnastics has now launched an independent investigation. It says it "__________ ________ any behaviour which is harmful to the well-being of our ____________ ______. Such behaviours are completely __________________ to our standards of safe coaching". It added, "We have worked particularly hard in recent years to ________________ that our athlete and coaching culture is ________________."

For Nicole, the effects of how she was coached has had a long __________________ impact.

NICOLE: It still __________________ my everyday life. I still hate __________________ I look; I still feel like I'm ________________. These coaches see us as ________ ________ and they just don't realise ________________ that it's going to have on the rest of your life.

Dictation

Elsewhere, with a different ... "... British Gymnastics."

Translation

1. I was doing a full pirouette on bars and blacked out.
2. Children were banished to a cupboard for hours on end as punishment.
3. Our athlete and coaching culture is transparent, fair and inclusive.
4. Too often the line between tough coaching and abuse is blurred.

Post-class task

Retell this story about the abuse scandal of UK gymnastics.

92. Importance of Sculpture

JULIE: And finally as Sarah has just shown us, the human body is capable of amazing things, and has captivated sculptors throughout time. Britain's most famous master of the art Antony Gormley has already fired the public imagination with his cast iron figures on the beach at Crosby on Merseyside, and of course the majestic Angel of the North outside Gateshead. Now he's doing it all over again with a new big display in London. For him, it's a statement of the importance of sculpture in a digital age, and once again representing that human body is at the heart of his art.

MARTHA: The human form is at the heart of Antony Gormley's work, but this is no retrospective. For his solo exhibition at the Royal Academy, there are new works, like "Clearing VII", a drawing in space that the public must find a route through. At his studio, Gormley says he wanted to question what sculpture can do, and make us feel.

ANTONY: It's about engaging with the total physical experience of moving through twelve rooms, each of which is inviting you to be in that room with those works in a very particular way.

MARTHA: This exhibition is designed to challenge the viewer to consider how we interact with the space we inhabit, but it's also posed a huge challenge to the Royal Academy to work out how to exhibit pieces like this.

The building has been reinforced to take the weight of "Matrix III", a suspended cloud of steel mesh; also we have "Host", where clay, seawater, and air fill an entire gallery and the 30-ton installation "Cave" where those who enter inside must feel their way through the dark spaces of a giant body.

MARTIN: It's not just about looking, it's also about squaring up to these works, even entering, being swallowed up by them and in so doing, you know, being slightly confounded. It's like disoriented, um ..., feeling your own body maybe more keenly.

MARTHA: Outside in the courtyard the sculpture of a tiny iron baby is already attracting attention. And in a world lived increasingly on screens, Antony Gormley believes sculpture is more relevant than ever.

ANTONY: I think sculpture in a digital age is critically important. It's still, it's silent, it doesn't need a roof. It can exist on the street, in the mountains, on top of buildings; and simply be there, and be a kind of acupuncture of our daily experience, saying what is ... or asking that question: What is a human life? Where are we going? How do we engage with our time? And maybe those questions are more relevant now than ever.

MARTHA: And he describes this exhibition as a test site to ask what art is for, and how it can shape our future. Martha Fairlie, News at Ten, at the Royal Academy. (*TTV-20190916*)

Notes

Angel of the North: 北方天使，英国最大的雕塑，坐落于纽卡斯尔的一个郊区，身长 54 米，200 吨重。

Crosby: 克罗斯比，默西塞德郡的一个小镇，其海滩有 Antony Gormley 创作的群雕 Another Place，由 100 个铁人构成。

Gateshead: 盖茨黑德，英格兰东北部一工业城镇。

Merseyside: 默西赛德，英格兰西北部一都市郡。

The Royal Academy (of Arts): (英国)皇家美术研究院，成立于 1768 年，坐落在伦敦市中心，每年举行优秀学员及艺术家作品展。

Words and Expressions

acupuncture *n.* 针灸
captivate *vt.* 使着迷
cast iron 铸铁
confounded *adj.* 困惑的
disoriented *adj.* 迷失方向的
fire *vt.* 激发
inhabit *vt.* 居住于
keenly *adv.* 强烈地;敏锐地
matrix *n.* 矩阵
mesh *n.* 网状物
reinforce *vt.* 加固
retrospective *n.* (艺术家作品)回顾展
square up to 勇敢面对

Questions

1. Where is the exhibition held?
2. How challenging is this exhibition to the venue?
3. What is Antony Gormley good at displaying?
4. Why is sculpture particularly relevant at the digital age?
5. Can you name some works of Antony's mentioned in this report?

Gap-filling

MARTHA: Outside in the courtyard the sculpture of a tiny ____________________ baby is already attracting attention. And in a world lived increasingly on ______________ ______, Antony Gormley believes sculpture is more relevant than ever.

ANTONY: I think sculpture in a(n) ____________________ age is critically important. It's __________________, it's silent, it doesn't need ____________________. It can exist on the street, in the ___________________, on top of buildings; and simply be there, and be a kind of _____________ of our daily experience, saying what is … or asking that question: What is a human life? Where are we going? How do we ____________________ with our time? And maybe those questions are more relevant now than ever.

Dictation

And finally as Sarah … the heart of his art.

Translation

1. Antony Gormley has already fired the public imagination with his cast iron figures.
2. This is no retrospective.

3. How do we engage with our time?

Post-class task

Discussion: Tell the class the most fascinating sculpture in your city.

93. Judith Kerr

HUW: Judith Kerr, the children's author who created the classic books *The Tiger Who Came to Tea* and the Mog series, has died at the age of 95. And fellow writers have been paying tribute to a remarkable woman who fled Nazi Germany and went on to publish dozens of books over a 50-year career. Our correspondent David Sillito looks back at her long and eventful life.

DAVID: "Excuse me, do you think I could have tea with you ...?" *The Tiger Who Came to Tea*. For Judith Kerr, it was the beginning of a 50-year career, and it all began when she and her daughter were feeling in need of a bit of excitement.

JUDITH: It got really very boring. I mean, you would go for a walk and have tea, and then that was it, really. And we wished somebody would come. And so, I thought, well, why not have a tiger come?

DAVID: And then came forgetful, accident-prone Mog. It was, for her friend and fellow children's author Lauren Child, trademark Judith Kerr.

LAUREN: Her work is beautiful because there's a lovely stillness to it. It never preaches, never tells you what to think. She's an extremely kind person, very thoughtful. But she's funny, really, really funny.

DAVID: But to understand Judith Kerr's own life story, you need to read *When Hitler Stole Pink Rabbit*. It was based on her own family. Her father was a Jewish theatre critic and they fled Nazi Germany in the 1930s. Talking to the author Michael Rosen, that refugee experience was the source of many stories.

MICHAEL: She was a wonderful, lively, witty, clever woman. She always had a new story and there was always another surprising story, whether it was from her childhood when the Nazis first came, or it was something about how she came to write a book. She was witty and clever and funny and loving and kind. She was a wonderful, wonderful person. I'm very, very sad today.

DAVID: She could make children laugh, but she would also tell the truth. The final Mog book is the story of how the lovable family cat dies. For someone who only began writing when she was 45, she leaves behind dozens of books that have become part of childhood for millions. Her life, her success, were, she said, a blessing. She always felt she was one of the lucky ones.

JUDITH: Escaping Hitler in the first place, I'm always conscious of the fact that millions of people would give anything to be in my shoes and just to have a tiny bit of what I've had. I've been ridiculously lucky.

HUW: Today's tributes to the wonderful author and illustrator Judith Kerr, who's died at the age of 95. (*BBC-20190523*)

Words and Expressions

accident-prone *adj.* 容易出事儿
be in one's shoes 处于某人的境地;设身处地
eventful *adj.* 多变故的;精彩的
forgetful *adj.* 健忘的
illustrator *n.* 插图画家
preach *vi.* 说教;宣扬
stillness *n.* 宁静
trademark *n.* 典型特征
witty *adj.* 风趣的

Questions

1. How did Kerr come up with the figure of a tiger?
2. What impression did Kerr leave to the people she knew?
3. How did Kerr think of her own success?

Gap-filling

DAVID: And then came forgetful, ________________ Mog. It was, for her friend and fellow children's author Lauren Child, ________________ Judith Kerr.

LAUREN: Her work is beautiful because there's a lovely ________________ to it. It never ________________, never tells you what to think. She's an extremely kind person, very ________________. But she's funny, really, really funny.

DAVID: But to understand Judith Kerr's own life story, you need to read *When Hitler Stole Pink Rabbit*. It was based on her own family. Her father was a Jewish ________________ and they fled Nazi Germany in the 1930s. Talking to the author Michael Rosen, that ________________ experience was the source of many stories.

Dictation

Judith Kerr, the children's author ... a bit of excitement.

Translation

1. Her work is beautiful because there's a lovely stillness to it. It never preaches.
2. She leaves behind dozens of books that have become part of childhood for millions.
3. Millions of people would give anything to be in my shoes.

Post-class task

Discussion: Tell your class the most inspiring book you read in your childhood.

94. Lady Hale

HUW: Now the President of the UK Supreme Court, Lady Hale, who retires next month, has warned that the lack of access to legal services for those people who most need them is a serious problem. She expressed particular concern for people going through the early stages of divorce. Lady Hale has been talking to our legal correspondent, Clive Coleman, during which she reflected on the momentous day in September when the court ruled that the Prime Minister had acted unlawfully when he advised the Queen to suspend Parliament.

CLIVE: It was a case of massive legal, constitutional and political significance.

HALE: The Prime Minister's advice to Her Majesty was unlawful, void and of no effect.

CLIVE: The Supreme Court ruling that the Prime Minister's advice to the Queen to suspend Parliament in weeks leading up to the Brexit deadline, was unlawful. Now, the president of the court is retiring, a time to look back on that momentous day.

HALE: There was a gasp in the courtroom, which was packed, when I said that it was the unanimous decision of us all, that's all 11 justices.

CLIVE: A time also for Lady Hale to reflect on the removal of legal aid in 2013 from a raft of areas, including debt, housing and most family cases.

HALE: Most people need legal services at the beginning of a difficulty and if they have them then, it will be sorted out and they won't have to go anywhere near a court, or they won't have their house repossessed or whatever, because somebody has managed to find a solution to the problem at an earlier stage. And it's that lack of initial advice and help which is a serious difficulty.

CLIVE: And when you are separating, as a couple, you are being, you know, taken apart emotionally and financially, many people would think that actually it's at that point the stage should be there.

HALE: It's unreasonable to expect a husband and wife or a mother and father to, who are in crisis in their personal relationship, to make their own arrangements without help.

CLIVE: The Government says it is improving early legal support to reduce the number of people going to court unnecessarily.

HALE: The prorogation was also void ...

CLIVE: But on the eve of her departure from the highest court in the land, the question everyone wants answered, was there any significance behind the spider brooch she wore on that day, even an incy-wincy bit?

HALE: I regret to have to tell you there was nothing behind it. I do almost always wear a brooch if I'm wearing a dress, or even if I'm wearing a suit. It's a way of livening up what is otherwise quite dull, and the particular dress that I was wearing has a spider on it. And I chose the dress; I didn't choose the spider.

CLIVE: As she leaves office, the first female president of the Supreme Court knows she has her critics—

HALE: The court will now adjourn.

CLIVE: —but also an army of admirers. Clive Coleman, BBC News. (*BBC-20191228*)

Words and Expressions

a raft of 许多
adjourn *vi.* 休庭
brooch *n.* 胸针
incy-wincy *adj.* 极小的;微小的
justice *n.* (尤指最高法院的)法官
lead up to (时间)临近;紧挨在……之前
liven up (给……)增色;(为……)添彩
prorogation *n.* 休会
repossess *vt.* (因买者未如期付款而)收回(房地产、商品等)
ruling *n.* 裁决
unanimous *adj.* 一致的
void *adj.* 无效的

Questions

1. How special is Lady Hale?
2. Did she intentionally wear the spider brooch on her dress when declaring the Prime Minister's action unlawful?

3. Why does she like wearing a brooch when appearing in court?
4. Why does she oppose the removal of legal aid for families?

Gap-filling

HALE: Most people need ________________ at the beginning of a difficulty and if they have them then, it will be ________________ and they won't have to go anywhere near a court, or they won't have their house ________________ or whatever, because somebody has ________________ find a solution to the problem at an earlier ________________. And it's that lack of ________________ advice and help which is a serious difficulty.

CLIVE: And when you are separating, as a couple, you are being, you know, ________________ emotionally and financially, many people would think that ________________ it's at that point ________________ should be there.

HALE: It's unreasonable to ________________ a husband and wife or a mother and father to, who are ________________ in their personal relationship, to make their own ________________ without help.

Dictation

Now the President ... to suspend Parliament.

Translation

1. The Prime Minister's advice to Her Majesty was unlawful, void and of no effect.
2. There was nothing behind it.
3. It's a way of livening up what is otherwise quite dull.
4. She has her critics, but also an army of admirers.

Post-class task

Retell the story of Lady Hale and explain what inspiration you can draw from her.

95. London's Future Skyline

ASAD: Well let's speak to Caroline Davis, though. There are some lovely views across London tonight, Caroline. But that's a view that's changed a lot in recent years.

CAROLINE: It is a rather spectacular view, isn't it, Asad? But if you would look over here ten years ago or five years even, it would have looked rather different. Now when most people think about skyscrapers, they do think about the city of London, or Canary Wharf. But 175 of these planned blocks are in outer London and 90% of them are for residential. So are these going to help with the housing crisis?

This isn't the first time we've looked up to find space for new homes.

(*These were the 12-storey blocks of flats at G street Finsbury, the first of Britain's skyscrapers.*)

Across London, there are more tower blocks to come. Ealing currently has two skyscrapers. They have 20 more in the pipeline.

MASON: Absolutely imperative that we put tall buildings in the right locations and that we don't allow them to spring up in parts of London where they're not appropriate. But, ultimately, if we cannot build out, we have to build up.

CAROLINE: Not all towers last. This was a council block in Ealing, knocked down to build new lower-rise homes. The same happened across London, partly because tower blocks are expensive to maintain, and the Grenfell Tower fire has made many even more aware of safety.

PETER: There will be problems in 30 years' time, when the elevators and all the wiring need replacing, as they do with tall buildings, and in 60 years' time the cladding will need to be replaced. Now no residential service charge will cover these costs. So we are building buildings and letting them on 125-year leases and they will be derelict before those 125 year leases are out.

CAROLINE: And, if they are expensive, there is a worry about who will live in them.

PETER: Tower blocks are great ways of selling views to very rich people who won't use the flats very much.

CAROLINE: But there is a possible solution. This is the East Village in Stratford. There are two skyscrapers opening here over this weekend and four more in the pipeline, but here these homes are not for sale.

All the flats in this block are for rent only. The hope is that more people will live in them, rather than buying and leaving them.

NEIL: You've got for-sale developments, where once it's sold the developer will leave and they're just reliant on the residents to organise things. Whereas, for us, because we own it, we are here for the long term.

CAROLINE: Some homes in skyscrapers will be affordable, but until they're built, it's difficult to know exactly how many and whether all will last for Londoners in decades to come.

Now the arguments on both sides about these tower blocks are pretty passionate. It might be difficult to shake off the idea that these are, as some have described them, safety deposit boxes in the sky for the internationally wealthy. However, there has been changes in taxation recently, which means it's more difficult for international investors to buy them. There's also arguments that particularly these blocks in further outer areas might be more affordable to Londoners. On the other side of the argument, people say that these blocks are not producing the sort of homes that suit everybody, and alternatively that they might create windy and cavernous cities. Our cities are evolving, our demand for housing is growing, and so are the height of our skyscrapers.

ASAD: Yeah, certainly. OK, Caroline Davis. Thanks very much for now. (*BBC-20190530*)

Notes

Canary Wharf：金丝雀码头，位于伦敦东部码头区（Docklands），原为水上运输中心，现为伦敦新金融城，全球公认的世界级金融中心，有着“伦敦曼哈顿”之称。金丝雀码头以摩天大楼林立著称，英国最高的三座建筑均坐落于此。

Words and Expressions

cavernous *adj.* 大而空的
cladding *n.* 覆面
derelict *adj.* 被弃置的
evolve *vi.* 逐步发展
imperative *adj.* 至关重要的
in the pipeline 在规划中
knock down 推倒（或拆掉、拆毁）建筑物
lease *n.* 租约
let *vt.* 出租
lower-rise *adj.* 低层的
passionate *adj.* 热烈的
residential *adj.* 住宅的
shake off 去除；摆脱
skyscraper *n.* 摩天大楼
spring up 突然出现
tower block 高层建筑

Questions

1. Why are there more and more skyscrapers in London?
2. Why are some tower blocks demolished?
3. What problems might tall buildings have?
4. Who are the potential buyers of the flats in tall buildings?
5. Why are the homes of some skyscrapers not for sale?
6. Is the present taxation policy attractive to international buyers?

Gap-filling

PETER: Tower blocks are great ways of selling ________________ to very rich people who won't use the ________________ very much.

CAROLINE: But there is a possible solution. This is the East Village in Stratford. There are two skyscrapers opening here over this weekend and four more in the ________ ________, but here these homes are not ________________.

All the flats in this block are ________________. The hope is that more people will live in them, rather than buying and ________________ them.

NEIL: You've got for-sale developments, ________________ once it's sold the ____ ______________ will leave and they're just ________________ on the residents to organise things. ________________, for us, because we own it, we are here for the long term.

Dictation

Now the arguments on both sides … and cavernous cities.

Translation

1. If we cannot build out, we have to build up.
2. In 30 years' time the elevators and all the wiring need replacing.
3. These blocks might create windy and cavernous cities.

Post-class task

Discussion: The pros and cons of living in high-rise buildings.

96. Mosquito Research

JANE: Now the buzz of a mosquito can be a familiar sound at this time of year, and researchers in London are studying it, to learn how the bugs communicate with each other. The team hopes that will allow them to develop systems to lure mosquitoes away from populated areas, or design devices to catch and kill them, helping to reduce the spread of malaria and yellow fever. Our science correspondent, Pallab Ghosh, has the details.

PALLAB: For us, the whining sound is annoying, but for the mosquito, it's a love song. The buzz helps the insects find mates and reproduce. So, what if we could learn to talk mosquito and sabotage their love lives? Malaria and yellow fever is spread through mosquito bites. The vast majority of cases are in Africa. In 2017, 200 million people had malaria. Nearly half a million of them died. One way to defeat mosquito-borne diseases is to turn their buzz against them.

JOERG: For me, it is a sound of utter sophistication. We could simulate these sounds, use them for new technological devices to perform attraction of mosquitoes, to lure them away from sites where they can transmit disease, for example from populations, from households, or also to catch them, kill them, so catch and kill devices could be designed, which are much more effective than the ones we are using right now.

PALLAB: The mosquitoes' buzz is created by the insects' wings. This is the sound of the female on the left. Look closely and you can see that her wing beat is slower than the male's and that is why the male's tone is slightly higher. In a breeding swarm, there are around 500 mosquitoes all buzzing away. Just five of them are female and somehow the males can hear and find them.

Mosquitoes can be lured away from populated areas. This swarm of males can be attracted by the buzz of a female.

Unfortunately, these audio techniques don't work on females, which are the ones that carry and spread malaria and yellow fever. So, in order to improve these audio traps, researchers here want to learn more about how mosquitoes communicate.

If we magnify this mosquito's hearing antenna, we can see how it opens up at sunset when it's time to swarm. Marta Anders is studying how it detects the sound of potential mates so that she can find ways of disrupting the process.

MARTA: Mosquitoes use their hearing to detect their mating partners. We are trying to find new ways to stop mosquitoes from hearing, using different drugs that then can be applied in the field to stop mosquito populations from reproducing and try to collapse them.

PALLAB: By disrupting their communications, the researchers believe that eventually they can rid millions from the menace of mosquitoes forever. Pallab Ghosh, BBC News. (*BBC-20190826*)

Words and Expressions

antenna *n.* 触角
-borne (构成形容词)由……携带的
breeding *n.* 繁殖
buzz *n.* 嗡嗡声;嗞嗞声
vi. 发出嗡嗡声
disrupt *vt.* 使中断
magnify *vt.* 放大
menace *n.* 威胁
reproduce *vt.* 繁殖
rid *vt.* 使摆脱(讨厌的人或事物)
sabotage *n.* 蓄意毁坏
simulate *vt.* 模拟
sophistication *n.* 复杂
swarm *n.* 一大群
vi. 成群地飞
whine *vi.* 哭哭啼啼;哀鸣
yellow fever 黄热病

Questions

1. What is the meaning of the buzzing sound to the mosquito?
2. What is the consequence of mosquito bites?
3. What is the difference in the wing beat between male and female mosquitoes?
4. Why must female mosquitoes be caught and killed?
5. What is the researchers' plan to completely get rid of mosquitoes?

Gap-filling

PALLAB: For us, the whining sound is ____________________, but for the mosquito, it's a love song. The buzz helps the insects find mates and ____________________. So, what if we could learn to talk mosquito and ____________________ their love lives? Malaria and yellow fever is spread through mosquito ______________________. The vast majority of cases are in Africa. In 2017, 200 million people had malaria. ____________________ half a million of them died. One way to defeat mosquito-____________ diseases is to turn their buzz against them.

JOERG: For me, it is a sound of ____________________ sophistication. We could ________

__________ these sounds, use them for new technological devices to ____________ ______ attraction of mosquitoes, to __________________ them away from ______ ____________ where they can ___________________ disease, for example from populations, from __________________, or also to catch them, kill them, so catch and kill devices could be ____________________, which are much more effective _________________ we are using right now.

Dictation

The mosquitoes' buzz ... of a female.

Translation

1. One way to defeat mosquito-borne diseases is to turn their buzz against them.
2. In a breeding swarm, there are around 500 mosquitoes all buzzing away.
3. The researchers believe that eventually they can rid millions from the menace of mosquitoes forever.

Post-class task

Discussion: How do you protect yourself from mosquitoes?

97. Netflix Expansion

SOPHIE: It's been heralded as a major boost for Britain's TV and film industry. The American streaming giant Netflix has signed a deal to take over much of the world famous Shepperton Studios, in Surrey, to turn it into one of its major production hubs. Shepperton opened its doors as a film studio in 1932. Since then, it's been the home of hundreds of films, from *Clockwork Orange* and *Alien* to *Star Wars* and *Bridget Jones*. Here is our media editor Amol Rajan.

NARRATOR: Everyone knows the best place for a clandestine meeting in London is and always has been St James's Park.

AMOL: *Good Omens*, based on the book by Neil Gaiman, is one of Amazon Prime's biggest ever productions, and it was made in Britain.

NARRATOR: Crowley and Aziraphale have been meeting here for quite some time ...

AMOL: Co-produced by BBC Studios, the series is an example of how a few American web giants are transforming global television.

CROWLEY: As if *Armageddon* were a cinematographic show you wish to sell in as many countries as possible.

AMOL: How has Amazon's entry into the UK market changed things for a director like you?

DOUGLAS: There's, I mean, in simple terms, more money to make things on a bigger scale. When we ... *Good Omens*' being made as a six and a half hour comedy, with a standard UK budget, we couldn't get it moving. We've now got the resources to actually make a world that is credible to the audience and that engages with the story completely, and now it's not just a pared-down adaptation.

AMOL: Of course, it's not just Amazon. There is a creative boom going on in Britain, driven by SVOD, or Subscription Video on Demand.

PHILIP: For Christ sake! Take the photo!

AMOL: Over the past ten years, there's been an exponential growth in the value of the film and TV industry in the UK and its growth has significantly outpaced that of the UK economy. TV today is marrying the best of the old with the best of the new. Shepperton Studios, owned by Pinewood, is where countless legendary movies were shot and Netflix is moving in. They believe that by investing in local studio space and hiring local staff, they can neutralise concerns about American dominance of the industry. The new Netflix production hub will include 14 sound stages and a total of 435,000 square feet.

No one in the history of film or television has caused so much disruption so quickly as Netflix, and the truth is, they're just getting started. The company is pivoting from an American distributor to a global production powerhouse, deeply embedded in local economies. Rivals might grumble about the dominance of an over-mighty Californian giant, but viewers aren't complaining. And anyway, that's showbiz!

TED: That's why we've invested so heavily here. That's why our original production in the UK is so big. This is about a $ 2.7 billion business, right, for the television market in the UK, that we hope to be a bigger and bigger part of. So, our productions have generated about 25,000 jobs already.

AMOL: There's a revolution going on in Britain's creative industries and this one will be televised. Amol Rajan, BBC News, Shepperton. (*BBC-20190703*)

Notes

St James's Park：圣詹姆斯公园，位于伦敦市中心，与林荫大道（The Mall）平行相隔，毗邻威斯敏斯特教堂、白金汉宫、圣詹姆斯宫，曾是国王亨利八世的猎鹿苑。

SVOD：订阅型视频点播。

Words and Expressions

adaptation *n.* 改编本
Armageddon *n.* 世界末日的善恶大决战
cinematographic *adj.* 电影摄影术的
clandestine *adj.* 秘密的
exponential *adj.* 飞速的；极快的
grumble *vi.* 发牢骚
herald *vt.* 称赞
hub *n.* 中心
marry ... with ... 把……同……结合起来
neutralise *vt.* 消除
pared-down *adj.* 简化的
pivot *vi.* 转变
powerhouse *n.* 豪门；巨头
showbiz *n.* 娱乐业
subscription *n.* 订阅；订购

Questions

1. Why do UK directors welcome American media companies?
2. Why does Netflix want to invest in the UK?
3. Do UK viewers complain about the dominance of American media giants?
4. What real benefits has American investment brought to UK citizens?

Gap-filling

AMOL: Over the past ten years, there's been a(n) ________________ growth in the value of the film and TV industry in the UK and its growth has significantly ________________ that of the UK economy. TV today is ________________ the best of the old with the best of the new. Shepperton Studios, owned by Pinewood, is where countless ________________ movies were shot and Netflix is moving in. They believe that by ________________ in local studio space and hiring local staff, they can ________________ concerns about American ________________ of the industry. The new Netflix production ________________ will include 14 sound stages and a total of 435,000 ________________.

No one in the history of film or television has caused so much ________________ so quickly as Netflix, and ________________ is, they're just getting started. The company is ________________ from an American ________________ to a global production powerhouse, deeply ________________ in local economies. ________________ might grumble about the ________________ of an over-mighty Californian giant, but viewers ________________. And anyway, that's showbiz!

Dictation

It's been heralded ... and *Bridget Jones*.

Translation

1. We've now got the resources to actually make a world that is credible to the audience and that engages with the story completely.
2. TV today is marrying the best of the old with the best of the new.
3. They believe that by investing in local studio space and hiring local staff, they can neutralise concerns about American dominance of the industry.
4. The company is pivoting from an American distributor to a global production powerhouse.

Post-class task

Discussion: Do you think SVOD is bound to replace free TV?

98. Supermassive Black Hole

REETA: Now astronomers are used to dealing in massive numbers when it comes to uncovering the mysteries of space. Today they've revealed the first ever picture of a black hole, which measures a whopping 40 billion kilometres across, and is 500 million trillion kilometres away! It was located by a network of eight telescopes located across the globe, and the hope is that this discovery will help space research, and particularly how galaxies came into being. With more, here's our science correspondent Pallab Ghosh.

HEINO: That. This is the nucleus of the galaxy M87 and this is the first-ever image of a black hole.

PALLAB: Unveiled to the world, this black hole is more than 3 million times the size of the earth. And devouring material that falls into it, it's been described as a monster at the heart of a galaxy. On top of the mountain in Southern Spain, seemingly touching the clouds, is one of the instruments astronomers used to take the picture. Pico Valeta is one of eight radio telescopes around the world that was pointed towards a distant galaxy, 300 million trillion miles away. Together, they scanned its centre for ten days and were able to take a picture of the gigantic black hole at its heart.

Astronomers have used a global network of dishes from all across the world and linked them together. No single telescope is powerful enough to see the black hole, but by adding together the information from each of them, the image gradually becomes sharper.

HEINO: We can actually see black holes! That's crazy! I always thought this is just way beyond what we can be doing. This is a super heavyweight champion among the black holes in the universe.

PALLAB: They're important because they're at the heart of every galaxy and probably the reason that stars and planets form around them. Gravity is so strong close to a black hole that it even alters how time flows, making it seem to pass slowly. It's not known what's on the other side of a black hole. Some speculate that they may be a doorway to parallel universes. This new image proves that black holes actually exist and it's hoped it will help astronomers learn more about space, time and our own existence.

LUCIE: I think that what's so exciting is that we're taking our knowledge of black holes, which is really focused on the theory, simulation, simulating how the environment of a black hole looks. Now having the data, seeing this, it turns the black hole into something tangible, into something that you can see, and there's so much we're going to learn from this.

PALLAB: Inside the telescope, the researchers are recalibrating their instruments, to take a picture of another supermassive black hole. This time, at the heart of our own galaxy, the Milky Way. Pallab Ghosh, BBC News, Pico Valeta in Spain. (*BBC-20190410*)

Words and Expressions

across *adv.* ……宽
alter *vt.* (使)改变
devour *vt.* 吞噬
galaxy *n.* 星系
gigantic *adj.* 巨大的
gravity *n.* 引力
parallel *adj.* 平行的
recalibrate *vt.* 重新校准
speculate *vt.* 推测;推断
supermassive *adj.* 特大质量的
tangible *adj.* 有形的;可感知的
the Milky Way 银河系

Questions

1. How large is the black hole compared with the earth?
2. How many telescopes have been involved in taking this picture? And for how long?
3. Why is it important to study black holes?
4. Why are scientist excited about the very first image of a black hole?

Gap-filling

HEINO: We can ________________ black holes! That's crazy! I always thought this is just ________________ what we can be doing. This is a super heavyweight ________________ among the black holes in the universe.

PALLAB: They're important because they're at the heart of every ________________ and probably the reason that stars and planets ________________ them. Gravity is so strong close to a black hole that it even ________________ how time flows, making it seem to pass slowly. It's not known what's on the other side of a black hole. Some ________________ that they may be a doorway to ________________ universes. This new image proves that black holes actually ________________ and it's hoped it will help astronomers learn more about space, time and our own ________________.

Dictation

I think that what's so ... the Milky Way.

Translation

1. I always thought this is just way beyond what we can be doing.
2. Gravity is so strong close to a black hole that it even alters how time flows.
3. Some speculate that they may be a doorway to parallel universes.

Post-class task

Write a short report about the image of the supermassive black hole in about 150 words.

99. Tackling Climate Change

HUW: Efforts to tackle climate change are way off track, according to the United Nations, which is hosting a major climate conference in Poland from next week. Last year greenhouse gas emissions reached a record high. And it's not just a matter of industrial pollution: food is also a factor. The global livestock population, for example, has reached 28 billion animals. And those animals produce methane, that's a potent greenhouse gas that's expected to increase by some 60% in the next two years. Our science editor David Shukman reports on how our food choices have an impact on the planet.

DAVID: Every breath from a cow, and especially every burp, releases methane, 600 litres every day, most from the front end, not the back. And because methane warms the planet, the more we eat beef and dairy products, the more the temperatures rise. At this farm, researchers encourage the cows to feed inside this hood so they can measure the methane.

CHRIS: So, a cow came in. She was eating ...

DAVID: Professor Chris Reynolds explains what they've found.

CHRIS: She had five eructations, or five belches.

DAVID: So each spike is a burp, is it, effectively?

CHRIS: It's a burp or a belch. There's been a huge increase in meat and milk consumption. That demand is going to continue, so I think we need strategies for sustainably producing that meat and milk.

DAVID: One option is adding special supplements to the feed. Some of these make the cows a lot less gassy. So technically it is possible to reduce the extraordinary amount of methane that cows produce, but on its own that won't be enough to head off the worst of global warming, so it comes down to the key and highly controversial question of what we all choose to eat.

Here at Manchester University, researchers study the climate cost of food. The fertilisers, tractors and processing all generate gases that cause more warming. So, add all that up, and these chocolates are responsible for up to 1.4 kilos of carbon dioxide and other gases. That's the equivalent of driving for 12 miles in a car. Producing this BLT sandwich involves a kilo of the gases—that's like driving for eight miles. And this serving of beef comes out top, creating more than 3.5 kilos of warming gases. That's like a journey of 30 miles.

ADISA: We have got to reduce our carbon emissions across different sectors, and the food sector is absolutely paramount to that because we all eat, and it has a significant contribution to our ... not just the UK emissions but globally, so we have to do something about it. And it won't be easy, and it won't be popular.

DAVID: So what does this mean for our everyday shopping? Well, Mike Berners-Lee helps supermarkets to work out their climate costs. The differences are striking.

MIKE: So making the switch from beef and lamb down to plant-based proteins is about one-50th of the carbon footprint.

DAVID: His advice is to eat more of this, and to check if the produce is British and in season, also to avoid fruit and veg that's been flown here.

MIKE: It's the tenderstem broccoli that's come from Kenya and that will almost certainly have gone on an aeroplane. There are some simple rules of thumb, so, is it either in season, or is it robust enough to have been able to have travelled from elsewhere in the world on a boat?

DAVID: Mike and other experts say they don't want to preach about low-carbon food, but they say, if we want to tackle climate change, we need to eat less of this. David Shukman, BBC News. (*BBC-20181127*)

Words and Expressions

belch *vi.* & *n.* 打嗝
BLT (= bacon, lettuce and tomato) 熏肉、生菜加番茄(三明治)
burp *n.* 打嗝
carbon footprint 碳足迹;碳排放量
dairy *n.* 乳制品
eructation *n.* 打嗝
fertiliser *n.* 肥料
front end 前端
gassy *adj.* (肠胃)胀气的
head off 防止
hood *n.* 罩
in season (水果和蔬菜)当令的
paramount *adj.* 最重要的
produce *n.* 农产品
protein *n.* 蛋白质
robust *adj.* 强健的;耐久的
rule of thumb 经验法则
spike *n.* 激增
tenderstem broccoli 嫩茎西兰花

Questions

1. Why do our food choices have an impact on the planet?
2. How much methane does a cow release every day?

3. What can farmers do to reduce the amount of methane released by cows?
4. What suggestions have been offered to food consumption in order to tackle climate change?

Gap-filling

ADISA: We have got to reduce our carbon emissions ________________ different sectors, and the food sector is absolutely ________________ to that because we all eat, and it has a significant ________________ to our ... not just the UK emissions but globally, so we have to do something about it. And it won't be easy, and it won't be ________________.

DAVID: So what does this mean for our everyday ____________? Well, Mike Berners-Lee helps supermarkets work out their climate ________________. The differences are ________________.

MIKE: So making the ________________ from beef ________________ down to plant-based ________________ is about one-50th of the ________________.

DAVID: His advice is to eat more of this, and to check if the ________________ is British and ________________, also to avoid fruit and veg that's been ________________ here.

Dictation

Efforts to tackle climate change ... have an impact on the planet.

Translation

1. Efforts to tackle climate change are way off track.
2. The more we eat beef and dairy products, the more the temperatures rise.
3. His advice is to avoid fruit and veg that's been flown here.

Post-class task

Discussion: Are you going to make some changes in dietary habit after watching this report?

100. V&A Dundee

* * * * * * * * * * * * * * * * *

JANE: The V&A, the world's leading museum for art and design, is about to branch out beyond its London base. The V&A Dundee opens on Saturday, and it's the central part of a huge project to transform the city. Our Scotland correspondent, Lorna Gordon, is there. Hi, Lorna.

LORNA: Yes. Hello, there. You know, this is a first look at this new museum and it is spectacular. This building has pushed the boundaries of engineering and design. The architect behind it, Kengo Kuma, has described it as a living room for the city, a place for people to visit, to hang out in, to learn from, and to inspire.

It's the show-stopping centrepiece of £1 billion riverside restoration. The V&A Dundee, described as a sculpture as much as a building, with curves, sharp edges, and stone panels, a cliff face jutting out over the Tay.

KUMA: The total form of the building is very different from normal concrete box. There is organic movement to follow the wind flow. That is the basis of this design.

LORNA: With the Scottish Design Galleries, the meticulously restored Charles Rennie Macintosh Oak Room, and Scottish engineering, a feature of ocean liners exhibition, Scotland's design heritage features large.

SOPHIE: Ocean Liners is a major international show. And as part of that story, Scottish engineering, and the work that was done on the Clyde bank, is the central part of the exhibition. It's that aspect of how we approach design which is really important. We need to be appropriate to cite, and to allow Scottish design to really shine. But we want it to shine within an international context.

LORNA: The museum tells a global story and there is plenty of interest from around the world in its opening. Dundee is a city, though, with creativity at its core. And this addition to the city's cultural landscape has ambitions which lie closer to home.

HUNT: My hope is that we're going to create a new generation of designers, artists, coders, engineers and architects coming out of Dundee. I hope that thousands, and tens of thousands of people are going to come to Dundee to see this great building and this great collection. And we are going to help Dundee find some of that confidence which might have been lost in recent decades.

LORNA: This museum brings jobs, yes, but it's also a bold statement about Dundee's design heritage and Scotland's cultural clout. A destination not just for tourists, but for the people living here, too.

You know, this really is a big deal for this small city on the banks of the Tay. Half a million people are expected to visit the V&A Dundee in its first year, the first of those expected through the doors on Saturday. Jane.

JANE: Fantastic, Lorna, thank you very much. Stunning. Lorna Gordon there at V&A Dundee. (*BBC-20180912*)

Notes

Charles Rennie Macintosh：查尔斯·伦尼·麦金托什（1868—1928），苏格兰人，19 世纪末 20 世纪初具有广泛影响力的先锋设计师。

Clyde：克莱德河，位于苏格兰中西部，全长 170 千米，旧时以其沿岸造船业闻名。

Dundee：邓迪，苏格兰第四大城市，重要港口。

Tay：泰河，苏格兰最长河流，向东流经泰湖，在泰河湾注入北海。

V&A：（= Victoria and Albert Museum）维多利亚与艾尔伯特博物馆，位于伦敦，是世界上最大的装饰艺术和设计博物馆；始建于 1852 年，为纪念艾尔伯特亲王和维多利亚女王而命名。

Words and Expressions

centrepiece *n.* 最重要的项目
clout *n.* 影响力
curve *n.* 曲线
feature *vi.* 是……的重要特点（或重头戏）
jut *vi.* 突出；伸出
meticulously *adv.* 细心地；周密地
organic *adj.* 有机的
panel *n.* （门、墙等上面的）嵌板；镶板
restoration *n.* 整修；修复
shine *vi.* 表现突出；大显身手
show-stopping *adj.* 极精彩的

Questions

1. What does the designer of this museum hope it becomes?
2. What is the cost of this project?
3. What has been highlighted about Scotland in this museum?
4. How many visitors are expected to come the first year?

Gap-filling

LORNA: The museum tells a global story and there is plenty of interest from around the world in its opening. Dundee is a city, ________________, with creativity at its ______

____________. And this addition to the city's cultural ________________ has ambitions which lie closer ________________.

HUNT: My hope is that we're going to ________________ a new generation of designers, artists, ________________, engineers and ________________ coming out of Dundee. I hope that thousands, and tens of thousands of people are going to come to Dundee to see this great building and this great ________________. And we are going to help Dundee find some of that ________________ which might have been lost in recent decades.

LORNA: This museum brings jobs, yes, but it's also a(n) ________________ statement about Dundee's design ________________ and Scotland's cultural ________________. A destination not just for tourists, but for the people living here, too.

Dictation

Ocean liners is a … an international context.

Translation

1. This building has pushed the boundaries of engineering and design.
2. The V&A Dundee is described as a sculpture as much as a building.
3. Scotland's design heritage features large.
4. This addition to the city's cultural landscape has ambitions which lie closer to home.
5. The museum is also a bold statement about Dundee's design heritage and Scotland's cultural clout.

Post-class task

Do some research about V&A and write a report in about 200 words.

Glossary

a barrage of 一连串的/68
a burning issue 当务之急;亟待解决的问题/47
a catalogue of 一系列;一连串(坏事情)/86
a leap into the unknown 冒险举动/2
a raft of 许多/94
a thing of the past 成为历史/38
abuse 滥用/20
abuse 虐待/71
accident-prone 容易出事儿/93
accredited 官方认可的/89
acoustic 声音的/16
across ……宽/98
acupuncture 针灸/92
adaptation 改编本/97
address (着手)解决;处理/32
adhere to 遵守/29
adjourn 休庭/94
administer 管理/28
administer 施用(to)/79
adoring 崇拜的/78
advent (重要事件、人物、发明等的)出现;到来/77
adventurer 冒险家/8
advert 电视广告/25
aerial 空中的/1
afloat 漂浮在水上的/66
against the clock 争分夺秒/56
aggressive 富于攻击性的/90
aggressive 激进的/4
agonise (about) 为……伤脑筋/54
Aladdin's cave 阿拉丁的藏宝洞;宝库/86
algorithm 算法/77
alien 陌生的/74
alive and kicking 活蹦乱跳/28
all but 几乎/73
all the more 更加;格外/48
all too 很;极;非常/80
allegiance 忠诚;效忠/26
alter(使)改变/98
alternative 替代物/47
amass 积累;积聚/31
amateur 业余的/69
ambition 雄心/63
ambitious 雄心勃勃的;(计划、想法等)宏大的,艰巨的/63
amendment 修订/12
amid 在……之中/17
amnesty 赦免/71
ample 足够的/61
an army of 大群;大批/56
anatomy 结构/31
anguish 极度痛苦/45
animation 动画/81
anonymous 匿名的/36
antagonism 敌意/54
antenna 触角/96
antibiotic *n.* 抗生素
adj. 抗菌的/37
anticipate 预期/42
anti-fungal 抗真菌的/37
antiretroviral 抗逆转录病毒的/4
antiviral 抗病毒的/36
appalling 令人震惊的;使人惊骇的/19
appeal 呼吁;吁请/57
appealing 有吸引力的(to)/78

aquarium 水族馆/70
arable 可耕的/88
archaeologist 考古学家/43
archive 档案馆;档案室/57
Armageddon 世界末日的善恶大决战/97
artefact 历史文物/43
artery 动脉/50
article(协议、契约的)条款;项/54
artificial 人工的/27
as … as … gets 最……;极……/53
as much as 虽然;尽管/64
assemble 装配/30
asset 资产/22
asthma 哮喘/23
astonished 感到震惊的/49
at the sharp end 关键时刻/15
at the wheel 在驾驶汽车/41
audit 审计/87
austerity(经济的)紧缩/76
aviator 飞行员/1
awash 充斥的;泛滥的(with)/86
back 支持/44
backbone 支柱;基础/90
backdrop 背景/76
back-to-back 连栋的/60
bacteria 细菌/37
bacterial 细菌的/65
balcony 栏杆外平台/2
ballroom 舞厅/76
banish 赶/91
bar 乐谱的小节/32
bars 高低杠/91
bathtub 浴缸/46
bathyscaphe 深海潜水器/74
bay 湾;海湾/70
be around 存在/28
be big on sth. 非常喜欢/38
be credited with 归功于/78
be exposed to 接触/25
be in one's shoes 处于某人的境地;设身处地/93
be inundated with 泛滥/86
be king 最为重要;极具影响/3
beacon 灯塔/29
beam 波束/79
bearing 方向/57
beat 节拍/32
beefburger 牛肉汉堡包/61
behind the wheel 在驾驶汽车/38
beige 米黄色的/13
belch 打嗝/99
belch 喷出;吐出/83
beluga whale 白鲸/70
bereaved 丧失亲友的/28
beyond one's means 入不敷出/34
billiards 台球/76
biodiversity 生态多样性/88
bio-engineer 生物工程制造/27
bird of prey 猛禽(捕食其他动物的鸟,如鹰、隼和猫头鹰)/84
birth defect 先天缺陷/42
black out 昏厥/91
blackout 断电;停电/52
bladder 膀胱/42
blessing 赞同/7
blockade 屏障/ 82
BLT = bacon, lettuce and tomato 熏肉、生菜加番茄(三明治)/99
blur (使)难以区分/91
boastful 自夸的/9
bone marrow 骨髓/4
bonfire 篝火;营火/35
bonnet 引擎盖/51
booming 飞速发展的/28
boost 改善;提高/49
-borne 由……携带的/96
borough 行政区/23
boundary 边界/14
bow 船头/46
bowel 肠/33
brachiopod 腕足动物/31

brazenly 厚颜无耻地/86
breach 违背;违犯(法规等)/23
breakaway 脱离/15
breathhold 屏气潜水/70
breathtaking 动人心魄的/38
breed (动植物的)品种/10
breed (人的)类型;种类/1
breeding 繁殖/96
breeze 轻而易举的事/49
brick phone 砖块手机(早期粗重手机的谐称)/71
Brit 英国人/6
brooch 胸针/94
bulge 凸起/42
bulimia 贪食症/91
bulk-buy 批量购买/20
bulldog 斗牛犬/51
bulldoze 推平/60
bully 霸凌/71
bump up 提升/33
bundle 捆/47
bunker 地堡;掩体/76
burn bright 火烧得正旺(本文喻指东北虎极为耀眼)/48
burp 打嗝/99
burrow 钻/65
bus lane 公共汽车专用道/40
busker 街头艺人/3
buzz *n.* 嗡嗡声;嗞嗞声
vi. 发出嗡嗡声/96
bylaw (地方)法规/2
by-product 副产品/10
C of E = Church of England 英国国教/3
caesarean section 剖宫产/50
calf 崽;幼兽/70
call for 号召;呼吁/57
campaigner 运动倡导者;活动家/23
canine 犬/21
cap 使达到高潮;使圆满结束/29
captivate 使着迷/92
captive 被关起来的;被困住的/70
captivity 囚禁,关押;圈养/70
capture the imagination of ... 使……着迷;受……关注/29
carb = carbohydrate 碳水化合物/33
carbon footprint 碳足迹;碳排放量/99
cardboard 硬纸板/30
carriage (火车的)客车厢/58
carry the day 胜利;成功/12
carton 硬纸盒/85
cartoonist 漫画家/45
cash cow 摇钱树/14
cash in 把……兑为现金/63
cashless 非现金交易的/75
cash-strapped 资金短缺的/34
cast iron 铸铁/92
casualty 伤亡者/39
catalogue 登记/24
cathedral 大教堂/7
cautiously 谨慎地/85
cavernous 大而空的/95
cavern 大洞穴/76
Celsius 摄氏的/68
centenarian 百岁老人/29
centrepiece 最重要的项目/100
cereal 谷类食物/44
ceremonial 礼仪/76
cervix 子宫颈/79
chamber 会议厅/12
champion 捍卫/9
chance 偶然的/57
charisma 个人魅力;感召力/72
charismatic 有超凡魅力的/72
charm 取悦/78
chill 凉意/45
chilli 辣椒/49
chock-a-block 水泄不通的/182
chorus of 齐声/35
chorus 合唱团/32
chronic 长期的;慢性的/49
chubby 胖乎乎的/73

chunk 相当大的量/34
churn out 大量生产/47
cinematographic 电影摄影术的/97
circular 环线/14
circulate 传播/35
circulation 流通/75
circumference 周围/60
circumnavigate 环绕……航行/56
City Hall 市政厅/82
cladding 覆面/95
clandestine 秘密的/97
clarity 清晰/28
class 把……分类/25
Classics 古希腊与古罗马的文化研究/78
cling (to) 紧握(本文指"顽强地活下来")/48
clinical 临床的/27
clinician 临床医师/77
clock 达到(某速度)/51
close-up 特写/81
clout 影响力/100
clueless 一无所知的/83
clumsiness 笨拙/49
cluster 群;组/59
clutch 紧握/2
coal-fired 用煤作燃料的/83
cocker spaniel 长耳猎犬;可卡犬/21
cockpit 驾驶舱/1
cockroach 蟑螂/89
coffin buffer 擦亮棺材的人/72
coincide (with) 同时发生/15
cold comfort 于事无补的安慰/58
collaboration 合作/9
collagen 胶原蛋白/27
collapse 倒闭/13
collateral damage 附带性破坏;附带损害/64
combination lock 密码锁/76
combustion 燃烧/47
come as no surprise 不足为奇/37
come of age 成熟;发达/57
come 当……到来时/18
come thick and fast 铺天盖地而来/30
come to terms with 接受(令人不快的事物);适应(困难的处境)/53
come up with 想出;拿出/5
comfy = comfortable 舒适的/20
commemoration 纪念;纪念仪式/26
commend 赞扬;称赞/48
commentary 评注;是……的反应/48
commission 任命军职/1
commission 委员会/25
committed 坚定的/83
committed 忠于职守的/72
commonplace 普遍的/2
commute 通勤/80
commuter 通勤者/58
compelling 引人入胜的/48
compliance team 加盟店守法情况检查组/89
compliant 符合的/14
comply 遵从;服从/47
composition 创作/48
concrete 混凝土/67
condemn 谴责/91
confer 赋予/4
confidentiality 保密性/77
confounded 困惑的/92
congested 拥挤的/23
congestion 拥堵/14
congregation 教区全体教徒/7
conjure up 想象/1
consensus 共识/80
conservationist 环境保护主义者/19
considerably 非常/73
consistent 前后一致的;一贯的/85
consultation 商讨;磋商/55
contactless payment 非接触支付/3
contain 控制/52
contender 角逐者/66
contentious 有争议的/44
controversial 有争议的/50
conventional 传统的/37

cookery 烹饪/61

coronation 加冕典礼/76

coroner 无主珍宝调查官/24

corridor (连接两地，尤指有特色或通往特殊地区的)通道；连接地；走廊；地带/80

cosmetics 化妆品/86

cosmologist 宇宙学家/75

costly 昂贵的/82

cosy 小而温暖舒适的/47

cottage 小屋/47

counterfeit *adj.* 假冒的
vt. 制假/86

counterterrorism 反恐怖主义/84

courier 快递员/87

course 疗程/65

crack down on 严厉打击/20

crackdown 严厉打击/41

cramped 拥挤的/58

crater 火山口；坑/74

creaking 嘎吱作响的/74

crease 压褶/30

cricket pitch 板球场/68

cricketer 板球运动员/82

cripple 严重毁坏(或损害)/86

criteria 标准/75

critical 危险的；严重的/82

cross one's mind (念头)闪现，掠过/32

crowd 使……拥挤/59

crown 给予荣誉；授予称号/22

crucial 至关重要的；关键性的/4

crucially 关键是/87

cruiser 巡洋舰/66

crushing 毁坏性的/74

cube 立方块/44

cuddly(儿童玩具)柔软的；适于拥抱的/30

cupboard 储藏室/91

current 水流/8

curve 曲线/100

custodian(建筑物的)管理员；看门人/76

cut down on 削减/61

cut out 剪出/35

cycle lane 自行车专用道/5

cycle route 自行车道/5

cycle superhighway 自行车高速路/5

dairy 乳制品/99

dangle 悬垂/46

dank 阴冷潮湿的/14

daredevil 冒失鬼/2

day in day out 日复一日/12

day-to-day 日常的；日复一日的/58

deactivate 关闭/20

dead 非常；绝对；极度/58

debilitating 虚弱的/65

decarbonise 降低……的碳排放/30

decent 体面的/80

decibel 分贝/16

deck house 甲板室/46

deem 认为/25

defective 有缺陷的/41

definition (图像或声音的)清晰度/83

deliver 分娩/50

delivery 递送/30

densely packed 鳞次栉比的/60

deploy 部署；利用/21

deposit 存放/85

derelict 被弃置的/95

descendant 后裔；后代/56

descent 血统/4

designer 名牌的/86

despair 绝望/19

desperate 非常需要的；非常想要的；极想/16

desperate 极严重的；极危险的/87

detain 拘留/35

detectorist 爱好使用金属探测器的人/24

deteriorate 恶化/46

detox 戒瘾/71

detrimental 有害的；不利的/55

devaluation 贬值/18

develop 患(病)/4

developer 开发商/67

devour 吞噬/98
diamond jubilee 钻石大庆;60 周年庆典/76
diesel 柴油;柴油车/14
digestive 消化的/33
dilemma 困境/80
dilute 稀释/21
dimension 大小;尺寸/30
dip 下跌/18
dire 极糟的;极差的/34
discern 觉察出/51
disheveled 头发凌乱的/78
disorder 失调;紊乱;不适;疾病/90
disorderly 目无法纪的/35
disoriented 迷失方向的/92
dispose 丢弃;处理/85
disrupt 使中断/96
disruption 中断;混乱;扰乱/52
disruptive 扰乱性的;破坏性的/84
distinctive 独特的;特别的/21
disturbing 令人不安的/71
divine intervention 上帝之祐/7
division lobby (英国议会的)分组表决厅/12
do one's bit 做贡献;尽力/85
dock 扣除/34
dockyard 船坞/57
dolphin 海豚/70
domestic 家用的;家庭的/47
dominant 主导的;占优势的/57
donor 捐赠者/4
dose 剂量/79
down the line 以后/80
down the years 这些年/45
down to 由……引起(或造成)/10
down under 在澳大利亚/56
downside 缺点/20
drain 导管/42
droppings (鸟、小动物的)粪/89
drum sth. into sb. 向……反复灌输/38
due 适当的;充分的/89
dugout 球员席/17
dwell on 唠叨/1
dwindle (逐渐)减少/10
dynamics 动力/51
dynamism 活力/88
ear-splitting 震耳欲聋的/16
eat away at sth. 侵蚀;逐渐毁掉/46
eccentric 古怪的/2
eclectic 不拘一格的/66
edge 徐徐移动/34
editor in chief 主编/9
Edwardian 英王爱德华七世时代的(1901—1910)/76
eel 鳗/74
elastic 有弹性的/2
eliminate 清除;消除/36
elite *adj.* 精英的;最优秀的/91
Elizabethan 伊丽莎白女王一世时代的(1558—1603)/57
embrace 拥抱/48
embryo 胚胎/50
eminent 卓越的/56
emission 排放/14
emoji 表情符号/45
empower 赋能/77
endeavour 努力/8
endorsement 支持/69
enduring 持久的/26
enforce 执行/47
enforcement 执行/47
engage 参加;参与/7
engagement 约会;约定;安排/13
engaging 有趣的;令人愉快的;迷人的/66
enter administration 进入破产管理状态/34
enthusiasm 热情;热心;热衷的活动/16
enthusiast 爱好者/46
enthusiastic 热心的;热衷的/40
enticing 诱人的/22
envious 羡慕的/73
epic 艰苦卓绝的;漫长而艰难的/1
epilepsy 癫痫/90
episode 疾病的发作;发病/82

equity 财产价值/55
equivalent 等量/44
eradicate 根除;消灭/36
eructation 打嗝/99
eternal 永恒的/6
EV = electric vehicle 电动车/40
evaporate (逐渐)消失;消散/15
eventful 多变故的;精彩的/93
evolution 演化/31
evolve 逐步发展/95
excavation 发掘/56
exceed 超过/44
excess 过度的/44
excruciating 极痛苦的/49
expedition 远征;探险/74
exploit 英勇的行为(通常用复数)/56
explosive 爆炸物/21
exponential 飞速的;极快的/97
extinction 灭绝;绝种/64
extrapolate 类推出/25
exuberance 精力充沛/78
fabric 基本结构/75
fall from grace 失去恩宠/3
fall victim to 成为牺牲品/51
fallout 不良影响/17
fantasy 梦幻的;虚拟的/60
fare worst 情况最糟糕/23
farmstead 农庄/66
far-reaching 影响深远的;广泛的/80
fatigue 疲劳/65
faulty 有缺陷的/90
feasible 可行的/59
feature 是……的重要特点(或重头戏)/100
fed up (with) 厌烦/16
feel the pinch 感到手头有点紧/18
feel-good factor 快乐感;满足感/78
fell 小山/10
fella 小伙子/73
fencing 击剑运动/15
fertilise 给(土壤、土地)施肥/88
fertiliser 肥料/99
festering 愈益恶化的/85
fiasco 惨败;彻底搞砸/58
fictional 虚构的/75
file 排成一行行走/26
filthy 肮脏的;污秽的/89
finalist 入围决赛者/48
finances 财力/34
fine 很细的/47
fire 激发/92
fixture 体育赛事/11
flake 碎片/85
flexibility 灵活性/52
flight lieutenant(英国空军)上尉/1
flip side 反面;对应面/18
florist 花店店主/14
flourishing 繁荣;蓬勃发展/86
fluke 偶然/4
follow suit 仿效/20
footage 影片片段/35
footprint 足迹(指个人或机构活动对环境的影响)/88
footwear 鞋类/13
for all intents and purposes 实际上;差不多等于/67
for life 终生/27
forgetful 健忘的/93
formula 方案;方法/13
fortuitous 幸运的/15
fossil fuel 化石能源/83
foster 助长;培养/91
fraction 小部分;少量/40
fragment 碎片/19
frantic 紧张忙乱的/57
frivolous 愚蠢的/83
from cradle to grave 从生到死;一辈子/90
front end 前端/99
frontier 前沿;新领域/74
frontman 头面人物/78
frustrated 沮丧的/71
fuel 维持/8

fuel 增加;刺激/25
fundraiser 募捐活动/69
galaxy 星系/98
galling (因不公平而)使人恼怒的;使人感到屈辱的/56
game-changer 规则改变者;在很大程度上改变形势的产品(或事件)/30
garden centre 园艺品店;花卉市场/47
garnish (食物上的)装饰菜/87
gas boiler 燃气锅炉/47
gassy (肠胃)胀气的/99
gateline 检票通道/82
gateway(通往其他地区的)门户/76
gear 设备;用具/86
gear up 做好准备/63
gene sequencing 基因测序/90
generically 一般地;通用地/85
generosity 慷慨/3
genome 基因组/90
genomics 基因组学/90
get around 出行/23
get away with 受到从轻发落/2
get behind 支持/69
get the wrong end of the stick 完全误解/45
getaway 短假/55
ghostly 幽灵般的;奇异的/74
gigantic 巨大的/98
gilded cage 镀金鸟笼(指豪华但不自由的环境)/72
give way to 让位于/56
go according to plan 按计划进行/81
go bust 破产/18
go down well 反应很好/3
go into administration 进入行政接管程序/13
go some way to doing sth. 对于做某事很有帮助/69
go-ahead 批准/14
golf course 高尔夫球场/7
GP = general practitioner 全科医生/23
grace 荣登;使荣耀/9
gravity 引力/98
graze (在草地上)吃青草/10
greenhouse gas 温室气体/83
grief 悲伤;伤心/19
grieving 悲痛的;伤心的/26
ground-breaking 创新的/79
grumble 发牢骚/97
guideline 指导原则/23
gut 消化道/27
gymnast 体操运动员/91
gymnastic 体操的/91
gymnastics 体操;体操训练/91
habitat 栖息地/10
hailing app 手机招车软件/55
halve 使减半/55
hand oneself in 自首/35
handler 驯兽员/70
hang about 闲荡/44
harassment 骚扰/35
hard sell 强行推销/71
harness 利用/21
haul 视频购物分享;直播带货/20
haul over the coals 严厉训斥某人/89
haunting 使人难忘的/45
have a go 尝试/45
have seen better days 已经衰败;今不如昔/62
havoc 灾祸/84
head off 防止/99
headlight (车辆的)前灯/51
head-on 正面地/41
healing 治愈的/37
health regime 养生法/63
hectare 公顷/59
hedgehog 刺猬/88
heels 女高跟鞋/13
heightened 增强的/70
helter-skelter 螺旋滑梯/7
Her Majesty 陛下/29
herald 称赞/97
heritage 遗产/10
HGV = heavy goods vehicle 重型货车/47
hide away 隐藏/31

high street 大街;主要街道/13
high-end 高档的/13
highlight 突出;强调/64
high-profile 引人注目的;高调的/13
hike（价格、花费等的）大幅度提高;猛增/58
hit 风靡一时;轰动/69
hoard 秘藏/24
hoist 吊起/70
holiday 度假/22
hood 罩/99
hoodie 带帽夹克/86
hop 快速旅行;冲/66
hordes of 一群群/86
horizontal 横的;水平的/43
hostile 恶劣的;不利的/74
house 给……提供住处/59
houseboat 船屋/59
hover fly 食蚜虻/88
hub 中心/97
humble 卑微的/72
humbling 惭愧的/8
hurdle 障碍/27
Hurricane 飓风式战斗机/1
husbandry 保护/43
hygiene 卫生/87
hysterectomy 子宫切除术/50
iceberg 冰山/46
Icelandic 冰岛的/70
iconic 符号的;标志性的;偶像的;非常出名或受欢迎的/10
idyllic 田园式的;诗情画意的/59
illustrator 插图画家/93
immense 巨大的/8
immunity 免疫力/4
impactful 有效的;有影响力的/21
imperative 至关重要的/95
implant 将……植入/36
impose 强制实行/57
in a bid to 试图/41
in awe 满怀敬畏/29
in custody 在押;被拘留/35
in formation 编队;列阵/57
in line with 与……一致/91
in place 到位的;就绪/5
in remission 康复期;病情好转/36
in residence 常驻/32
in season（水果和蔬菜）当令的/99
in succession 连续地/52
in the order of 大约/59
in the pipeline 在规划中/95
in the red 负债;有赤字/34
in the wake of 随……之后而来;跟随在……后/80
incentive 刺激;激励/40
inclusive（团体或组织）可以包容各种人的/91
incy-wincy 极小的;微小的/94
indelible 消除不掉的/65
indication 暗示;迹象/74
infestation（昆虫、老鼠等）成群侵扰;滋生/89
infrastructure 基础设施/52
ingrain 使……深深印在脑中/51
inhabit 居住于/92
initially 起初/2
initiative 倡议;新方案/40
injury time（英式足球等运动）伤停补时/17
innovator 创新者/2
inscribe 书写/45
insider 知内情者/28
insight 深刻见解;洞悉/48
instant food 速食食品/61
instant gratification 即时满足/71
instigate 发起/25
instinct 本能/72
instruction manual 指导手册/90
intact 完好无损/46
intelligence(机密)情报/76
intensification 增强/64
interference 干涉/54
interim 暂时的/17
intervene 出面;介入;干预/62
intervening decades 几十年间/51

intestine 肠/27
intimate 温馨的/48
intolerable 无法忍受的/16
intrigue 吸引力/34
intruder 闯入者/84
invasive 侵入的/64
investiture 授衔仪式/29
irrelevant 不相关的/19
irresistible 富有诱惑力的/45
isolation bearings 独立基础/67
issue（杂志或报纸的）一期；期号/9
IVF = in vitro fertilization 体外受精/50
jackpot 头奖/24
jaw-dropping 令人惊愕的/77
jellyfish 水母/8
jeopardise 危害；损害/64
jetpack 飞行背包/39
jobbing 打零工的/72
jog 慢跑（尤作为锻炼）/69
juggle 同时应付/75
jumper 针织套衫；毛线上衣/86
junction 交叉路口/38
justice（尤指最高法院的）法官/94
jut 突出；伸出/100
keen 渴望/8
keenly 强烈地；敏锐地/92
keep sth. off sb. 使……远离某人/37
kerosene 煤油/39
kick sth. stone dead 完全扼杀/55
kick-start 快速启动/62
kidney bean 菜豆/33
knight 封（某人）为爵士/29
knock down 推倒（或拆掉、拆毁）建筑物/95
knock-down 低廉的/62
knock-on effect 连锁反应/52
label 标签/32
Labrador 拉布拉多猎犬（常用于导盲）/21
ladies' man 爱和女人调情的男子；有女人缘的男人/72
lampoon 嘲讽/45
landfill 废物填埋/85
landmark 有重大意义或影响的/33
larger-than-life 有传奇色彩的/78
laxative 轻泻药/91
lead 铅/56
lead up to（时间）临近；紧挨在……之前/94
leaky 渗漏的/56
lease firm 租赁公司/40
lease 租用/39
lease 租约/95
legendary 传奇的/17
legion 大量；大批/72
legislation 法规/25
lentil 兵豆/33
let 出租/95
let sb. off 从轻处罚/2
LGBTQ 性少数群体/66
liaise（为双方合作而）建立工作关系；联络/89
license plate 车牌/16
ligament 韧带/50
like 点赞/71
like-minded 想法一致的/67
limelight 公众注意的中心/29
limousine 豪华轿车/28
line 一行字/45
line up 排成一行/12
linear 线形的/60
lining tissue 黏膜组织/27
livelihood 生计/55
liven up（给……）增色；（为……）添彩/94
livestock 牲畜/10
loads of 大量；许多/69
loathe 厌恶/16
lockdown 封锁/63
log 记录/31
log 原木；木材/47
longevity 持久/15
lookout 望风者/86
loot 战利品/25
lottery 抽彩给奖法/24

lower-rise 低层的/95
lunar 月球的/81
luxuriant 茂盛的;浓密的/65
macular degeneration 黄斑变性/77
magnetic field 磁场/79
magnify 放大/96
maiden voyage 处女航/46
mainstream 主流/50
majestic 雄伟的;壮丽的/70
make of 理解;看待/89
make out 看清;辨认清楚/56
make sense 是明智的;合乎情理;可行/63
malaria 疟疾/21
mammography 乳房 X 线照相术/77
mammoth 极其巨大的/31
mandatory 强制的/41
manipulate 操纵;控制/49
map 绘制/90
marine 海洋的/70
marry ... with ... 把……同……结合起来/97
martyr 殉道者/49
massage 按摩/53
massive 巨大的/11
mastermind 策划/17
mastery 控制权/1
maternal 产妇的/53
matrix 矩阵/92
mayfly 蜉蝣/64
mechanism 机制/49
medic 医护人员/69
medieval 中世纪的/7
membrane 膜/42
menace 威胁/96
merit 价值/2
mesh 网状物/92
mess up 弄糟;毁掉/80
methane 甲烷/83
meticulously 细心地;周密地/100
metro 地铁/82
microbe 微生物/46
midwife 助产士/53
mileage 里程数/14
milestone 里程碑/81
mineral 矿物质/37
minicab (须电话预约订而不能自由揽客的)出租汽车/55
mint 铸造/24
mishap 小事故/78
miss out on 遗漏;错过/33
mitigate 减轻/65
mobilise 动员;调用/31
moderate 节制;克制/71
moist 潮湿的/65
molecule 分子/4
momentous 重要的/12
monoculture 单种栽培/88
monorail 单轨铁路(通常为高架)/60
moor 系泊/59
mooring 停泊处/59
morgue 停尸房/72
mortal 致命的;极度的/1
moth 飞蛾/64
motor function 运动神经功能/42
motorist 驾车者/16
motorway (英国)高速公路/60
mount 发起/57
mourn 哀悼/72
MRI = magnetic resonance imaging 磁共振成像/79
murky 污浊的;隐晦的/71
muscle contraction 肌肉收缩/27
muscular 肌肉的/27
musty 陈腐的/3
mutation 变异/4
National Grid (英国)国家电网/52
naturalist 博物学家/19
nave 教堂正厅/7
near miss (尤指两架飞机)侥幸避开的相撞/84
nebulizer 喷雾器/23
nerve tissue 神经组织/42
nervy 紧张的/18

neural 神经的/42
neutralise 消除/97
news presenter 新闻主播/69
nickname 给……起绰号/13
nightingale 夜莺/88
nightmare 噩梦/72
nine holes 九洞高尔夫球/7
nitrogen dioxide 二氧化氮/14
nominate 提名/75
non(法语)不/54
Norman 诺曼人的/24
nuisance 麻烦事/16
number plate (汽车)牌照/40
nylon 尼龙/21
obesity 肥胖症/44
obsession 痴迷/51
odour 气味/21
oesophagus 食管/27
off the bat 毫不耽搁/39
offence 违法行为/35
old wives' tale 无稽之谈;迷信/21
on end 连续地/91
on hand 在场/53
on one's doorstep 离……很近/22
on suspicion of 涉嫌/35
on the brink of 濒于/13
on the cards 可能发生的/84
on the spot 当场/41
on top of 除……之外/55
oncologist 肿瘤专家/79
opponent 反对者/55
opt out 决定退出/54
opulence 财富/76
orbit *n.* 轨道
vt. 沿轨道运行/81
orchestra 管弦乐队/32
ordain 任命为牧师/7
organ rejection 器官排异/27
organic 有机的/100
organism 有机体;生物/74
ornate 华美的;豪华的/46
out of fashion 过时/13
out of the blue 出乎意料/53
outer 外围的/5
outfit 全套服装;装束/13
outlet 专营店;经销店/87
outsize 极大的/6
overheads 营运费用/28
overlap 与……重叠/11
overpowering 强烈的;令人无法忍受的/89
override 超控/38
overriding 最重要的/52
overrun 超过;肆虐/19
oversee 监督/80
oversize 过大的/30
oversized 过大的/30
over-the-counter 非处方的/37
overwhelm 击败/57
overwhelming 压倒性的;难以辩驳的/48
package 将……包装好/20
packaging 包装材料;外包装/30
packed 挤满人的/68
pain threshold 痛觉阈/49
painkiller 止痛药/49
pancreas 胰腺/79
panel 金属板/51
panel (门、墙等上面的)嵌板;镶板/100
parachute 降落伞/84
parallel 平行的/98
paralysis 瘫痪/42
paramedic 急救医士/39
paramount 最重要的/99
parched 晒焦的/68
pared-down 简化的/97
Parkinson's (disease) 帕金森病/21
particle 颗粒;微粒/47
pass 关口;关隘/72
passionate 热烈的/95
pasty 肉馅饼/78
pedal 骑自行车/5

peddle 兜售/86
peer(英国)贵族成员/76
penetrate 穿过/74
penicillin 青霉素;盘尼西林/75
pensioner 领取养老金的人/41
peregrine falcon 游隼/88
perfume 香水/86
perk 额外待遇;特权/40
pest 害虫/64
pesticide 杀虫剂/64
petition 请愿书/75
petrol forecourt 加油区/47
petrolhead 车迷/16
phase out 逐步淘汰/47
phony 假的/86
photocard licence 含驾驶人照片和签名的塑封卡片式驾驶证/41
pick up 付账/85
pin one's hopes on 寄希望于/78
pinpoint 明确指出;确定(位置或时间)/43
pinprick 针刺/49
pint 一品脱啤酒/11
pint 品脱(容量单位,约 0.568 升)/47
pioneer 开创,开发;倡导/20
pioneering 开创性的/79
pirouette 单脚尖旋转/91
pitch 推销/13
pitch 球场/34
pivot 转变/97
plague 折磨;使受煎熬/91
plaudit 褒扬/72
plight 苦难;困境/48
plough 犁/88
plunge 骤降/74
poacher 偷猎者/70
poignancy 哀伤/26
poignant 悲惨的;酸楚的/48
poised (to do sth.) 准备好/13
polarised 两极化/9
pollinate 授粉;传粉/64
pollinator 传粉昆虫/37
pollutant 污染物/14
popularity 受欢迎;普及/15
porridge 粥/33
port of entry 入境口岸/21
porthole 舷窗/46
potent 强烈的/83
powerhouse 豪门;巨头/97
preach 说教/93
precast 预制/67
predisposed 更倾向于;更有可能/73
pre-eminent 超凡的;卓越的/43
prehistoric 史前的/43
premature 过早的;提前的/61
Premier League (英国)超级联赛/11
prepaid 预付费的/28
prescribe 给……开(药)/37
prevalent 普遍存在的/65
preventative 预防(性)的/4
prime time (广播与电视的)黄金时段/25
principal conductor 首席指挥/32
prioritise 优先考虑(处理)/63
private-hire vehicle(须电话预约而不能在街上招停的)私人租用汽车/55
privileged 幸运的/17
probe 航天探测器/81
processional 列队行进时用的/76
proclaim 宣告;声明/37
produce 农产品/99
profile 概况/34
profile 形象/78
profound 巨大的;深远的/77
progressively 日益增加地;逐步/91
promising 有前途的/27
prompt 促使/15
propel 推动/39
prorogation 休会/94
prostate 前列腺/21
protagonist 主角/75
protein 蛋白质/99

prototype 样机/16
prototype 原型/51
pulse 豆子/33
punishing 艰难持久的/68
purple emperor butterfly 紫蛱蝶/88
put off 使反感;使疏远/22
put on hold 搁置/65
put on weight 增加体重/73
put one's money where their mouth is 用行动证明自己的话/63
putting (高尔夫球)轻击入洞;推杆/7
pyramid 金字塔/74
quadruple 成四倍;翻两番/25
quarters 住处;宿舍/46
quid 一英镑/2
quota 限额/73
radiotherapy 放射疗法/77
rage 迅速蔓延/68
raid (警察的)突击搜查/86
rammed 拥挤的/82
rash 皮疹/65
reaffirm 重申/54
realm 领域/39
reassurance 令人安心的保证;清除疑虑/85
rebrand 重塑……的形象/5
recalibrate 重新校准/98
recession 经济衰退/51
reckon 想;认为/37
rectum 直肠/79
recyclable 可回收利用的/85
redress 纠正/32
referendum 全民公投/54
refine 改进;改善/39
reflective 深思的/78
refund 退款/20
refurbish 翻修一新/89
regenerate 使振兴;使复兴/62
regeneration 复兴/10
regenerative medicine 再生医学/27
regulate 约束;控制/25
regulator 监管机构/52
rehabilitate 使……恢复正常生活/70
rehearsal 排练/32
reign 主宰/17
reign 君主统治时期/24
reinforce 加固/92
reinter 移葬/56
reinvigorate 使再振作/17
rekindle 重新激起;重新唤起/51
relay satellite 中继卫星/81
relegation 降级/34
relish (doing sth.) 喜欢;享受/78
reluctantly 勉强地/12
remains 遗体;遗骸/56
remedy 疗法;药品/37
remission 缓解期/4
renew 延长……的期限;使续期/41
replica 复制品;仿制品/26
repossess(因买者未如期付款而)收回(房地产、商品等)/94
reproduce 繁殖/96
reprogram 为……重编程序/36
reservoir 水库/68
residential 住宅的/95
resilience 快速恢复的能力;适应力/52
resistant 抵抗的/4
resonance 共鸣/45
resort 度假胜地/68
restoration 整修;修复/100
resurface 再次露出(水面或地面)/74
retailer 零售商/13
rethink 重新考虑/63
retina 视网膜/77
retire (to) 离开(去另外的地方)/70
retrofit 翻新/82
retrospective(艺术家作品)回顾展/92
rev(发动机)加快转速/16
revelation 内幕揭秘/87
revenue 收益/55
reverence 崇敬/72

revisit 重新考虑;重提/60
revitalise 使恢复生机;使复兴/62
revoke 撤销;吊销/41
revolutionize 彻底改变/20
rewilding (大片土地的)野化;恢复原始样貌/10
rid 使摆脱(讨厌的人或事物)/96
ring 圆形标记;圆环,圆圈/65
rival 竞争对手/11
roar 轰鸣声/16
robust 强健的;耐久的/99
rogue 反常的;胡作非为的/84
role model 模范;榜样/32
roll on(时间)流逝/68
roll out 推出(新产品、服务等);实行(新制度)/47
root around for sth. 翻寻/3
root cause 根本原因/80
root out 根除/80
rose-tinted 极为乐观的/60
roughage 粗纤维/33
roundabout 环行交通枢纽/5
routinely 惯常地/20
rugged 崎岖的/81
rule of thumb 经验法则/99
ruling 裁决/94
runaway 轻而易举的(本文有双关意)/69
rust 锈/46
sabotage 蓄意毁坏/96
sack 解雇/17
safeguard 保护/89
sanctuary 避难所;庇护所/70
sarsen 砂岩/43
satirist 讽刺作家/6
saving grace 可取之处/84
savior 拯救者;救星/21
savour 享受/48
say 发言权;决策权/75
scaffold 支架/27
scales 磅秤/91
scatter 撒播/26
scenario 可能发生的事;可能出现的情况/15
scent 气味/48
scheme 计划;方案/3
school 教育/78
school run 接送学童上学(或放学)的行程/23
scores of 大量/86
Scotland Yard 苏格兰场(英国大伦敦警察局的总部)/35
scrap 取消/58
scrappage 为报废旧车提供金钱补偿/40
scratchcard 刮奖卡/25
scrutiny 详细审查/34
sculpture 雕塑/22
seal of approval 批准;认可/13
seasoned (木材)风干的;晾干的/47
see the back of 结束/70
see things 出现幻觉/39
seed 在……播种/27
seethe with 布满/8
segregate 隔离;使分开/5
seizure 发作/90
server 服务器/83
session(训练活动的)一节/91
set one's sights on 以……为奋斗目标;决心做到/78
set sail 起航/46
set the record straight 澄清事实;纠正误解/45
settle on 选定/48
shake off 去除;摆脱/95
shambles 混乱局面/7
shatter 粉碎;破灭/80
shattering 令人震惊的/51
shave 削减/39
shine 表现突出;大显身手/100
shortlist *n.* 入围名单
vt. 把……列入入围名单/66
showbiz 娱乐业/97
showcase 展示/20
show-stopping 极精彩的/100
side effect 副作用/79
sift through 细查;详查/56
sign up 签约;加盟/87

signing 签约球员/17
simulate 模拟/96
simulation 模拟/39
single-seater 单座机/1
skinny 极瘦的/73
skull 颅骨/31
skylark 云雀/88
skyscraper 摩天大楼/95
slap bang 恰好/62
slap 拍/8
slash 大幅度削减/39
slim 苗条的/73
slip road 匝道/41
slipper 拖鞋/46
slot machine 投币式自动赌博机/25
slur 含糊地说/65
smash 粉碎;打破/69
snail fish 狮子鱼/74
snarl 咆哮;怒吼/72
sniffer dog(训练来嗅查毒品或炸药的)嗅探犬/21
sniffly 抽鼻子的/37
sociable 易于社交的;气氛友好的/60
solar 太阳的/81
soothe 安慰/46
sophisticated 复杂的/38
sophisticated 先进的/82
sophistication 复杂/96
sort out 解决;处理/19
source 找出……的来源/86
souvenir 纪念品/43
space 把……分隔开;以一定间隔排列/26
spark 引发;激励/40
speak for itself 不言而喻;有目共睹/39
specialist 专业的;专门的/51
specialist junction 专用枢纽/5
specimen 标本/31
speculate 推测;推断/98
speechless(尤指由于震惊或强烈感情而)一时讲不出话的/29
speed up (使)加速/37
spell 一段时间/68
spike 激增/99
spina bifida 脊柱裂/42
spinal cord 脊髓/42
spinal fluid 脊椎液/42
Spitfire 喷火式战斗机/1
sponsor *n.* 赞助商/11
spook 特工/76
spring up 突然出现/95
sprout 球芽甘蓝/44
squad 小队;特别行动组/39
squander 浪费;挥霍/19
square up to 勇敢面对/92
squiggly 弯弯曲曲的/45
stalactite 钟乳石/46
stalled 停滞的/85
stand 看台/11
stand up to 勇敢反对/44
star 担任主角/75
starboard 右舷/46
stardom 明星地位/72
stark 明显的/31
starring role 主角/75
steal the show 吸引更多的注意;抢风头/6
steam engine 蒸汽机/75
steelwork 钢制品/67
steer 引导/9
stem cell 干细胞/27
sticky 难办的;棘手的/38
still 定格画面/35
stillness 宁静/93
stint 工作期限/78
stitch (sb.) up 诬陷/78
strain 压力;重负/37
stranded (人或交通工具)被滞留的/52
strategy 策略;行动计划/23
streaming service 流媒体服务/6
stretched 手头紧的/47
strewn 布满……的;……遍地的/81
strip 拆卸/51

strip 狭长地带/67
strip … of … 剥去/27
strip … of … 剥夺/41
stunning 极漂亮的/8
stunt 特技;惊险动作/2
subarctic 亚北极的/70
submarine 潜艇(缩写为 sub)/74
submersible 水下使用的/46
submit 提交/52
subscribe (to) 向(某个基金、项目或慈善事业)捐款/29
subscriber 追随者;粉丝/20
subscription 订阅;订购/97
subsidence 下沉/67
subsidised 有补贴的/71
subterranean 地下的/76
suburbia 郊区/60
successor 继任者/54
summit 峰会/23
super sub 超级替补/17
supermassive 特大质量的/98
surge 暴增/6
surgery 诊所/23
surrender 交出/41
suspend 悬挂/27
suspend 停赛/34
suspension bridge 悬索桥/2
sustainable 可持续的/30
swamped 疲于应对/77
swap 换掉/44
swarm *n.* 一大群
vi. 成群地飞/96
swearing 脏话/24
sympathetic 同情的/73
symphony orchestra 交响乐团/32
symptom 症状/21
synthetic 合成的/64
take a hit 受到严重影响/22
take its course 任其发展;听其自然/88
take on 决定做/8
take on 呈现/32
take sb. at his/her word 对某人深信不疑/54
take shape 形成/51
take shelter 躲避/57
take to 喜爱/38
takeaway 外卖餐馆/87
takeaway 外卖的饭菜;外卖食物/89
take-home message 主要信息,要点;得到的教益/73
takeover 收购;接管/34
tangible 有形的;可感知的/98
tantalising 诱人的;令人向往的/4
taste bud 味蕾/44
tee off 发球/7
tee up 将(高尔夫球)置于球座上;准备击球/7
teething problem 初期问题;萌芽期的困难/11
teller 计票员/12
telltale 泄露秘密的/65
tenderstem broccoli 嫩茎西兰花/99
territory 领地/48
tether 拴住;系住/67
the bowels 内部最深处/67
the envy of 忌妒对象;羡慕目标/73
the Milky Way 银河系/98
the toast of … 有口皆碑的人/6
the Treasury (英国)财政部/86
the waves 大海/76
there we are 别无他法;无计可施;只能这样了/19
thermal camera 热感摄影机/68
thrash out 反复讨论/85
thrilled 非常激动的/29
thriller 惊险剧/6
thrive 茁壮成长/74
throwaway 用后丢弃的;一次性使用的/85
thruster 推进器/81
thumbs-up 批准/11
tick all the right boxes 一切如愿;众口皆调(本文一语双关)/30
tick 蜱/65
tick over 维持原状;稳定运行/37
tier 层/11

Tinseltown 星光熠熠之城(好莱坞的谐称)/6
titanium 钛/74
to date 迄今为止/91
to sb. 's liking 中某人的意/60
toiletries 洗漱用品/30
top-flight 第一流的/34
top hat 高顶礼帽/2
touch down 着陆/81
touchdown 着陆;触底/74
toughen up 加强;强化/34
tower block 高层建筑/95
toxic 有毒的/23
track athlete 田径运动员/69
track record 业绩记录/17
trademark 典型的;特有的/13
trademark 典型特征/93
traffic 数据流量/83
trafficking 非法买卖;贩卖/86
trailblazing 开创性的/9
trainer 运动鞋/86
tranquil 宁静的/59
transformational 彻底改变的;革命性的/90
transparent 透明的/91
transplant 移植/4
transplantation 移植/27
treasure trove 无主宝藏/24
trench 海沟/74
triage 确定治疗顺序/39
trial 试用/16
tribute 致敬/45
triceratops 三角龙/31
tricky 难对付的/7
triumph 获胜/6
troop 列队行进/12
tuck 收藏;把……藏入/31
tumour 肿瘤/79
turmoil 动乱;混乱/34
turn away 拒之门外/82
turn up 被发现;突然出现/57
turnover 营业额/34
turnstile 旋转栅门/11
turtle dove 斑鸠/88
two-seater 双座机/1
ultimately 根本上;归根结底/91
ultimately 最终/27
unanimous 一致的/94
under way 已经开始;在进行中/16
undercover 暗中进行的;秘密干的/86
undergrowth 下层灌木丛/65
underneath 在……下面/45
undulation 起伏/74
uniform 一致的;统一的/85
unprecedented 前所未有的/12
unsalted 未加盐的/33
unscrupulous 无耻的;肆无忌惮的/28
unsettling 令人紧张(不安)的/15
unveil 公布;推出/5
up to sth. 能胜任/78
upkeep 保养费/59
uplifting 鼓舞人心的/48
upside 优点/20
urban myth 都市传奇(街谈巷议的传闻或趣事)/56
uterus 子宫/50
valid 有效的/50
value for money 物有所值/22
value 估价;定价/89
veg = vegetable(s) 蔬菜/33
vegetation 植被/65
vein 静脉/50
versatile 多才多艺的/72
vertical 竖的;直立的/43
veteran 老兵/1
viable 可实施的;切实可行的/62
vicinity 周围地区;邻近地区;附近/84
vicious cycle 恶性循环/91
vie 争夺/66
vigilant 警惕的/65
village blue 市民天地/59
virtual 虚拟的/25
vitamin 维生素/37

vlog = video log 视频博客/20
void 无效的/94
voluntarily 自愿地/44
voucher 代币券/63
vulnerable 脆弱的;易受……伤害的/25
ward off 防止/15
watch 留心;注意/73
watch the space 拭目以待/69
water vole 水鼠/59
waterborne 经水路的/59
wax lyrical 盛赞/37
way 大大地;远远地/31
weird 怪异的/8
well-being 幸福/5
well-trodden 常有人走的/78
well-wisher 祝福者/8
what have you 等等/72
whine 哭哭啼啼;哀鸣/96
white bread 白面面包;精粉面包/33
wholegrain 含全谷物的/33
wholegrains 全谷物;全麦/33
wholemeal(面粉或面包)全麦的/33
wholesale 批发的/28
wholewheat 全(小)麦的/33
whopping 极大的;异常大的/33
wind farm 风力发电场/52
winding 蜿蜒的/38
windmill 风车/7
winner 制胜的一记入球/17
with a bang 有强烈影响地;令人难忘地/68
with intent (to do sth.) 故意犯罪的/35
with regard to 关于/36
withdrawal 退出/12
withstand 承受;经受住/67
witty 风趣的/93
womb 子宫/42
wood burner 烧木柴的炉子/47
woodlark 森林云雀/88
work out 算出/2
worst-case 最不利的/15
worth every penny 物有所值/28
worthwhile 有益的;值得做的/69
wrap up 圆满完成/12
wreath 花圈/26
wreck 沉船/46
yacht 游艇/59
yellow fever 黄热病/96
yield 产生;提供/90
yogurt 酸奶/44
zero-emission 零排放的;无污染的/40